D0771142

The Undersea Discoveries
of Jacques-Yves Cousteau

THE WHALE
Mighty Monarch of the Sea

The Undersea Discoveries
of Jacques-Yves Cousteau

The Whale
Mighty Monarch of the Sea

Jacques-Yves Cousteau
and Philippe Diolé

Translated from the French by J. F. Bernard

ARROWOOD
PRESS

Copyright © 1972 by Jacques-Yves Cousteau
Translated from the French by J. F. Bernard

All rights reserved. No part of this work may be
reproduced or transmitted in any form or by any
means, electronic or mechanical, including photocopying,
recording, or any information storage and retrieval
system, without permission in writing from the
publisher.

Published in 1987 by

Arrowood Press
166 Fifth Avenue
New York, NY 10010

This edition published by arrangement with The Cousteau
Group, Inc., 38 Eleven O'Clock Road, Weston, CT 06883.

Library of Congress Catalog Card Number: 87-71045
ISBN: 0-88486-014-0

Printed in Hong Kong

Contents

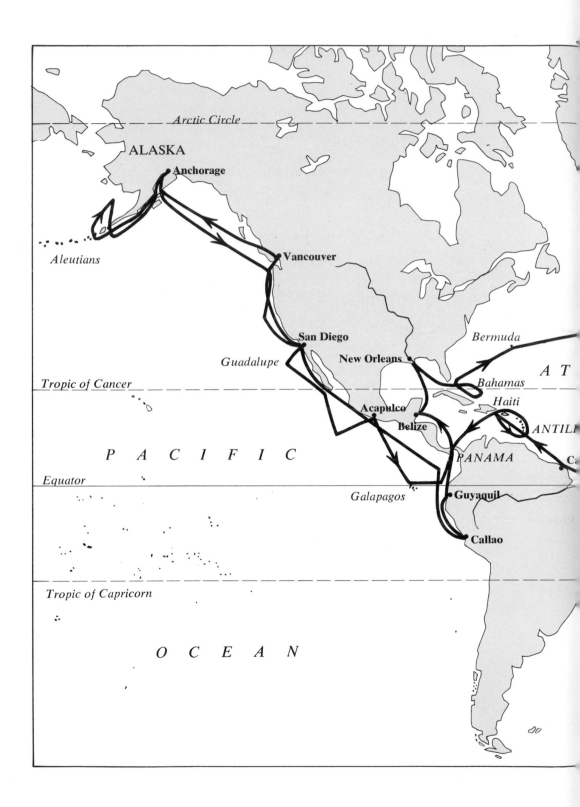

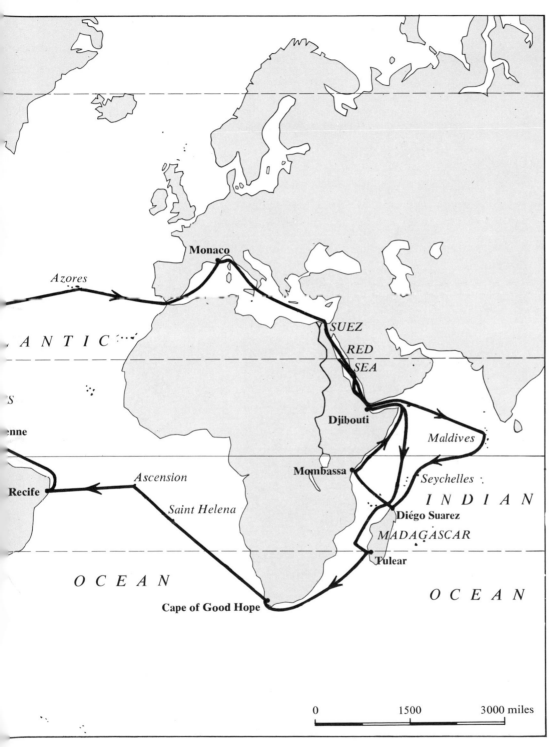

Calypso's itinerary, February 1967 to September 1970.

ONE

Meeting a Whale

The seas of the earth are vast. But, paradoxically, in that vastness there are few chance encounters. The waters, like the land, are covered by a network of paths and highways. Every species of life in the oceans has its route, and there are routes for every season. Nothing in this elaborate web of traffic has been left to chance. It has all been worked out in detail. It is all rigorously controlled by biological factors. And it works out greatly to the advantage of seafarers like ourselves whose mission it is to observe, and try to understand, the creatures who inhabit the seas.

In March 1967, *Calypso* was following one of these great underwater highways. Years before, during the spring, we had sighted sperm whales, or cachalots, here in the Indian Ocean near the equator. And again in 1967, during an extended course of observation in the Red Sea and the Indian Ocean, we had seen them once more. I knew, therefore, that we could count on sperm whales being here again at this time of the year.

(Left) Captain Cousteau forward on *Calypso.*

The sighting of great underwater mammals — cachalots, killer whales, pilot whales, and so forth — is always a great adventure for everyone aboard *Calypso.* Now, we have had some experience with all the animals of the sea. We have studied a huge number of species, fish of all kinds, both small and large. We have fed groupers, eels, octopuses, and even sharks. To be sure, these contacts and these tentative efforts at understanding, domestication, and communication were rewarding. But contact with whales — with those enormous warm-blooded beings who bear such a strong resemblance to man, with their lungs, their intelligence, and their talent for communication — this is a uniquely exciting experience.

It is also a uniquely difficult experience. When dealing with fish, we can attract as many as we want simply by offering them food. The effect of such an offering on a whale that weighs perhaps a hundred tons, however, is nil. There seems to be no set formula for establishing a relationship with a whale, and we have to rely upon experience gained from hit-or-miss attempts. For all of our thirty years of living on and in the sea and trying to understand its inhabitants, our experience is still woefully inadequate.

It is astonishing to recall that, after centuries of whale hunting, man knows very little about these giants of the sea.* Until recent years, man had not succeeded in crossing the boundary that separated him from the world of marine life. He had never observed whales, sperm whales, and killer whales in their natural habitat. We are the first to seek them out, in a spirit of friendship and curiosity, in the depths of the sea.

A Marvel of Nature

The relations of man and animals are always mysterious. The gulf separating the two seems virtually unbridgeable. But the most difficult creatures of all in the sea to approach and understand are the great mammals.

Face to face with this mountain of flesh, with the tens of tons of living tissue that constitute a cetacean, man's perplexity has been considerable; and his attitude, variable.

The first emotion was, understandably, terror. And, as always when fear plays a part, legends about whales multiplied. The Leviathan of the Bible story about Jonah† bears witness to man's fear when confronted with a being

---

*It should be noted, however, that certain whalers — William Scoresby, for instance, — gathered considerable information on cetaceans.

† The narrative is in the second chapter of the Book of Jonah.

so tremendous that it defies human understanding. And the age of Jonah and long afterward was a time when natural phenomena were expressed in myths, or in terms of religious or poetic significance.

Upon the heels of this relatively innocuous era, there came another, less innocent: the age of the hunt. And then, still another, even less harmless: the age of butchery. At this latter stage, whales were regarded as an economic factor, an industrial product; and so avidly were they pursued that, with the development of modern weapons and the tilting of the scales in favor of the hunter, several species of whale were threatened with extinction. The harpoon cannon not only destroyed myth, legend, poetry, and Moby Dick, the white whale; it also brought into question the very survival of the largest beings on the face of the earth.

In the twentieth century, whale hunting has been limited and controlled by national laws and international agreements. This was done at first, for obvious economic reasons, at the insistence of whale hunters themselves. Later, public opinion, catalyzed by more humane reasoning, began to insist on the preservation and protection of whales. Nonetheless, it seemed impractical to leave the whalers unemployed; and so, a certain amount of whale hunting is still allowed. Whales, in other words, are still being killed. And they are being killed, as ridiculous as it may sound, so that dogs and cats may be fed "seafood platters."

Ships of the Soviet Union and Japan hunt whales in order to obtain whale oil. American, British, Dutch, and Norwegian ships, however, have practically ceased all whale hunting. Whaling by French ships — usually at Gabon and Madagascar — has always been at best sporadic. Some were killed during a short period after World War II, when fatty materials were otherwise in great demand and in short supply.

Despite the continuance of whale hunting — which, at least so far as the Western world is concerned, is hardly justifiable from an economic standpoint — the relations between man and whale have changed; and this evolution, which is primarily psychological in nature, is irreversible. The whale is no longer fair game. He is no longer, in man's mind, merely a colossal prey, the handsomest trophy of all. By the same token that it is no longer a sign of virility to fell an elephant with a single explosive shell, it is no longer a manly act to destroy a great whale with a shot of cannon. What has happened is that man has become convinced — and we hope to be able to reinforce that conviction — that the whale is the greatest and most intriguing of nature's marine marvels, the most stupendous form of animal life in the seas.

In Melville's time, it was fashionable to emphasize the "ferocity" of whales. Today, we are astonished at the gentleness of whales, at their extraor-

(Left) The entire team watching for whales from *Calypso*'s bow.

(Right) A Zodiac and a launch attempting to encircle a sperm whale. *Calypso* is in the background.

(Below) Falco and Bonnici chasing sperm whales in the Zodiac.

dinary diving ability, at the fact that they have the ability to communicate with one another. And we are touched by their highly developed maternal instinct.

Aboard *Calypso*, we have learned much from our experiences with whales. We know especially that contact with whales is not impossible. We are not forever cut off from our brothers, the mammals who, eons ago, chose the sea rather than dry land for their world. In order to attain even that knowledge, however, it has been necessary for us to tempt fate, to take chances, to run risks; and we have done so. In the course of our contact, the observation that emerges most clearly is this: it is very rare that a cetacean, even one that we have disturbed, or surrounded, or chased, shows any sign of aggressive action. Of course, everything depends on the species of whale, and on circumstances. But, even so, we can say that, up to now, not a single man of *Calypso* has been harmed in any way during our sometimes hazardous encounters with whales. Indeed, we can assert that whales have shown every sign of being docile creatures, every indication of wishing to spare man — and particularly divers — from harm.

This having been said, I must emphasize that there is a great mystery in this apparent respect of whales for man. For there is nothing simple about any aspect of the relations between the monarch of the sea and the ruler of the lands of the earth.

effect of their tail movements upon the water — water vibrations, or what old-time seafarers called *glip*.

The whales remain underwater, swimming along at a depth of twenty-five or thirty feet — even though they are capable of going down as far as perhaps three thousand feet — and surfacing only when they have to come up for air. Once, they stayed under for twenty minutes. What wind they must have!

In spite of everything, we manage to get a few shots. Albert Falco ("Bebert") has taken out the Zodiac — which is faster and more maneuverable than the launch — and is able twice to head off the herd. With him are Deloire, with his movie camera, and Sillner, our photographer, and they capture a whale on film before it gets too far away. The second time, there is enough time to focus the cameras, and Deloire and Sillner manage to get a few good photographs and some excellent frames.

Obviously, we are going to have to find some less timid whales if we are ever going to get good shots. What happened? So far as we can see, there is nothing to account for the difference in behavior between yesterday and today. And yet, yesterday, the whales were indifferent to our presence, while today they are most unapproachable.

We continue the watch all afternoon until dark, but without seeing a sign of the school.

The tail of a sperm whale diving.

(Right) Falco and Bonnici prepare to confront a sperm whale.

(Below) A diver has jumped out of the Zodiac and is going to latch onto a young sperm whale.

Thursday, March 16. Today, nothing. We are into the fringe of a storm from the northeast. There is a wind, and the sea is rough — force 4, which is not dangerous, but is rough enough to make whale watching impossible. It is too easy to confuse the spout of a whale with the crest of a wave in this kind of weather.

I have worked out and distributed a plan for filming. Barsky, Deloire, Marcellin, Dumas, Bebert, and Didi are reading it, and I have asked them to let me know their comments after they've had a chance to think about it.

We must get to work on the sequences that we have already filmed, and begin to plan others. I am not overly concerned about this aspect of it, though. Barsky is a true artist with his camera, and I have the greatest confidence in him. And Deloire is simply unbelievable. He manages somehow to plan every aspect of his work in the most minute detail, and yet remain so flexible that he is never unprepared when something unexpected turns up. Yesterday, for example, when he went out with Bebert and Sillner in the Zodiac, he lay down in front of the raft with his camera cradled in his arms. Then, as soon as Bebert told him "Go!" he simply rolled into the water, practically on top of a whale, and began shooting instantly. This kind of thing seems to be his cup of tea. He simply radiates contentment and good humor.

March 18. The squall from the northeast is not so rough, and we have once more taken up our watch for sperm whales. We will reach the Maldives, our next port of call, at the earliest on March 20.

The past two days have been taken up entirely with our hunt for whales. There have been many fewer than during the month of April, both in 1954 and 1955, when we were sailing along the equator, north of the Seychelles. We hope to see some more before reaching the Maldives — and I've deliberately charted a crooked course in order to add ten days to our cruise. Even so, there is no certainty that it will have been worth it.

I am struck, as always, by the incredible fertility of the sea. Whales seem to exist in all parts of it. And Japanese fishermen* seem able to drop their lines at just about any spot and haul out tuna and swordfish bigger than the fishermen. Whales, tuna, swordfish — it is no wonder that the waters of the earth abound with such a variety of life forms. Think what resources are necessary to sustain these huge (and hungry) creatures.

We have taken steps to cope with the next whales we sight. We know that sperm whales are able to attain speeds of up to 20 knots, while *Calypso* struggles along at eleven knots. And so, I have had two 40-horsepower outboard motors mounted on one of our launches. This should make it possible for our team to keep up with the great mammals. The problem is that, if the sea is even a little rough, a launch traveling at that speed is in for trouble. Everyone aboard — our divers, cameramen and pilots — are thrown about mercilessly and are in constant danger of ending up in the water.

**Calypso had the opportunity to observe these fishermen at work in the Indian Ocean.

(See *Life and Death in a Coral Sea,* Chapter Two.)

It is true that it is often easy to get fairly close to whales — a phenomenon that always surprises me. The trouble comes when we want to capture them on film. It seems that we no sooner get our cameras in focus than the whales dive and are lost to sight. Several times, Deloire, clutching his camera, and another diver, jumped into the water right in front of a sperm whale; but, as soon as the whale sensed their presence, it disappeared. "If one has a great deal of patience, it is possible to film a whale's tail," André Laban says, but without a trace of bitterness. And that is only a slight exaggeration. Even so, it seems to me that a whale's tail is well worth the effort.

From aboard *Calypso*, at any rate, it is this enormous tail that we see most clearly when a whale, having drawn himself up to dive, plunges with a mighty burst of speed into the deep. We see it then, a flat, triangular expanse of living flesh, curving into what seems an ironic salute, for a second before it too disappears where no man can follow. An awe-inspiring sight. Sometimes, an infuriating one. And, occasionally, in spite of ourselves, we burst out laughing.

April 6. We are at anchor off the island of Funidu, one of the Maldives group, in order to take on fresh water. This evening, a party from *Calypso* went ashore to do a bit of exploring, and turned up a few objects of interest: some drums, and a superb dagger the hilt of which is made of whale's tooth. This shows that there are indeed whales in these waters, and that the natives are able to kill them — but how?

A First Meeting.

April 9. This morning, after breakfast, Bonnici, Bebert, and Barsky go to the Zodiac and have a great time romping with a troop of dolphins. The dolphins, who seem to love this sort of thing, make a game of rushing at the Zodiac, at full speed, and then diving just when it seemed that they could never turn away in time. We almost captured a magnificent spectacle on film: a troop of a hundred dolphins leaping along ahead of the Zodiac, seeming to be harnessed to it as Bebert, pushing the Zodiac to its maximum speed of 18 knots, never quite manages to catch up to them.

A Difficult Part to Play

The first thing to do, obviously, is to be prepared; and so, I set up a tight schedule. Our gear must always be ready: suited divers on the foredeck, with

The Zodiac catches up with a fleeing dolphin.

harpoons, nylon line, and buoy within reach. The Zodiac and the launch must be ready to be lowered into the water with their motors in place. Two underwater cameras must always be loaded and ready for use. And a cameraman must be standing by to go immediately to the observation room.

The use of the harpoon gun by our divers requires some explanation. It is

very rare that one is able to follow a particular whale, observe it when it dives, and then pick it up again when it comes to the surface for air. There is usually no way of knowing if the whale that comes to the surface is the same whale that you saw disappear fifteen or twenty minutes before; for one cachalot looks very like another, at least to human beings. Therefore, it is almost impossible to judge the speed of a certain whale by measuring the distance from the point of disappearance to the point of reappearance, unless there is some way of making sure that the whale, in both cases, is the same whale.*

So far as I know, there is only one way to be certain, and that is to "mark" the animal. And for that we intend to use the same method that worked for sharks in the Red Sea. That is, we try to attach a metal marker to at least one whale's dorsal fin — if we can get close enough to those enormous cylinders of shiny black flesh that are spouting and rolling all around *Calypso*.

The job of attaching this marker is reserved for Albert Falco. It is not a task to be undertaken lightly, or to be carried out without trouble; but if there is one man in the world who can handle it, it is Falco. He has been with us since he was fifteen years old. He has shared everything with us, every danger and every risk, for twenty years. But Falco is not only an extraordinarily capable diver and a dexterous athlete; just as important, he is a man with a gift for handling animals. Somehow, he is able to succeed in making himself accepted by marine animals. Others on our team have developed the same talent to some extent — Delemotte, Raymond Coll, Canoë Kientzy, and my son Philippe; but Albert Falco was the first who deliberately undertook to make friends with life forms in the open sea, and he remains the practitioner par excellence of that difficult art.

This aspect of Falco's talent is especially important at this time. The relationship between man and whale is precarious and uncertain. It is true that whale hunting is now practiced on a much smaller scale than formerly, and that whales are no longer looked upon as "ferocious monsters." But we have not yet been able to work out a new relationship, to devise a new approach to these sperm whales which, only yesterday, were considered "Leviathans" existing in a kill-or-be-killed relationship to man. It is very difficult for man to go directly from butchery to sympathy.

April 10. As soon as it is daylight, I am up and on deck checking to make sure that the television camera and the automatic camera are set up and ready to roll in the observation room. By 7:30, Barsky is ready on *Calypso*'s diving platform, at water level, camera in hand, waiting for a chance to shoot some flying fish. And Simone is up in the crow's-nest, keeping a sharp lookout for sperm whales. Then, just at the moment when René Haon climbs up to relieve her, the alarm sounds: Whales!

---

*Whalers were the only ones who ever had the opportunity to keep track of the duration of a cetacean's dive, or of its speed. They, however, observed whales only when the animals' behavior was abnormal; that is, when they were being closely pursued.

Calypso swings about, and our team is galvanized into action. The Zodiac, with its new 33-horsepower motor, is lowered into the water, as is the launch with its twin 40s. Bebert and Bonnici set out in the Zodiac with the harpoon — a weapon designed to mark the whale without harming it, for its spearhead is short and light and it is incapable of going deeper into the whale than its layer of blubber. Maurice Leandri and René Haon pull away in the launch.

The first group of sperm whales comprises four animals, and, in addition, there are two other groups nearby, each with three whales. *Calypso* gets to within fifty yards of them — and they dive. We are too late.

Thirty minutes later, the three groups reappear, but a little more widely dispersed. This time, Bebert is prepared. He fires. One of the whales is hit! Apparently bewildered, it remains motionless a few feet below the surface, and its companion whales stay with it. A good shot, apparently. But then, with a flick of their great tails, all three are gone, and Bebert dejectedly reels in his spear. It seems that the harpoon became entangled in the line, struck the whale at an angle, and then fell out. So near, and yet so far. Everyone is disappointed, except, no doubt, the whale.

Nonetheless, we continue the chase all morning, until at half past noon, the whales disappear for good and we are left facing an empty sea. I reset our course for Mahé in the Seychelles, our next port of call, and everyone turns in for a siesta — everyone, that is, except those on watch on the observation platform.

It would seem that, from dawn to about ten or eleven o'clock in the morning, sperm whales are sleepy, or sluggish, and are easy to sight and approach. Beginning at eleven o'clock or noon, however, they liven up and begin to travel; and then is when we lose them. It is even difficult to see them when they blow. Is it because there is less condensation in midday than early in the morning? Perhaps there is some connection between this phenomenon and the fact that most marine life tends to rise or swim toward the surface during the hours between sunrise and sunset. It is possible that whales prefer to hunt at night, when they are able to find food without diving to great depths. That would explain why they appear to be tired and listless early in the morning. And, of course, we have no way (for the time being) of observing whales except in daylight.

April 11. I am adopting a zigzag course in order to increase our chances of sighting sperm whales.

Our team is aware that they are going to attempt to do something that has never been tried before; and that they are going to attempt it in perilous circumstances. This is the kind of challenge that we love, and everyone senses

Two gray whale spouts. Canoë Kientzy, in a Zodiac piloted by Bernard Delemotte, is getting ready to throw his harpoon.

that our task requires not only special skills, but also special attitudes and a particular kind of morale. Even Raymond Coll, our almost speechless Catalan, who has never wasted a word in his life, has suddenly come to life and is talking (for him) madly. This is important, for Raymond has an "in" with the great animals of the sea; after all, he was the first man ever to hitch a ride on the back of a whale shark.

Caught in the Trap.

April 16. At dawn, we are where we were years ago, at the "meeting place of the sperm whales." And we are not disappointed. By seven o'clock, Frédéric Dumas has sighted a disturbance in the water on the horizon, an up-

Michel Deloire, our cameraman, prepares his equipment before diving to meet a whale.

heaval like those that we saw here in 1955. Fifteen minutes later, I can make out clearly, dead ahead at about a half mile, the shape of a huge cachalot. To make sure that nothing is able to get by us, I send Bebert, Bonnici, and Barsky out in the Zodiac. They are to stay two miles off our portside. Meanwhile, the launch, with Maurice, Omer, and Deloire, is at the same distance off our starboard. For all practical purposes, nothing can get by us along an eight-mile front.

As it turns out, we still have a lot to learn. It is my intention, thanks to our unsurpassed team of divers, to do what man has never done before: to sail with the whales in the open sea, to come face to face with them in the same way as we have confronted sharks, eels, and groupers. Our encounters with these latter, it is true, gave us a greater familiarity with them than had ever been possible before. What we had forgotten, however, was that even the largest sharks we saw measured around 15 feet — which is quite sizable — while our eels were about 9 feet long, and our groupers, at most, 6 feet. And none of these could begin to compare with a whale 60 feet long. How does one become friendly with a body that weighs over 60 tons? That, of course, is the question that this expedition is intended to answer.

The alarm bell rings. Frédéric Dumas — "Didi," our oldest friend and companion-in-adventure — up in the crow's-nest, has sighted a blow. Apparently, the whale is sleeping. It blows twice more, without showing its back on the surface, and then disappears for eight minutes. The Zodiac goes forward — but is slowed down by engine trouble. After a half hour spent in determining the whale's location, in observing from a distance, and in following slowly, the Zodiac now attempts to close in on the whale. But the animal has awakened and moves eastward at a good speed, closely followed by the Zodiac. We can see the whale's back now, as streamlined as the hull of an atomic submarine, but with a ridiculously small and slanted dorsal fin. The whale is making 12 to 15 knots, and the Zodiac is managing to keep the gap between them at no more than seven or eight yards. In a few seconds, it will be close enough for Bebert to fire his harpoon. Now!

And, at that precise moment, the Zodiac's motor conks out.

Bebert is beside himself with rage. So am I.

Fifteen minutes later, the Zodiac's motor has been changed and the chase begins anew. But the spirit of the thing has been lost, and, although we continue on, we know in our hearts that it is useless.

The reasons for today's fiasco are three: first of all, the breakdown of our new 33-horsepower outboard; second, the sea itself, which, while not really rough, is no longer so smooth as to make use of the Zodiac and the launch very easy; and, finally, *Calypso* herself is slowed down by the absence of her starboard propeller.

After nightfall, I consult my charts in order to try to work out a schedule. It is no use. We must make Mahé, our port of call in the Seychelles, and so our expedition has every chance of having ended with today's failure.

(Facing page above) A sperm whale aground in the Bering Strait. (An engraving from *Histoire des Cétacés*, by Lacépède.)

(Facing page below) André Laban suits up on *Calypso*'s deck.

(Following page) A gray whale, with Canoë's harpoon in its blubber, makes a vertical dive.

The animal that we encountered this afternoon was probably a finback whale, or rorqual. When he breathed, we were able to locate him by his blow; but we could see neither his back, nor his little dorsal fin. He breathed twice every eight minutes, but virtually without moving forward. Once the Zodiac began chasing him, however, he seems to have panicked. He tried to lose the Zodiac by swimming at a speed of 12 to 15 knots — but hardly below the surface; and then he was breathing more heavily, and we could see him very well. His real defensive means became apparent when he began to dive. For an hour he demonstrated the efficacy of his Asdic (sonar), for he obviously knew exactly where *Calypso*, the Zodiac, and the launch were at any given moment, and he always came to the surface where we were not.

I have the impression that the rorqual is somewhat more highly developed and clever than the sperm whale, and that our only chance of getting close to him would have been to catch him by surprise at some point during the first fifteen minutes of the chase.

I must admit that I am discouraged by today's events. Our whale hunt, twentieth-century style, is, it seems, nothing more than a dream. I want to be alone for a while, so I do not go in to dinner with the rest of the team. There is no one I want to see, or to talk to. But there is nowhere I can go in this crowded ship. On the forward deck, one can be seen from the bridge. Sillner and Sumian are on duty in the crow's-nest. And the rest of *Calypso* is one huge resonance chamber for diesels and ventilators. I resign myself to my cabin. I write, I read. And finally I lose myself in a crossword puzzle.

April 18. I am awake at five o'clock and go up on deck to see the sunrise. But everyone else is already there, eager for the sign of land, of islands, of trees. Still smarting from yesterday's fiasco, I find it difficult to share their gaiety.

It does not help that the sea today is what it should have been yesterday, calm as a pond. And here we are, between the islands of Bird and Denis, virtually trapped for the next three days — perhaps the last three days of calm of the entire season. How frustrating. For the next three days I intend to go into a state of suspended animation, and I will not breathe again, so to speak, until we leave these miserable, beautiful islands.

It is two months today that the *Calypso* sailed from Monaco.

The Speargun Sinks

April 20. We left Mahé at 7:30 this morning, and we were no sooner out into the open sea than the helmsman, pointing to a nearby squall, shouted, "There are the trade winds, and they're going to last for six months." This was precisely what I was afraid would happen — that the winds would come, and that that would be the end of our whale hunt.

I set a course for the African islands to take a look at the northern end of the Amirantes. But, as soon as Mahé was below the horizon, the alarm bell sounded. And suddenly it had all been forgotten — the disappointments and failures and discouragement — and I felt a surge of joyous hope. For there was a blow — and another, and another. And the closer we came, the more there seemed to be, slender columns of vapor against the blue of the sky. And best of all, there was no doubt that these were sperm whales, for the spouts were oblique, at an angle of about 45°. And of all the great whales, only the sperm whale has a single blowhole, rather than two.

I order *Calypso* to cut her speed. We must take no chance of a collision that might injure one of our giant friends.

Slowly, cautiously, we draw nearer to the whales. We can see their great backs turning among the waves of the Indian Ocean.

The cachalots are not in a hurry. The noise of our engines — which they no doubt hear very clearly, given the perfection of their auditory sense — does not seem to frighten them or even to disturb them. And yet, they have every reason to be wary of man and his ships.

I check off everything in my mind to make sure that we are prepared for any eventuality. Everyone seems ready, the divers and the cameramen, as well as our sound engineer who will tape, both above and below the surface, the sounds of the whales.

We are now very near. Indeed, *Calypso* is in the midst of them. The Zodiacs are being launched — but ever so cautiously, so as not to frighten the animals. In one of them are our cameramen. They will try to film the whales in the water. I watch from the bridge as they move slowly away from *Calypso*; and at that moment I begin to wonder whether this whole project is not senseless. From the bridge, I can see our tiny men, in their tiny boat. And, at the same time, I see the incredible size of the sperm whales, their mighty backs, the great flat tails that propel these phenomenal creatures. I see their dark silhouettes beneath the surface, more like mountains than mammals.

The men in the Zodiacs, however, seem troubled by no such doubts. I see Falco holding his speargun, to the tip of which a buoy has been attached. His nylon line is neatly coiled in its bucket. In the other Zodiac, Bebert is standing as far forward as he can get, held erect by a special harness so that he may fire his speargun from a standing position even at high speeds.

But now the whale shows signs of being disturbed by the noise from the outboard motors, and begins to swim away. The Zodiac shoots forward, and Falco is very close to the animal. He aims his speargun, and fires.

Aboard *Calypso*, no one breathes. For a few moments, we do not know what has happened. Then we see the other Zodiac skirt around the whale and slow down. Raymond Coll jumps into the water. He is trying to catch hold of one of the whale's fins! This means that Falco's shot was good! And, sure enough, we then see that the spear is in place and that the whale, when he moves, is trailing a red buoy behind him.

The whale's reaction seems initially one of surprise at all the unwelcome commotion around him. Since he is unable to outdistance his pursuers on the surface, he takes the only way out: he dives. We see his huge triangular tail above the surface for an instant, then it is gone. Apparently, our friend is going straight down: a deep dive. The red buoy disappears into the deep at an astonishing speed. This is the critical moment. The line attached to the whale is 3000 feet long — a length that, for all practical purposes, seemed sufficient. But what is practical for us is not necessarily so for sperm whales. The line uncoils, uncoils . . . then reaches its end and snaps like a thread.

Our whale is gone, buoy, buoy line and all. We will have to start all over again.

The main problem is to attach, or implant, a piece of iron, in the form of a spearhead, into the blubber of these animals. Their blubber is so elastic that a harpoon fired from a speargun — or even from a powder-operated gun — penetrates it only with difficulty. And it often penetrates so superficially that the barb cannot hold. I am certain that we shoot as straight as the old-time whale hunters, and from at most the same distance as they did. Why, then, do we fail where they succeeded? The answer, of course, is in our speargun. Our "harpoon" is ridiculously small and light compared to theirs. And yet, we dare not use anything larger or heavier, for fear of harming the whale.

We have learned a few things from our experiences today. We know, for instance, that it is not enough to slow down the animal so that we can film him from the front; we must also be able to guess the direction in which he is going to swim. The trouble is that, once a sperm whale is harpooned, his conduct becomes totally unpredictable. Or rather, in a sense it becomes too predictable: he dives, and that is the end of harpoon, buoy, and line. And the end also of our chance to film him.

Once a cachalot has disappeared beneath the surface, he will not appear again for anywhere from five to fifteen minutes. In the meantime, he is traveling beneath the surface. If we follow him at top speed, we can usually see him when he returns to the surface for air; but, by the time we can get close enough for it to do any good, he has already filled his lungs and dives again.

Watching a sperm whale, one has the impression that he does not move very fast. That impression is wholly incorrect. Watching a whale dive, all of the animal's movements — the movement of the tail, especially — seem desultory, almost casual. What we sometimes fail to take into account is the power in that tail, and the fact that its movements are extraordinarily well co-ordinated and graceful.

Given the whale's speed once it decides to move away, or to dive, all that we can do is to space out our team along the route that we guess the animal will take. Our cameramen wait, cameras in hand, to film whatever (if any) part of the whale they can, either full face or in profile, as he swims. Then, the Zodiac picks up its men, tries to speed past the whale, disperses them in the water once more, and the whole thing begins again. This is not an easy technique; but everyone seems to enjoy it, even the helmsmen of the Zodiac who must maneuver the craft at the direction of the cameramen.

All in all, the whole operation resembles a bullfight more than a filming session. The trouble is that, in this case, the matador's — that is, the team's — courage and skill are largely wasted. It is not a question of accumulating "points" for daring or technique, but of getting some meaningful film footage of whales in their natural habitat. From that standpoint, I must say that whales are considerably more troublesome than sharks. Using the *corrida* technique with sharks is highly dangerous, of course; but at least there is some return on the risks involved.

Such were our first contacts with sperm whales in the Indian Ocean. We were soon to meet animals even larger than these, for it was not our intention to limit ourselves to close-range observation whenever *Calypso* happened to come within the proper distance to a whale. We set out for the express purpose of making a systematic study of whales in any and every part of the sea. We were going to follow their migrations, and we would observe them mating. We would see whale calves nursing. We would record their cries, their language, their "songs"; and the whole range of sounds emitted by these surprisingly loquacious animals.

The first phase of that project is now complete. It extended over a period of years, and took us from the Bahamas to Alaska to Baja California. And I would like now to report on that expedition.

TWO

Fragile Giants of the Sea

During the nearly two days that we remained virtually in the midst of a school of sperm whales in the Indian Ocean, we are able to gain some insight into the scale of life of these giants. It is a scale possible only in the vastness and depths of the sea; for only in the sea could such monstrously huge bodies have evolved, and only there could they exist. There is, therefore, between man and the whale, a difference in scale; a chasm that separates us from them, and that makes them seem not only strange to us, but truly alien.

The whales swimming and spouting around *Calypso* were not a group of unknowing beings, not brutes. They were creatures bound together by ties, by relationships among themselves. Some of them even had distinctive characteristics—they were more daring, or more timid, or more intelligent than the others. Was this intuition? Instinct? Perhaps. But how does one find out when one is dealing with dozens of beings, each one made up of from 30 to 60 tons

(Left) After a long voyage, *Calypso* arrives within sight of the Maldives lying low in the water.

of bone, muscle, and fat?

In the water around *Calypso,* separated from us only by a few planks, there was a fantastic ballet taking place; or rather, a measured, calculated activity that seemed fantastic to us because the performers were a dozen Leviathans. We could see their glistening backs, their tails as large as the sails of a ship, and, rarely, their massive heads. If we had been able to interpret their language, we would very likely have discovered that these turnings and wheelings were not at all random movements, the result of chance, but that the entire school was following a carefully reasoned pattern of behavior. And, indeed, the hydrophones that we used to record their sounds revealed that these whales "spoke," sometimes in dialogue, by means of a series of clicks and vocal sounds.

Strangely, this observation of whales, interesting as it was, had a depressing effect upon me. We found what we came for, it is true, and there were whales all about us. But the very sight of them brought home to me the conviction that we—men and whales—were separated from each other by an impossible gulf, by a too-great disproportion in size between them, cavorting in the sea around a ship hardly bigger than they, and us, who were clustered on that ship like ants adrift on a plank.

In spite of all our techniques, despite our outboards and our Zodiacs and our launches, notwithstanding all the expertise of our teams, it seemed that we were hardly more than specks alongside those islandlike giants swimming, diving, and floating around us. On the surface, they were acceptable by human standards, because we could see only a part of their bodies. But when they dived, they were so immense, so long, and often so fast, that, watching from beneath the surface, it was impossible for us to take in the entire mass of a whale's body at one glance.

I have often felt a sense of bitterness, or rather of impotence, when confronted with the thought that in the final analysis, these marvels of nature are beyond us, beyond our senses, beyond our experience—not because they live in the sea, but because they belong to a race of giants that requires of man an intellectual and emotional flexibility, an understanding, a willingness to break away from traditional concepts, that is perhaps beyond him.

We are trying, with all the means at our disposal—our launches and Zodiacs and divers—to establish contact, to achieve a *rapprochement* with these marvels of marine life. But we are attempting to do so in the sea; and that limitless stretch of water and those great depths are not our natural environment. It is that of the giants we are observing. It was proportionate to *their* size and to *their* strength, and not to ours.

It is difficult to explain what a man's reactions are when he first comes face to face with a whale in the water, with that great living, moving, shining cylinder of black and gray. The first feeling is one of stupefaction at the size of the animal. The whale's dimensions go beyond man's experience with life forms, and beyond his expectations—so much so that incredulity follows upon astonishment. The mind rebels, and the diver wonders whether he is not dreaming, or deluded. On this point, all of our divers agree. The first sight of a whale in the water is terrifying. There is no experience on dry land that can compare with it. Another point on which there is universal agreement is that, when seen from the surface, these animals do not appear to be moving very rapidly; but for a diver in the water to touch a whale, or to grab hold of it, becomes an athletic experience —or a nightmare.

In dealing with such phenomenal beings, we have been able thus far to work out only one technique. As I have already mentioned, it involves the use of two Zodiacs. One Zodiac attempts to get ahead of the whale and, by moving directly in front of it, to slow it down. The other Zodiac puts our cameramen and divers into the water, in front of the whale to watch (and hopefully to film) the creature as it swims around them, or under them, or over them. Nothing that they can do hinders the whale's progress in the slightest. They can climb on its back, grab hold of a fin—nothing seems to bother it; it continues to move forward as though it were alone in the sea. Then, the Zodiac returns, picks up the men, and the game begins all over again. This, unfortunately, is our only method of observation; and, as empirical as it is, and as clumsy, it has had a few good results. That is, we have learned many things.

We have understood, for example, that, if we want to observe a whale for any length of time, or especially to film it, we must by all means slow it down. "We chase it, we jump into the water, we wait a second or two for our masks to clear, and begin shooting," explains André Laban. "And then when we run the film, we see that the only thing on it is the whale's tail — and then only if we were lucky. What happens is that, by the time the water settles after we have jumped in, the whale is gone."

In our attempts to slow down a school of sperm whales, or at least to isolate a single animal, we have tried different tactics with our Zodiacs and lauches. But, so great is the disproportion in size between these cachalots and our craft that we are virtually doomed to failure from the start. It seems that, in the sea, nothing can hope to prevail against these moving mountains of flesh.

An additional difficulty is that there is nothing about a whale, no reaction, no movement, no flick of a fin, no motion of the tail, that man is able to interpret with certainty. We have no idea at any given moment whether a

The virazeou technique: a Zodiac literally runs circles around a sperm whale

The whale, disturbed by the noise, tries to pass under the Zodiac.

(Facing page) The sperm whale charges the Zodiac and will overturn it.

whale is delighted or furious, or neither. When a dog snarls, or a lion roars, or a rattlesnake rattles, you know what to expect. But a whale? A sperm whale could be in a frenzy of rage for an hour before he decides to put an end to us with a flick of that incredible tail, and we would have no way of knowing it. There is no reaction that we are able to interpret as meaning that we have gone too far. For the diver, only the sight of that monstrous square mouth, with its row of glistening teeth, gives warning of what could happen. . . . And yet, we ignored even this, and for thirty-six hours we were able, with absolute impunity, to tease these apparently good-natured behemoths.

In all of this, we have had at least one satisfaction: our method of "marking" whales has been successful. "Bebert" Falco has proved, as we all expected, to be our most daring and effective marker. The helmsmen of the Zodiacs have also risen to new heights of derring-do with their little boats. For example, in maneuvering for an advantageous position for our cameramen, they have learned how to skirt over the back of a semi-immersed whale — the trick being, at the very last moment, to raise the outboard motor

so that its propeller blades do not injure the whale.

Fortunately, the sea is calm and the weather marvelous. Despite that deceptive squall, the trade winds, it turns out, are not yet upon us. And so, we continue our whale hunt and our efforts to mark a whale for observation, using the same technique as before. And we are successful. Our divers manage somehow to jump into the water right in front of the whales. (It is usually the whale who maneuvers to avoid the diver. Is this because he sees the man, or is he forewarned by his echo-location system? We do not know.) And the cameramen are now diving with tanks of compressed air on their backs. This extra weight slows down their movements, but it is necessary for them to use scuba equipment, since a harpooned whale will often dive to anywhere from fifteen to sixty-five or seventy feet. And, of course, the cameramen and divers follow him down. There is something reminiscent of a circus in this; and, as in every animal act under the big top, there is a large element of risk involved.

After one successful marking, we have been able to keep the cachalot near *Calypso* for twenty-four hours, which is a record for us. During that time, the rest of the school — about ten sperm whales — remained in the neighborhood, apparently waiting for their captive companion. Our hydrophones picked up a continual exchange of signals between the marked whale and the others during this period. The waiting whales were not scattered around *Calypso*, but swam a short distance ahead of us, usually to starboard. We could see their spouts rising at regular intervals.

It happened several times to Laban to be able to film the head of a sperm whale; literally to stick the camera into his face. Laban had the impression that the animal, despite its size, was frightened. The noise from the Zodiac's motor no doubt had something to do with it.

There has been no indication of any aggressiveness on the part of these whales during the time that we have been filming them. There are, however, certain signs that may — or may not — indicate nervousness on their part: brusque movements of the head, motions of the tail, and erratic dives.

It seems that the most frequent reaction of a sperm whale, when we try to slow it down, is to continue moving forward and to join its school. He is obviously far more inclined to flee than to confront the Zodiac — though that light craft would be an easy victim.

An Invention: The Virazeou

Bebert Falco has found a way to do what we have been trying to do since the beginning of this expedition: to stop whales long enough for us to be able to observe and film them. Bebert himself has devised a name for this technique. He calls it *virazeou* — a Provençal word that is incomprehensible unless one is familiar with the melodious accents of the South of France, but which Bebert assures us means merely "turn-turn." In any case, thanks to Bebert's virazeou, my morale is much better. This technique — which Bebert has tested on dolphins and grampuses — is fairly simple. He takes out a Zodiac, and with the outboard motor running wide open, he circles around a sperm whale, and circles, and circles. . . The whale finally is enclosed in a circle of noise and bubbles from the Zodiac's wake. His initial reaction seems to be one of annoyance, but he is quickly confused by the noise and the wake. Little by little, he becomes quiet, as though in a stupor.

Sperm whales, like all cetaceans, are creatures with very highly developed hearing. It is likely that the wall of sound with which Falco surrounds him becomes unbearable. Apparently, he reacts much in the same way to the disturbance caused by the Zodiac's wake. In any case, the whale slows, almost stops; and, for the first time in our efforts to approach these giants, we have gained an advantage.

The whale could, no doubt, have chosen to dive, to disappear into the depths in order to elude his tormentors. But he seems paralyzed by the technique of virazeou. I say "seems" paralyzed. For the first time that Falco tried it, we learned otherwise. All seemed to be going well. The Zodiac was circling, the noise was deafening, the water was boiling from the motor's wake, and the sperm whale was lying almost still in the water, just below the surface. Then there was a sudden, monstrous movement in the water. We saw the Zodiac and its passengers thrown up into the air like toys, while the motor, the cameras, and other equipment were all spilled into the sea.

The Zodiac fell back right side up, and Maurice Leandri, who was in the stern, was thrown overboard by the force of the impact, but he succeeded in climbing back aboard.

What had happened was very simple. The whale, whom we thought to be "in a stupor," had tired of the noise and the bubbles, and with one twist of its tail it had sent the Zodiac and all its occupants flying into the air. He could have done much worse. He could have attacked with his great mouth, or crushed the craft and its men with one casual stroke of his tail. Instead, he chose to give a "measured response," but an effective one. And then he continued on his way very calmly, as though the incident were already forgotten.

This power that is so sure of itself, and that little resembles the malevolent aggressiveness of a Moby Dick, is undoubtedly one of the advantages of being a giant. When one is sixty feet long and preternaturally strong, what is there to fear? In my opinion, the so-called "ferocity" of whales, and of sperm whales in particular, is a characteristic invented by man to justify his butchery of the species. Certainly, in our experience with whales, there has been not the slightest sign of any inclination to aggressive violence.

A Delicate Giant

The most striking characteristic of the great whale is its fragility. For its life, its strength, and its effectiveness as a life form, it depends entirely upon the sea. Out of the water, it has no hope of survival. A whale aground in the open air, washed up on a beach, is condemned to death. He has not the

One of the hammerhead sharks that has come to join the school of dolphins.

Our kytoon, inflated with hydrogen, is decorated with aluminum butterflies so that we can pick it up on radar.

strength, nor the limbs, to regain the life-giving water. He smothers; and it is his very size and mass that kills him. All of his power, great though it is, is not sufficient to fill his lungs, to move the tons of blubber that cover his body. And he dies of asphyxiation.

The reason for this relative dependency and delicacy goes back far in

Calypso's radar can follow the kytoon night or day.

geological time into the Miocene era. Whales first appeared in the Tertiary Era, about 25 million years ago, although their ancestry goes back much farther than that. They were at first land animals — a fact that paleontologists no longer contest. Before becoming lords of the sea, they held a more modest position on dry land. Unfortunately, no one has ever found a fossil trace of the ancestor of whales who walked the earth on four feet; and this point is the only doubtful one in the theory. On the other hand, a good number of complete whale skeletons have been discovered, in fossil form, which are anatomically very close to land mammals. They were considerably smaller than the cachalots and finback whales of today, measuring no more than 18 or 20 feet in length.

The skeleton of the present-day whale shows traces of its land-bound ancestors. There are rudimentary femurs and tibia, and the remains of a pelvic girdle, all surrounded by muscle and not connected to the spine. Moreover, the skeleton of the pectoral fins reveals that the front limbs that are now modified into flippers were once endowed with five fingers. The tail fin is not like that of the Pinnipedia (seals, walruses, and related forms), which evolved from the lower members of a terrestrial ancestor, but is a member found only among cetaceans and *Sirenia* (e.g., the mantee and the dugong).

In its long past, Earth has known creatures of enormous size, particularly in the Secondary Era, when monstrous reptiles roamed the continents — the Diplodocus, the Brontosaurus, the Brachiosaurus, the Gigantosaurus. These were the largest beasts that ever lived on land. But none of them ever approached the 130 tons of the blue whale. None of them, it appears, ever exceeded 30 or 35 tons, for the length of their bodies, though considerable, included a disproportionately long neck and tail, and thereby reduced the weight per foot of length.

These earth-bound giants were reptiles, not mammals. They dominated the life forms of earth during the Secondary Era, which is therefore called (justly) the Age of Reptiles. But, even so, their size and weight compelled them to spend their lives in the water, or at the edge of the water, for a huge amount of energy was required merely to move, on land, a mass of flesh and bone weighing 30 tons. Only in the water could a living being of such size be spared the necessity of using every ounce of its energy to move from place to place.

Among the great Sauria of the Jurassic age, a few species seem to have attained the length of the modern whale — that is, 60 to 75 feet — and still managed to exist on land. The explanation, however, is that, even though they equaled the whale in length, their body mass was much smaller — at most one fourth that of the whale. Nonetheless, a few species — the Brontosaurus, for example — still chose to live in the water; and, for that reason, its nostrils were on top of its head, as are the blowholes of the whale today.

Obviously, for these enormous quadrupeds to be able to move, it was necessary that they have enormous legs. It has been calculated that if an elephant weighed twice as much as it actually does, its feet would have to be so big that they would be wider than the elephant's body. But an elephant weighs only three to six tons — which is the approximate weight of the tongue of some whales. So, one can imagine what sort of legs and feet an animal like the Brontosaurus had.

Dinosaurs disappeared from the face of the earth with a suddenness that has always mystified paleontologists. It is possbile that their very gigantism was the cause of their downfall, for size entails numerous and important disadvantages. In any case, the giants of the Secondary Era were, so to speak, one of Nature's mistake — a mistake that was not perpetuated. Or, at least Nature was able to correct her mistake by transferring her giants to the sea and allowing them to become extinct on dry land.

The problems faced by these enormous monsters on land were virtually insoluble. And movement was not the only such problem. Even breathing was a great effort. To open its thoracic cage, which meant raising a part of its body, a creature of this size had to make an effort that presupposed extraordinarily powerful muscles and a skeleton constructed in a peculiar manner. And this is the reason why a whale out of water, even though it is an air breather, dies very quickly. Despite its incredible power, it simply does not have sufficient strength to breathe in the open air. Its skeleton is not capable of sustaining the weight of its muscles and blubber in the air, although it serves very well in the dense medium of water. On one occasion, we took a whale calf out of the water in order to nurse it, and it was necessary to place its body on a stretcher, or litter. Otherwise, its very weight would have caused even its relatively small body to "collapse."

Another problem faced by the great reptiles of the Secondary Era was that of food. In order to nourish a body such as that of the Brontosaurus, a very large amount of food was necessary. Even an elephant consumes between three and four hundred kilos of food every day. But the Brontosaurus was almost incapable of consuming what was needed, for the reason that its head was ridiculously small in proportion to its body. A beast weighing 30 tons, with a head the size of that of a horse, obviously must eat without stopping if it is not to die of malnutrition.

Both baleen whales and toothed whales have no problem in this respect, since they all have enormous heads and mouths to match. The baleen whales,

The head of the finback whale seen in the water was a pleasant surprise for us.

since they have no teeth, nourish themselves by straining millions of tiny sea animals through the rows of whalebone (baleen) hanging from their upper jaws. This requires no particular effort on their part. They simply swim with their mouths open, collecting their prey on the whalebone plates while the water runs to waste.

Pursuit is more complicated, and more arduous, in the case of the sperm whale, which has teeth in its lower jaw. This whale's natural prey includes the giant squid that live near the bottom of the sea, at depths of 1500 feet and over. In this case, the whale's size is a considerable advantage. One can imagine the amount of energy that is necessary for that massive body to propel

A finback whale's huge tail—with two divers above it.

itself to the bottom for a combat to the death with a squid that may measure more than thirty feet from tip to tip.

The size and power of whales make them monarchs of the sea. But are they monarchs without enemies? That is a moot point. Certainly, man has long preyed on whales, and even on the very largest species, such as the blue whale and the finback whale. The Basques, those early hunters of whales, pursued and killed so many right whales *(Eubalaena glacialis)* — which are particularly vulnerable because of their lack of speed (three knots) — that the species became virtually extinct along their shores.

Until the nineteenth century, however, man's career as a killer of whales was limited by the relatively primitive means of pursuit and slaughter at his command — ships propelled by sails or oars, hand winches, flimsy ropes, and hand-thrown harpoons. At this time, size was a decided advantage to a whale, for man could attack and kill only the smaller specimens. With the invention of the harpoon gun in 1864, however, the balance of power shifted. Man was now able to hunt any whale, regardless of its size; and gigantism was no longer an advantage.

But man is not the whale's only enemy. It has foes in the water as well as on land, and, among these, the most formidable is one of its relatives, the killer whale* — also known as the orc *(Grampus orca)*. The killer whale is a toothed relative of the sperm whale. It is smaller than either the baleen whale or the sperm whale, but what it lacks in size it makes up for in ferocity and in strength, and particularly in its almost diabolical intelligence. Traveling in schools, these killers do not hesitate to attack even the largest baleens.

The Ideal Solution: A Balloon

April 13. At seven o' clock in the morning we set sail toward Shab-Arab, but following a deep curve toward the end of the gulf. We do not hold to that course for very long, for, very soon, three white whales are sighted about twenty-five yards off the starboard. They are perhaps Belugas, or "white whales." We bring *Calypso* around, but are unable to locate these mammals. Then the alarm bell rings again. Sperm whales! It is incredible what one can find in the Gulf of Aden at this time of the year.

*Chapter Ten is devoted to the killer whale.

(Following page) A diver has just jumped out of the Zodiac and is about to climb onto the finback whale's head.

The pursuit of the whales begins rather badly. Rather than risk losing sight of them, I decide to try to approach them with *Calypso* while the Zodiacs are being launched. Falco therefore has to fire his harpoon from a greater distance than usual. It is a hit — but the harpoon slides off the slippery flank, taking a piece of the whale's skin with it.

Meanwhile, Bonnici is out in the Zodiac and has succeeded in reaching a group of three whales. He manages to isolate a young whale for a few minutes; but the calf's parents will have none of this, and they quickly position themselves to either side of their offspring and lead him away.

We continue trying, in vain, until early afternoon. Then, at two o' clock, there is a new alert. A very young cachalot calf has been sighted, swimming alongside its mother. As *Calypso* approaches, she is sighted by the calf — who leaves its mother's side and makes straight for the ship! I order the engines to be cut immediately. It is just in time, for no sooner have the propellers stopped revolving than the baby whale is contentedly swimming along right next to the hull. The whale mother follows its calf and remains at a cautious distance from *Calypso*, but close enough to be able to protect her baby if there should be any sign of danger.

The Zodiac goes out in an attempt to mark the mother with a light harpoon, but she seems to suspect our intentions and quickly swims away. The calf then joins its mother, and together they return to the school and we lose sight of them.

Immediately after dinner, I have a meeting with Bebert, Laban, Dumas, and Marcellin to discuss our situation. We all feel that we must have more time for whales, and so we decide to abandon our plans for Shab-Arab and devote three additional days to the pursuit of the sperm whale.

When my four friends are gone, I remain alone in my cabin to reflect a bit on our problems. And then, surprisingly, a solution occurs to me: a kytoon!* In other words we will no longer simply attach a buoy to the whale, but a balloon — something that will not merely float on the surface but actually rise into the air. This balloon will be much easier to see from *Calypso*, and especially from the Zodiacs; and we can attach a bit of aluminum to it so that we can pick it up at night on radar.

April 14. Simone is absolutely inexhaustible. She is like a worker bee in a hive. She is not only in charge of our food supply and of the wardroom, but she is spending more and more time on watch for whales. And when she is in the crow's-nest, nothing gets by her. I hope that her luck holds out; I am very eager to try out the kytoon.

---

* *Kytoon,* for all its exotic appearance, is a term composed from two English words: *kite,* and *balloon.*

The Beauty of the Finback.

Our first sighting on April 14 was not a sperm whale, but a rorqual, or finback whale *, which, after the blue whale, is the largest of the cetaceans. Here are my journal notes for that day:

Early this morning we sighted a large school of dolphins very near to *Calypso*. And, swimming around in the middle of the school, were a large number of hammerhead sharks!

During the morning, we sailed around Cape Guardafui, at the entrance to the Gulf of Aden. After having watched our two Zodiacs cavort with three schools of dolphins for a while, we heard Bebert yell: "A whale! Leave the dolphins alone, and let's go!"

The sea is very calm, and the Zodiacs are able to get up to 15 knots of speed. For two hours, they pursue the whale — a finback, apparently, between 35 and 45 feet long. Speed is absolutely necessary, of course, because the whale stays on the surface for only a short time — long enough to breathe; and then it dives and stays out of sight for ten to twenty minutes at a time. Finally, exhausted by the chase, it slows down, and it begins surfacing at shorter intervals.

Experienced whalers have no difficulty in distinguishing between the sperm whale and the finback because of the sperm whale's oblique spout. For us, however, there is a much easier way: the dorsal fin of the finback whale is large and hooked, while the only protrusion from the sperm whale's back is a sort of low and irregular crest about two thirds of the way down its length. One can also distinguish between the two species by the way they dive. The sperm whale goes straight down, so that the last thing we see before it disappears is its tail protruding from the water; but the finback whale dives at an angle. Moreover, sperm whales seem usually to travel in schools; and our finback whale appears to be alone. Apparently, they travel singly, or in groups of two or three.

Bebert's Zodiac is now in place, almost against the whale's blue-gray flank. He fires, and hits his target. The whale bolts — and we watch the harpoon line unwind at 15 knots. When the 1500 feet of polypropylene are gone, there remain another thousand feet of blue nylon line, which unwind with astonishing speed. We will soon know if the harpoon will hold.

---

* In order not to encumber the text with descriptions of the characteristics of the various species of whales, we have relegated such information to the appendices and glossary. The reader is referred especially to Appendix I for the essential distinction between baleen or whalebone whales (Mystacoceti) and toothed whales (Odontoceti).

Bebert has returned to *Calypso* and begins to secure the Zodiac when, suddenly, the harpoon line goes slack. The harpoon has not held.

Everyone is disappointed, even disheartened. But that does not keep us from getting back to work immediately. As the cameramen's Zodiac and *Calypso* continue the chase, Bebert rewinds his 2500 feet of line and reloads the harpoon gun. By the time we are within sight of the whale again, he is ready. He raises the gun, fires, and hits the whale — but the spear does not penetrate its blubber. He grabs the rubber crossbow and fires — but the steel bowstring breaks. Finally, he picks up the old-fashioned hand harpoon.

By now, the whale is tired and has slowed to eight knots. It can be seen clearly from the Zodiac, only a few feet beneath the surface. And Falco's craft approaches it easily when it rises to the surface to breathe as Bonnici, in his Zodiac, blocks the animal's way. (Bonnici's part is not as easy as it sounds. When he cut in front of the whale after it had surfaced, its great triangular tail struck the water only inches from his boat.) As soon as Falco is close enough, he fires and sticks the finback in the left flank. The spearhead penetrates — but the handle of the spear bends like a straw as soon as the whale dives. It bends — but holds. Falco allows 1500 feet of the line to run, and then he attaches a large red buoy to it. The preceding four hours' work has been only a preliminary. Now, the chase begins in earnest, with Laban and Deloire in the water shooting footage of the whale swimming by and Barsky filming from the surface. Aboard *Calypso*, we are busy making notes on everything that the whale does.

The finback is evidently bothered by the Zodiacs buzzing around her like mosquitoes. And, in view of its size, Falco's little harpoon has about the same effect as a moquito bite. It is constantly changing direction. The two Zodiacs keep the whale between them, with the cameramen on the right and the divers on the left. They jump into the water ahead of the animal and film it as it swims past. The whale is breathing very frequently now, about every fifteen seconds. Despite the heat and the dry air, the vapor of its spout can be seen from a distance.

Late in the afternoon, the cameramen's Zodiac returns to *Calypso*. Falco is already aboard, preparing the kytoon for use. The balloon is filled with hydrogen, and to its top is attached an aluminum butterfly to serve as a radar guide. Then the entire apparatus is attached to the buoy by means of a line.

As this is going on, another ship, no doubt attracted by the kytoon floating in the air, has been drawing nearer and nearer to the whale. *Calypso* diverts her by means of a few maneuvers.

Marcellin and Dumas take their sound equipment and, in one of the Zodiacs, follow the whale very closely. One of their tricks is to hang a

In pursuit of two gray whales, who have a bagful of tricks for getting away from curious humans.

microphone at the end of a pole and hold it over the whale's blowholes. We are rewarded by a tape of the whale breathing — like a series of muffled cannon shots.

This finback whale is truly an exceptional subject. Exceptional, first of all, because of its size, for it is larger than any of the sperm whales that we have seen on this expedition. It is also more handsome, with its marvelous head (which appears rather serpentine when the mouth is closed), and with a body less massive than that of the sperm whale. There is no neck discernible. Altogether, it is a perfect body from the viewpoint of hydrodynamics, and a graceful and elegant one. Its color is also lighter, more silky and "luxurious" than the sperm whale's.

Aboard *Calypso*, everyone is delighted with "our" whale. It is the consensus that finbacks are much more easily approachable than cachalots. This, no doubt, has something to do with the fact that this particular whale is traveling alone. It does not belong to a group from which it would be unwilling to be separated.

"There seems to be only one thing that sperm whales want," Michel Deloire, says, "and that is to get away from us so that they can rejoin their school. They would even push us aside in order to get back to their friends. Our whale, however, is much more casual about the whole thing. She seems to have all the time in the world, and has no appointment to keep with her friends. And, aside from that, this whale is a truly remarkable animal; ten times, or a hundred times, more beautiful than a sperm whale. I could swear that, with its flat head, it looks as though it is always smiling. If you see a finback directly from the front, it looks like one big smile — as though there were something friendly about it, or as though it has a sense of humor. In fact, this whale of ours is the only animal I have ever seen that really astonishes me."

During the night, a duty team remains in the Zodiac to keep an eye on the buoy and the kytoon. Naguy has installed a blinking light on the kytoon so that it is easily visible. All through the hours of darkness, we were aware of what the whale was doing. At times, she halted completely. And sometimes she would sprint forward at six or seven knots.

Saturday, May 13. Today we have organized our time so as to be able to take advantage, as much as possible, of our whale's presence. At dawn, Barsky and Deloire are at work taking pictures of the kytoon and *Calypso*. This is followed by underwater photographs of the whale, using the same technique with the Zodiacs as yesterday. That is, the Zodiac pursues the whale. The whale dives, reappears slightly to the north, and begins swimming eastward. All this Deloire films from a Zodiac with an underwater camera. Barsky is in the other Zodiac with a regular camera.

Everything is going very well. Too well, I suspect, for it to last. And, sure enough, the unforeseeable occurs. The finback executes a half turn around one of the Zodiacs and the harpoon line becomes entangled in the propeller blades of one of the Zodiacs. An extraordinary scene follows: the whale dives, and begins dragging the Zodiac down with it. One can imagine how much power is required to submerge a large inflatable raft like the Zodiac! Fortunately, Falco, with great presence of mind, knows exactly what to do. In an instant, just as the Zodiac is beginning to go down, he quickly hands all the cameras and equipment to the other Zodiac and then cuts the line. The whale is now free — but the alternative would have been to lose the Zodiac.

Perhaps yesterday we were guilty of a bit of anthropomorphism in describing our whale as "friendly." Obviously, she cares very little for us; and right now, no doubt, she is swimming merrily on her way without giving the slightest thought to us.

Falco, however, is more faithful than his whale. As soon as the line is untangled from the Zodiac's propeller, he sets out in hot pursuit — and succeeds in implanting another harpoon. We are back where we started yesterday, as *Calypso* follows as best she can the gyrations and maneuvers of Zodiacs and whale.

Deloire, taking no chances, is now using his Tegea in the water, and the results are sensational. For the first time, a finback has been observed and filmed under the surface. It is a great moment for Michel. Also for Bonnici, who has jumped into the water, latched onto the whale's dorsal fin, and is being towed as by some nightmarish locomotive. Another first! And Barsky, not to be outdone, joins in the fun and films Bonnici's acrobatic exploits.

Laban and Bebert, meanwhile, are in the water with their still cameras. The results show a long, supple body. At one point, they were so close that they saw an enormous eye staring at them from only three feet away.

Late in the afternoon, Barsky's Zodiac starts back to *Calypso* — and once more the harpoon line becomes entangled in its propeller. This time, Falco is taking no chances. He cuts the line immediately and Barsky — by now standing on *Calypso*'s deck — films our farewell to the valorous finback as it swims away on our portside, as indifferent to us as ever (or at least so we think).

After dinner, Bebert, Dumas, Laban, and the cameramen meet to go over their shots and sequences and to determine what remains to be done. "The finback," Laban says, "is more impressive than the sperm whale because it is bigger. This one must have been fifty feet long. And, for a diver, the sperm whale's big square head has something monstrous about it — it makes up almost a third of the whale's body. It looks like someone made a mistake in judging proportions, and then gave up before finishing the job. But that well-shaped and handsome finback head — that comes as a pleasant surprise when you are used to sperm whales."

The finback whale's apparent gentleness is also in its favor. Regardless of whether or not it is naturally gentle, the fact remains that it cannot really bite, since it has no teeth. The divers took advantage of this to the extent that they approached the finback more freely, and treated it more familiarily, than they would have a cachalot. They were not deterred, as they always are in dealing with sperm whales, by the sight of those great teeth gleaming in the water. Even so, the finback is not a helpless creature. It has a weapon, and a terrible weapon, for use against sharks and killer whales: the enormous flukes of its tail — what Bebert calls its "fly swatter." This fly swatter is capable of crushing a man with one blow.

"As long as you stay in front of the animal," Deloire says, "there is nothing to be afraid of. Its front part is not frightening at all. Once half of its body has swum past you, though, you must begin to be careful, and remember that you move more slowly in the water than on land. When you see that huge tail waving in the water and covering a large area of it, it's time to get out of the way. Otherwise, it's like being hit with a ton of bricks."

Humpback Whales and Gray Whales.

All whales do not look alike in the water. There are differences, even among the giants. Finback whales, as we just observed, are enormous — and indifferent. Humpback whales — such as we already filmed in Bermuda — are endowed with a suppleness and a grace that are reminiscent simultaneously of a swallow and a Boeing 707. Their flippers are white and very long and, in the water, look like wings. The humpback uses them to turn. These whales do not swim, like the finback, in a straight line. And, unlike sperm whales, they are easily approachable and sometimes brush against divers as they swim around, turning and circling back, probing with their long cylindrical heads and slightly receding chins. What the humpback whale does not have, however, is a humped back. They got the name from their practice of showing the napes of their necks and their backs when they dive.

It should come as no surprise that our divers have favorites among the different species of whales. They have lived with whales, and they found some species disappointing; and others, delightful and admirable.

The whale that our team has the greatest affection for is the gray whale of California, with whom we lived for several months.

"The first time I saw a gray whale," Philippe Cousteau says, "I jumped into a Zodiac and grabbed a camera. As soon as I was in front of the whale, I dived into the water — forgetting to put on my diving equipment. I practically landed on top of it, but it didn't seem a bit disturbed, and didn't try to turn away. I could see, somewhat fuzzily, its immense mouth — a mouth unlike any that I had ever seen before. And then I saw its body as it swam past me. Its movements seemed incomparably supple; they were not separate motions, but one beautifully co-ordinated action. I was struck by the hydrodynamic perfection of its power, by its invincibility . . . It disappeared, finally, because I simply could not swim fast enough to keep up with even its casual pace. I climbed back into the Zodiac and put on my mask, and then dived again. But the spell had been broken. I had to worry about the camera, about angles, about my breathing equipment; I could no longer give myself over

The bleak mountains of the African coast around Cape Guardafui. *Calypso*'s aft is in the foreground.

entirely to the feeling of admiration. But, for a brief time there, it had seemed that whale and I had reached a perfect understanding."

Approaching a whale *beneath* the surface of the water — that is, while diving — is very different from doing so on the surface. Zodiacs, spearguns, and buoys no doubt have an effect upon an animal's reaction to man, even though we do not know exactly what that effect is. We do know, however, that whenever we approach a whale in his own element, without such apparatus and equipment, we experience a feeling of understanding, or sympathy, or empathy.

Philippe states categorically that he has never encountered a whale that showed the slightest sign of hostility. But then, we must add that no whale encountered by Philippe had just been harpooned, even by a light spear such as that used by Bebert. (Understandably, Philippe dislikes the idea of "marking" whales. At Bermuda, for example, he was strongly opposed to our doing so to the humpback whales we saw there.)

"I could swear that they know how weak we are," Philippe says. "One stroke of the tail, or of a fin, or a bump with the head — that would be it as far as a man is concerned. But they've never done anything like that. The impression I've always gotten is one of extraordinary gentleness. They usually try to avoid us, but when they swim away they move slowly, gently — not suddenly, the way that fish do. . ."

It is not impossible that there is an element of sexuality in a whale's behavior. Once, Philippe encountered a gray whale who was behaving rather strangly, swimming back and forth and turning over on her back. She was obviously not pregnant, but her sexual organs were turgid, inflamed, she was possibly "in heat." Perhaps she was hoping for sexual contact with these strange new forms of marine life — the diver, or the Zodiac. (We have recorded the same phenomenon with Dolly the Dolphin, whose sexual appetites were, to say the least, obvious.)

In any event, I can say that, in these underwater encounters, there exists an element of attraction to one living being from another, from one mammal to another. Despite the great difference in size between man and whale, we are not indifferent to one another.

THREE

When Whales Travel

Whales love to travel. A very strong instinct leads them to winter in equatorial seas, where the water is warm, and to summer in the arctic and antarctic regions.

Whalers used to take advantage of these migratory habits to attack schools of whales, and succeeded in slaughtering large numbers of the animals. Despite this contact, we know very little about the details of these migrations or about the behavior of cetaceans while traveling thousands of miles through the oceans.

It was our intention to follow the whales and, making use of every means at our disposal, to get as close to them as possible — not only with our Zodiacs, but by diving among them — and to film them.

The gray whales of California, who leave the Arctic in January for a southward migration to Baja California, where they mate and give birth, seemed to us to offer a splendid opportunity for the observation of whales in migration.

Here is a transcript of Bernard Delemotte's account of one of the most

A gray whale tries to elude its pursuers by diving.

dramatic episodes of this three-month expedition to the Pacific:

"*January 23, 1968.* It is 2 P.M. The Zodiac is in the water and the cameras are in place on their foam-rubber pads. Yves Omer is our cameraman on this occasion. He has already suited up and taken his place in the Zodiac, on the portside, ready to grab his camera and dive at a moment's notice. Falco is all the way forward.

"We set out after our subject, a large gray whale who, unfortunately, is swimming very fast. So much the worse for us. We must still try; for in two hours there will no longer be enough light for underwater filming.

"We manage to keep up with the whale by maintaining a speed of five or six knots, and then accelerating whenever she comes up to breathe. Yves has already been over the side three times, but conditions have not really been ideal. In order to get full shots of the animal's head, we have to time ourselves almost to the split second. If the diver goes down too soon, the whale turns aside to avoid him; and if he dives too late, the film will show only the body and tail.

"We have decided not to dive from the Zodiac unless we are absolutely certain of our timing, even if this means missing a few opportunities offered by the whale's surfacing.

"The chase continues. Very exciting — despite the fact that, whenever we hit a wave, it is like running into a stone wall. Each time the whale surfaces, we are in a slightly better position. Now, we are only 150 feet away.

An accident: the gray whale charges the Zodiac while Bernard Delemotte tries to protect Yves Omer by pulling him toward the rear.

"She surfaces, and I speed up, We are almost even with her. She dives — but we can still see her. She can't be more than 25 or 30 feet beneath the surface, and we can make out the movements of her enormous body.

"Bebert Falco, from his vantage point forward, can see her better than I. He guides me by gestures so that the Zodiac can remain directly above her. Yves already has the camera in his hand, for the whale will have to come back to the surface to breathe at any moment now. And we intend to be there when she does.

"She is quite obviously bothered by the Zodiac's engine noise. She turns first to the right, then to the left. She speeds up, then slows down. Thanks to Bebert's sharp eyes, I am able to keep the Zodiac directly over her. Now the whale seems to be rising. I cut the motor and immediately Yves Omer is over the side, camera clutched in his hand.

"Then I hear Bebert's yell: 'Watch out ! . . .'

"But it is already too late, I hear an incredible sound, like a giant waterfall. Is it the whale spouting? Is it merely the water that she is displacing as she breaks the surface?

"I see a gigantic, monstrous head above the water, only ten or twelve feet from the Zodiac and looming up over it. Then I see a great black mass rising next to the boat, and, somewhere between me and the whale's body, I catch a glimpse of one of Yves's legs. . .

"I never did figure out exactly what caused the roar of water that I heard.

The next thing I knew, the whale's body had struck the Zodiac and Omer and I were both thrown violently into the water. I could tell from the water pressure in my ears that we were going down, deep.

"I knew that I was still alive, and I had my eyes wide open. But all I could see was blackness. I tried to swim, but, somehow, I could not move a muscle. I was squashed flat against a living wall of flesh. Against my left cheek, I could feel soft skin. I was pinned against the whale's body. But that was only on one side of me. I was being held there — by what?

"I realized what must have happened. The Zodiac and I had gone down together; and we were both trying to get to the surface at the same time and from the same place. I was trapped beneath the Zodiac and the whale's stomach.

"My first reaction was one of anger. I was furious to think that, after surviving a head-on collision with a whale, I might drown because an inflatable raft was holding me *under* the whale.

"Then, suddenly, my arms and legs were free. I kicked, and began to move. I rose straight up, as though I were climbing a ladder. It seemed to take forever, and I needed desperately to breathe.

"Finally, my head was above the surface, and I heard a yell: 'My leg, my leg!' It was Yves. He had been hooked to the Zodiac by a line, and had risen to the surface with it. But now he was thrashing around about thirty feet from the Zodiac, entangled in pieces of clothing and a coil of line.

"I yelled back, 'Hold on, I'm coming!' I grabbed his hand with one of mine and, with the other, pulled myself onto the Zodiac. Then I helped him climb aboard. All the while, I avoided looking at his legs. I was afraid to see one of them crushed. . . or missing. Fortunately, it was not nearly that bad. At the moment of impact, Yves's leg was caught between the whale and the Zodiac; but it was an inflatable section of the Zodiac, and the air had cushioned the leg somewhat. Even so, it was quite a blow; but there seemed to be no broken bones.

"Bebert had been just a bit more lucky. He had had time to jump overboard — but he had forgotten that he was also tied to the Zodiac by a harness. He had been dragged along for about sixty feet, until the snap hook had broken because of the violence of the traction.

"The second Zodiac soon picked us up and towed us back to *Calypso*. Our friends, somewhat pale, were waiting for us on deck. They had been able to see everything that was happening in the water, while we had been otherwise occupied. They saw the whale leap out of the water and fall back with an immense splash. When the water had calmed, they said, there was nothing to be seen on the surface. No whale, no Zodiac, and no men. At least fifteen

Canoë Kientzy, ready for a dive.

Bernard Delemotte, Philippe Cousteau, and Jacques Renoir during our stay with the gray whales.

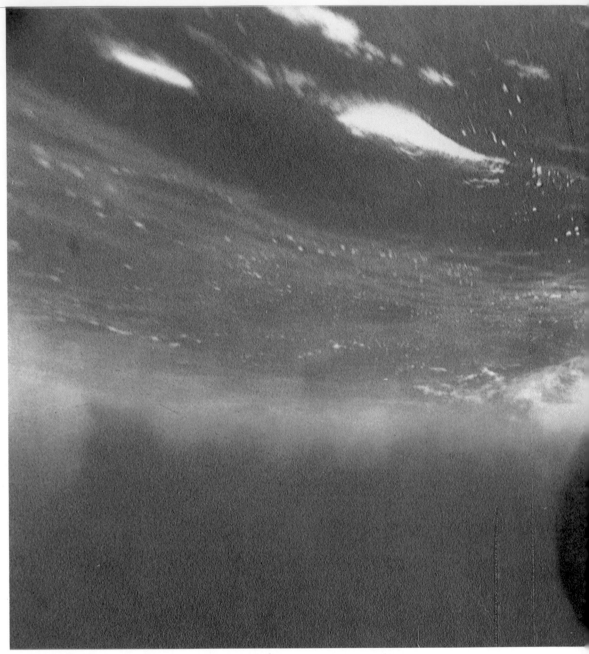

A diver has succeeded in grabbing onto the tail of a finback whale.

seconds had passed before the Zodiac reappeared, 150 feet away from where it had gone down. Then one head appeared above the surface. Then another. And then another.

"We are being very offhand about the whole thing, but we are all rather shaken.

"The final tally shows that Yves Omer has a dislocated knee. The Zodiac: an inflatable section has been ripped off and punctured, the flooring has been reduced to kindling, and the gas tank has been smashed flat."

The Salvation of a Species

One may gather from Bernard's account that whale chasing is not always a safe occupation. Up until then, the whales we encountered had always seemed rather gentle; but, on this occasion in the Pacific, we were dealing with gray whales.

At the beginning of 1968, my son Philippe had heard some talk about these gray whales, *Eschrichtius glaucus*. This species, threatened with extinction during the nineteenth century and at the beginning of the twentieth, is now protected by international agreement. The measures taken have been so effective that the species is now flourishing — so much so that, in the past few years, hunting permits have been issued for 600 gray whales. The total number of these whales, worldwide, is estimated at 20,000 specimens.

Gray whales winter in the Arctic, feeding on plankton off the Siberian coast, in the Bering Sea, and in the waters of Korea and northern California. In winter, they migrate to the warm waters of Baja California, off the Mexican coast.

Since gray whales swim close in along the California coast, their migrations have been observed more carefully than those of other species. And there are always crowds of people who gather to do so. It is known as the "Moby Dick Parade," and it is undoubtedly the best free show On the West Coast: 40, 50, and sometimes 75 whales a day swim by on their way to Baja California.

In San Diego, interested persons have formed an association for the conservation and defense of the species, and also to lead them back out to sea when they lose their way inside a port.

"Whale watchers" follow the course of the migration with great interest from watch towers, and help the whales whenever help is needed.

Gray whales migrate southward for a well-defined reason: some of them are going to mate, and others are going to give birth, in the shallow, warm water of the Mexican lagoons. In the nineteenth century, whalers — and particularly one Captain Charles Melville Scammon, who discovered the secret of the gray whales' destination — slaughtered many of these animals. But, since the species has been protected, both males and females have returned in large numbers to these sheltered lagoons. And it was there that we hoped to be able to observe them at close quarters.

Our rendezvous, it seemed to us, could be scheduled in advance, for one could almost set a clock by the gray whales' migratory schedule. On the same date of any given year, they are always at the same spot. And they always pass through the Bering Straits on the same day.

Philippe Reconnoiters

In February 1967, Philippe was in San Diego on the first leg of his reconnaissance of the gray whales. At that time, *Calypso* was in the Indian Ocean, and unavailable. Philippe therefore rented a Cessna. He then invited Wally Green, and Professor Ted Walker, a specialist in gray whales, to accompany him on a flight down the West Coast to Mexico.

Philippe's primary interest in this flight was to determine whether, and where, we could film the gray whales. In that respect, he gathered much useful data. It was too late in the migratory season, however, to mount an expedition to follow the whales, and Philippe concentrated on finding the lagoon in Baja California that seemed to be the most promising for observation and filming of the whales.

When his work was done, Philippe joined us aboard *Calypso* in the Indian Ocean, and he quickly persuaded me that it would be worth our while to organize an expedition the next year in order to film the gray whales of California. His enthusiasm was contagious.

We first planned to follow the whales from the time they reached San Diego, in January, during their migration southward. But *Calypso*'s heavy schedule made it impossible for her to be in San Diego at that time. I therefore decided to rent another boat, *Polaris III* — a small boat that seemed adequate for the expedition — and to turn the project over to Philippe.

It Begins

The *Polaris III* left San Diego on January 16, 1968. Aboard with the regular team was Ted Walker, a gray-bearded scholar with a passionate interest in whales, who was to be of great help.

The migrating whales were traveling in small groups, and generally were swimming in water not over 650 feet deep. The *Polaris III* was exactly on time, and it had no trouble in sighting many groups, all visible and recognizable by their spouts.

As soon as a group of whales realized that they had been seen, they all dived together. But this was a trick. While the group as a whole was making a 90 turn underwater, a solitary gray whale remained on the surface, directly in front of the *Polaris,* to lead the boat on a merry chase.

This strategem — which I do not find described in any of the accounts of the whalers — demonstrates an extraordinary amount of understanding and communication among the members of the group of whales. How else does one particular whale know that it is his responsibility to distract the pursuers while the other whales escape?

Even more surprising was the fact that this ruse was put into effect immediately, as though it had been rehearsed, or used, many times in the past.

Whales know more than one trick. It happened on one occasion that the decoy whale made a great show of diving and then reappearing to the rear of the *Polaris,* hoping no doubt to throw us even further off the track of the group. Sometimes, the whale would pop up to port, and then to starboard. There were many variations. It was by no means a fixed, invariable plan. The decoy whale's behavior seemed to be largely extemporized according to the requirements of the situation.

It seems to me that such varied behavior presupposes that whales are able, to a certain extent, to exchange abstract concepts, such as "left," "right," "up," and "down," and to communicate an order to maneuver — that is, to reverse their direction.

They Sleep, But Not Much

Faced with this new and clever species of whale, the *Polaris'* team had to start almost from scratch, forgetting what we had learned so painfully in 1967, in the Indian Ocean, about cachalots.

First of all, it must be said that no one ever succeeded in filming a gray

A gray whale spouts at the surface.

whale migrating toward Baja California. Every time a diver jumped into the water, the whale was somehow, and immediately, 35 or 45 feet away from him. It always takes about five seconds after a diver jumps into the water from the Zodiac for his mask to clear and for him to get his direction. And that is plenty of time for a gray whale to flick its tail and disappear, leaving the diver, to all appearances, alone in the sea.

The cruise down the California coast took a relatively long time. It took the *Polaris'* team a full month before they were able to mark a whale so as to slow her down and be able to track her during the migration. This particular whale was the source of some important data; for example:

That gray whales sleep in half-hour "naps," six or seven times a day;

That they swim all night long, without stopping;

That they eat while they are migrating — a fact that was in doubt up until then. There can be no mistake about it. When a whale starts swimming in circles in shallow water, where there is plankton on the surface, it is obvious that she is eating. It seems that the California coast has their favorite foods in abundance.

The tail of one of Matancitas Bay's gray whales.

To give an idea of the problems that Bernard Mestre's team encountered on this first gray-whale expedition, I would like to quote from the expedition's journal:

A Near Shipwreck

January 23. In the open sea off San Diego we have run into vast areas of kelp — that is, giant algae of the Pacific that measure no less than 65 feet in length. We have noticed that gray whales like to roll around in kelp, and there are two of them doing so at this moment.

We intend to film them, and we are very fortunate. The water is absolutely calm. A short distance away, we can see several spouts. The *Polaris* is proceeding at reduced speed. The Zodiacs are launched noiselessly and are rowed among the algae. Meanwhile, the whales are still rolling around, showing not the slightest intention of running away. This will be a great scene on film.

January 24. At 9 A.M. a whale passes under the *Polaris,* and every amateur cameraman on board is hanging over the railing.

Around 10 A.M. we begin pursuing an isolated whale swimming southward. Falco manages to sink a harpoon to which is attached a bag of fluorescein. The fluorescein will allow us to track the animal and even to know beforehand where she will surface. This is a new device that we are trying to perfect.

The whale's dives are becoming shorter and shorter: 35 seconds now. She is worried and nervous. Going past Minson Bay — a large beach near San Diego — we had a scare: we thought that she would go aground in 20 feet of water.

At a given moment, the Zodiac catches up to the whale's tail by going forward at full speed, and then cutting the motor and letting the boat's momentum carry it the last few feet. The men can see the whale below them in the water, 10 or 12 feet below the surface. She is almost absolutely still. Then, suddenly, she moves upward toward the Zodiac and turns on her side. Delemotte and his men can see her eye, which appears to be watching them. It even seems that there is a flicker of interest in that shining orb. Then she rises a few more feet until she is up against the Zodiac, as though to get a closer look at its occupants. Next, using her left flipper, which she has slipped under the Zodiac, she raises the craft, and the men, three feet out of the water — and then suddenly pulls away the flipper. The Zodiac comes crashing down; but the men foresaw the attack and lay down in the boat, and were able to keep from being thrown overboard. In fact, there is no damage at all.

Jacques Renoir, aboard the other Zodiac, was filming the whole spectacular scene.

January 25. We continued southward almost the whole night; and, at the first light of dawn, the *Polaris* was surrounded by whales!

About a mile to the south, we can see a whale jumping. At least once her entire body was out of the water.

We begin by pursuing a group of four whales, who react, as usual, in an apparently disorganized manner, This is around 8 A.M. and we hope that, by the end of the morning, we will have harpooned one of them.

The shoreline has changed its appearance considerably since yesterday. Then, we were sailing along an inhabited coast; but now the shore seems empty, desolate — but beautiful nonetheless. We must be in Mexican waters. The land seems flat, but directly in front of us are some islands, high out of the water, among which we will have to maneuver in order to follow our whales.

At 10 A.M. we notice a group of five whales in the water, swimming about in all directions, surfacing often, and showing their flippers more than they usually do. Ted Walker, stroking his salt-and-pepper beard, explains that they are probably trying to mate — "trying," he says, because it is not easy for whales to do so.

We try to get in closer and harpoon one of the females; but the animal shakes off the harpoon within ten seconds, after having twisted it into a pretzel.

We have often discussed why our harpoons always seem to become dislodged. Is it because the barbs are too short? Or too long? Yet, the harpoon does sink into the whale's blubber.

In this particular instance, the harpoon entered at an angle, and was probably pulled out by the traction of the water. After quick consultation, it is decided to continue using this type of harpoon and gun.

Philippe wants to try the harpoon himself, and we begin pursuing another group. (We have a wide selection to choose from.)

The sky is now cloudy, and the sea absolutely still. It will probably rain tonight. We are only about a quarter mile from shore, and a crowd of porpoises is accompanying us.

At 4 P.M. Philippe has his chance and throws the harpoon. It appears to be a miss, and the whales disappear. When we retrieve the harpoon, however, we see that it was not a miss at all. The head penetrated the whale's side, but then came out without the barbs being able to fasten into the whale's blubber. It is possible that the barbs are not spread out enough. It seems that we are jinxed.

An hour later, we see another group, this one with four whales, and we try to catch up with them. But it seems that we may have already tried this group. (How do you tell one group of gray whales from another?) In any case, they will not let us near them.

The *Polaris* is now in shallow water, over a rocky bottom. The Zodiac is close by. We are using sonar, and moving very slowly and carefully to avoid an accident on the rocks.

At 5:20 we are informed by radio that Canoë has shot a harpoon, but that the line caught in the Zodiac's propellor and was cut. Ted Walker says that a 40-hp motor is too loud and too fast, and so it is impossible to come to a quick stop — hence, today's accident.

January 26. This morning the weather is gray and chilly. There is a large swell from the southeast that sprang up during the night, and it is doing some minor damage — broken dishes, etc.

Several groups of whales are swimming in front of us at 170°.

We spent the night at anchor near a small island called Saint Martin. This island is inhabited by birds — millions of birds, especially pelicans and cormorants — and by a colony of sea lions. There are a few human residents, too: a few fishermen, who inhabit the end of the island where there are no birds or sea lions. It is an edifying example of peaceful coexistence.

Despite the unpleasant weather, Canoë scores a hit with his harpoon, and we see the red buoy bouncing along on the surface. But, once more, the line breaks — perhaps cut, this time, by barnacles, the parasites that attach themselves to the backs of gray whales and give them a mottled appearance.

We add 250 feet of new line and decide to try again. We pass within touching distance of a submerged bank where the water is only five feet deep. It is easy to tell where these are: there are breakers.

Thousands of birds are perched on a tiny spot of land in the water. When they see us, they take wing with a deafening screech.

The Hand Harpoon

We follow a group of five whales, and then a group of three. It is a fine shot — but the harpoon does not hold. Everyone on board, all the harpooners or aspirant harpooners, vow never again to use our Norwegian harpoon gun — or, at least, never again today. It is decided that we will use the good old

(Right) A diver exploring the kelp forest off San Diego Cape.

hand harpoon that nineteenth-century whalers used. We have one aboard the *Polaris*.

Ted Walker who, I believe, has never run across such a totally committed team, is very enthusiastic about the experiment.

A group of eight whales appears in the distance — at about two miles — and is immediately pointed out by the men on watch. The Zodiac is on their trail at once, and tries to keep one animal always in sight. At 2:15, Canoë, standing forward in the Zodiac, in the traditional harpooner's stance, throws his weapon — with such force that he breaks the harpoon's stem and almost falls overboard onto the whale's back. Even so, the harpoon's head remains embedded in the whale, and we can see a trail of red ribbons — another one of our tracking devices — streaking through the water. But the ribbons do little good. The whale dives, taking her ribbons with her into the mysterious depths. Perhaps we will see her again in a lagoon of Baja California, still with the ribbons.

January 27. We are now near the lagoons. We can see the high sand dunes, that give this area its desert appearance, along the coast. Immediately in front of the channel into Scammon Lagoon, there is an island looming high out of the water: Cedros. We anchored off of Cedros last night.

At seven o'clock, we are under way, going south, past the mountains of Cedros whose red and yellow cliffs look like copper in the morning sun. The crests of the mountains are hidden by billowing white clouds.

The whale chase begins for the Zodiacs. But we are distracted. A friendly and photogenic sea lion wants to play, and Philippe and Bernard Delemotte cannot resist him. They cut the motor in sufficient time not to frighten him by its noise, and they dive and cavort with the animal for a while. It is a fine sequence — but, unfortunately, not the one that we came to Baja California for.

It seems that the island of Cedros is the point at which the migrating gray whales divide into two groups. Some of them swim between the island and the mainland and almost all enter Scammon Lagoon. Those who continue swimming in the open sea go on to the Matàncitas lagoon or the Bay of Magdalena. A few of them even go down to the southernmost point of Baja California.

The *Polaris* follows those who are going farther south, and we inaugurate a new tactic for the Zodiacs. We sneak up on the whales, as it were, without ever accelerating the motor or racing it, but by maintaining the same speed even when the whales slow down. This seems to be working very well. A Zodiac gets to within 25 or 30 feet of a whale — the closest it has ever been. But then the Zodiac's helmsman becomes nervous and speeds up. The result is instantaneous: the whale disappears.

Another tactic: we cut the Zodiac's motor and try to row to two whales not very far off. But they see us, or sense us, and are gone in a flash.

At one o'clock we head back to the *Polaris,* tired, hungry, and a little discouraged. Have we come all this way for nothing? No, we decide, we have not. This afternoon, come what may, we are going to harpoon a whale.

And we do. By the middle of the afternoon, we have had a successful shot. The harpoon penetrates into the blubber, and the whale streaks off with the buoy trailing behind it. The line holds — for all of two minutes.

Our "jinx" is beginning to curb our enthusiasm a bit.

A Tap on the Head

If there is a man aboard the *Polaris* who is a part of everything that we undertake, it is Ted Walker. By his advice and his almost intuitive knowledge of whale behavior he has become indispensable. Philippe and his friends find him untiring, always pleasant, and always ready to answer questions. Moreover, his affection for whales is contagious.

To our young divers, Professor Walker is an "elderly gentleman," a respected authority on a mysterious subject. But Ted is also an expert on putting people at ease and making them forget the generation gap.

He does not seem to mind at all that we are all jammed into the *Polaris* like sardines into a can. I think that the sight of a whale spouting makes him forget everything else in the world.

Ted, no doubt to warn our divers against taking foolish chances, has told them the story of his friend Rick Grigg, who almost lost his life diving. Rick had gone down with an aqua-lung one day, and when he surfaced he saw a gray whale so close that he could simply stretch out his hand and touch it. And he did. He felt the flesh quiver, like a horse's flesh; and then the sea exploded into blackness.

The next thing Rick Grigg knew, he was lying on the deck of his diving companion's boat, with a serious wound on his forehead. He still has the scar from that light tap of a whale's tail — a tail encrusted with barnacles.

Techniques of Marking

The kind of marking that the *Polaris* was trying to accomplish among the gray whales of Baja California was exactly the same kind that we succeeded in doing with cachalots in the Indian Ocean. It is a very superficial kind of

A finback whale tows a diver holding onto its dorsal fin.

wound, that does not harm the animal in the slightest. In fact, the harpoon markers that we use do not penetrate the whale's skin as deeply as those used by the International Whaling Commission; and even the Commission's harpoons do not do any damage to the whale. These harpoons have been found not only buried in a whale's blubber, but even enveloped and hidden by new layers of blubber.

If we have had so much trouble making our harpoons stick and attaching a buoy to a gray whale, it is because we absolutely refuse to use any sort of weapon that might actually injure a whale. Instead, we use a very light harpoon — so light, it seems, that the whale is able to shake it off almost immediately.

Little by little, however, we are learning to do our marking as quickly, and as gently, as possible. We have discovered that the best method is to stay about forty feet behind a whale while it is under the surface, and then to wait until it surfaces. It is also helpful occasionally to cut the engine for a few seconds in order to confuse the whale as to the Zodiac's distance from him.

A sperm whale near the surface.

There is, however, no absolute rule in whale chasing. Everyone on the team brings his own particular qualities to it. Some have ingenuity; others, quick reflexes, and others, strength. What it requires of everyone, in addition, is nerves of steel.

The Parasites

Everyone aboard the *Polaris III,* including myself when I brought *Calypso* to join the expedition, ended up by developing a special affection for gray whales — and this despite all the tricks they played on us. It is difficult not to sympathize with beings of such intelligence — in the same way as we are attracted to a brilliant, but difficult, child.

Even so, we must admit that gray whales are not the handsomest of creatures. Their bodies, and the huge triangular tails, are covered with spots which are parasite scars.

The presence of parasites on whales is related to their migratory habits. In warm waters, they pick up barnacles, that look like (and are often mistaken for) mollusks. They are, however, small crustaceans: *Cirripedia*. These fauna drill deep into the delicate skin of the cetaceans in much the same way that a relative of these parasites, the acorn barnacle, attaches itself to rocks. But, as soon as the whales enter the colder waters of the Arctic, the parasites drop off. Fortunately, birds also help to rid the unhappy cetaceans of these "whale fleas."

Among these scars, there are other marks, semicircular in form, that seem to be left by lamprey bites.

Along the coasts of Siberia, some gray whales have found a clever method of ridding themselves of all kinds of salt-water parasites. They literally take showers at the foot of the cliffs from which fresh water pours into the sea.

Perennial Travelers

A common but erroneous belief is that whales have taken refuge in cold waters because they have been so much hunted by man. Actually, their migrations have to do with temperature and nourishment rather than safety. Plankton, the crustaceans favored by baleen whales, is plentiful in the Arctic and Antarctic during the summer. Tropical seas, on the other hand, offer ideal conditions during the winter for mating and giving birth. And in the Antarctic, during the summer, when the water is at a temperature of 0°C, cetaceans find an abundance of krill *(Euphausia superba)* which is their staple diet. The whales who go to the Antarctic, like their cousins who go to the Arctic during the summer, also, when winter comes, migrate; but they migrate northward, toward the warm equatorial waters.

"We now know," Professor Budker writes, "that there are two populations of baleen whale, one in the Northern Hemisphere, and the other in the Southern Hemisphere; and we know that the two groups do not mingle."

Humpback Whales

Humpback whales, remarkable for their large white flippers and their songs, have unusual migratory habits. Between January and March, they go to the Caribbean, in the area of Puerto Rico, the Bahamas, and the Virgin Islands. In April, May, and June, they are off the American coast near the

Carolinas, to the west of the Gulf Stream. They remain in the shallow water around Bermuda, where we have had the opportunity to film them and record their extraordinary sounds. This stopover in Bermudan waters allows them to rest in preparation for their migration to the northeast, which will take them toward Iceland and Norway.

Because their migrations are so predictable, humpback whales have suffered a great deal from whalers, particularly in the vicinity of Newfoundland, along the southern coast of Labrador, and around New Zealand and Australia.

Humpback whales have certain characteristics that leave them at the mercy of whalers. They swim slowly along in coastal waters, near to shore; and when they are feeding or mating, they do not flee when approached — as we learned at Bermuda.

Until recently, humpback whales were hunted relentlessly by whalers using helicopters, sonar, and harpoon cannons to destroy what is left of the last schools. And, as humpback whales tend to sink when they are dead, their carcasses are inflated with compressed air to keep them afloat. No group of animals can survive this sort of technological slaughter. If the humpback whale is to survive, it will only be because the whaling industry, in condemning a species to extinction, also condemns itself to extinction.

A 500-Horsepower Engine

In every account of an encounter with whales, as well as in the hundreds of photographs that we have taken, it is easy to see how important the tail is to all cetaceans. It is at once a weapon (which is sometimes used against divers), and a means of locomotion which enables them to migrate. It has been estimated that the tail of a whale is the equivalent of a 500-horsepower engine.

No one who has ever encountered a whale in the water will think that this is an exaggeration. A diver who brushes against a whale has the impression that he has just had an encounter with a speeding locomotive. Moreover, the passing of the whale's enormous body creates great turbulence in the water, while its tail stirs up a trail of waves in its wake. So much water is displaced that a camera cannot be used for several seconds after a whale has passed; it is knocked around too violently by the water.

Deloire has drawn a judicious distinction between the way that a shark swims and the motion of a baleen whale or a cachalot. The shark throws himself forward like a rocket, propelled by a twist of its whole muscular body.

A cetacean, on the other hand, goes forward smoothly, rhythmically. Its horizontal tail is so powerful that there is no need for violent motions; it beats slowly, gracefully, almost floating in the water around it.

One exception to Deloire's rule is the whale shark *(Rhincodon typus),* with whom we have had some experience in the Indian Ocean. The whale shark, which is not a whale at all but a shark, with a vertical tail, has the same slow, graceful rhythm of the cachalot. The reason probably lies in its size, for the whale shark is the largest of the sharks, measuring from 40 to 50 feet in length. For an animal of this size, regardless of whether the tail is vertical or horizontal, it is probably physically impossible to move the tail rapidly because of the resistance of the water.

One must have seen a sperm whale dive in order to appreciate the utter grace of its tail movements. Of all the cetaceans, the cachalot is the only one who, in preparing for a dive to the bottom, jackknifes and, as he goes beneath the surface, raises his tail, like two great wings, out of the water.

A Surface Leap

The whale's tail is used not only to propel it in the water, but also to propel it above the surface. In my journal of January 24, 1968, I have this notation:

"At the end of the day, when there was not enough light for filming, we saw a whale leap, twice, completely out of the water. It was an unforgettable sight; but, unfortunately, a brief one. We must keep constant watch, and never become discouraged — even when it seems that nothing will happen."

On this occasion, it is not a cachalot, but a baleen whale; and probably a gray whale. All of the large cetaceans probably dive in order to feed, and their horizontal tails enable them to go back and forth from the surface, where they breathe, to the depths, where they eat. The tail is, in fact, both a rudder and a stabilizer or stern oar placed flat in the water. An ideal appendage for a marine life form.

Whale Speed

The speed of a whale depends, among other things, upon the species of whale. We have had ample opportunity to clock the whales that we have encountered in the Indian Ocean and in the Pacific. Here are some of the data that we have gathered on the subject:

Sperm whales, again, are the speed champions of the world of whales. Left to themselves, they swim at only three or four knots; but, once they are disturbed or irritated, they speed up to ten or twelve knots. It is recorded that, in the Azores, a cachalot that was being pursued was capable of towing a boat at 20 knots.

A blue whale weighing 100 tons and 90 feet in length swims at a speed of 14 to 15 knots for two hours at a time; and he can sustain a speed of 20 knots for ten minutes.

Finback whales have been known to attain a speed of 18 knots.

It is reported that Sei whales* are capable of speeds of up to 35 knots, but we have never had any demonstration of this ability.

Humpback whales are relatively slow-moving animals. Their normal speed is 4 knots; if they are disturbed, they may exceed 10 knots.

It should be noted, however, that a female with a calf slows down in order not to lose her offspring; and that the school slows down to match her speed also.

The gray whale that we observed over a long period, from the *Polaris* and *Calypso* as well as from the Zodiac, normally moved at 4 or 5 knots. We ascertained, however, that when she was frightened she could swim at 10 knots, and perhaps more — in any case, at a speed greater than the 7 or 8 knots usually cited by cetologists.

Finally, we have calculated that, for a whale to leap entirely out of the water as they do (for reasons that we do not yet understand), he must be able to attain an accelerated speed of 30 knots. Males, apparently, leap more frequently than females; and the dive which follows a leap lasts anywhere from four to fifteen minutes.

Despite the power of their "engines" and their massive musculature, whales are far from being the fastest animals in the sea. Smaller cetaceans — the killer whale, the dolphin, the porpoise, for example — attain incomparably higher speeds.

*See Appendix I.

The spout of a gray whale off Baja California.

FOUR

The Breath-Holding Champions of the World

The Cachalot: Our Master

The cachalot, or sperm whale, is a marvelous diver. He is, in that respect, our undoubted master. Although cachalots are, like us, warm-blooded and lung-breathing, they seem immune to the physiological perils that are the lot of men in the sea: rapture of the depths, and decompression accidents. This immunity is, thus far, one of the mysteries of the sea. In trying to solve it, we may be able to better man's situation in the sea and expand the range and competence of the diver.

When a sperm whale dives, apparently using every muscle in his body and raising his great tail above the surface of the water, to what depth does he go?

Once more, I must have recourse to my journal and refer to *Calypso*'s expedition in the Indian Ocean:

Monday, May 22. We drifted only five miles last night. This morning, we set a course for Shab-Arab; but we did not get far. We soon made a detour to inspect a school of dolphins.

To be sure, dolphins are not what we are looking for. Yet, we have often had occasion to notice that there are spots in the sea where life seems to congregate — assembly areas which exist, no doubt, because food is abundant there. The food may consist of microscopic forms — plankton, or tiny crustaceans. Nonetheless, it seems to attract everything in the sea, even sperm whales. And this is the case today.

At 10:30 A.M. we sight a group of cachalots calmly going about their business. Instantly, Deloire is on the harpoon plaftorm; Barsky backs him up; Falco is at the prow with one of our new hand harpoons, which are heavy but, unfortunately, have weak heads. Li is in the observation chamber. And Jack and Alan are excitedly filming away with every camera they could find aboard the ship.

As *Calypso* picks her way toward the school of cachalots, we find our first subject: a young — or rather, an adolescent — whale. Falco sinks his harpoon in the youngster's side on the first try; but the whale reacts violently and succeeds in shaking loose the point.

The second subject is an adult, and he is well within range; but the harpoon strikes him sideways and bounces off harmlessly. Indeed, the trouble with our harpoons is that they are *too* harmless.

The third whale we select is enormous, the largest of the school. Falco throws the harpoon with all his strength. I am standing next to him, and I can see the harpoon strike the whale on the left side. Then we hear an extraordinary noise — a loud clap. The cachalot's skin has been split like that of a drum. And yet, it seems so tough and so thick!

I am certain that the harpoon's head has not reached the sensitive flesh underneath. It is embedded in the thick layer of blubber under the skin — a layer 20 to 25 inches thick, while our harpoon's point is only 16 inches long. The cachalot very likely is only vaguely aware of our harpoon. Even so, he stops swimming, and begins turning in a circle, his head held above the surface as though he is looking around to discover the source of that annoying pin-prick.

Then, he suddenly decides to leave, and begins moving away very rapidly. The polypropylene line uncoils so fast in its basket on the forward deck that it fairly whistles. When 1500 feet of the line have uncoiled, the red buoy attached to it is dragged overboard, and we follow it with our eyes as it leaps and bounds over the waves at high speed. A promising beginning.

Deloire sets out in the Zodiac with the 35 mm. Tegea, as we keep the whale in sight from the *Calypso*. He has been swimming toward his companions and, by now, has rejoined them. There are seven or eight whales altogether. When Deloire reaches the school, he jumps into the water in the middle of them, camera whirling. We should have some footage of the school as a whole.

For almost an hour, our captive cachalot swims quietly around the red buoy at the end of his 1500-foot leash. At first, his companions remain near him. But, after a while, they swim away, leaving behind, as company for our whale, another adult of almost the same size as the captive whale. But, before long, this one leaves too, and our whale is alone. We are somewhat surprised, and disappointed — prematurely, as it turns out — at this apparent lack of solidarity among the cachalots.

Our divers, who have already had a taste of broncobusting with whales, would like to try it again with a sperm whale. It seems easy enough: our cachalot is circling quietly around like a performing horse under the big top. But this one is no performer. He senses the divers approaching him, and, with a single stroke of that incredible tail, shoots sixty feet away from them. Then he goes back to his circling pattern.

The divers exhaust themselves trying to catch up to him. When they are ready to give it up, the Zodiac picks them up one by one. It would take ten divers, lying in ambush around the whale, for someone to be able to climb on his back.

By radio, I instruct the Zodiac to call the whole thing off. All of the divers are being worn out with nothing to show for it.

The Whale's Dive

Around four o'clock, the sperm whale decides to change his tactics. He dives. The 1500 feet of line disappear beneath the surface. Then the red buoy also disappears.

I should explain the significance of the buoy being dragged beneath the surface. Our buoys are actually balloons, made of thick plastic and inflated with air. The particular model we use was developed by Gaz de France for the purpose of holding up its underwater gas lines while they are being laid. On the surface, these buoys have a volume of 60 liters; therefore, in order for them to be dragged beneath the surface, a pull of at least 135 pounds is required. These buoys, however, are not crushed by water pressure. Since the plastic skin is flexible, they resume their form, and retain their floatability, when they return to the surface.

The whale therefore went down to at least 1400 or 1600 feet, and remained at that depth for about fifteen minutes He then rose to the surface

— and, a few minutes after, we see the buoy bouncing gaily on the water.

I immediately dispatch a Zodiac to attach a second buoy by means of 1000 feet of line. Then, we inflate a kytoon with helium and attach bits of aluminum foil to it so that we may track our whale by radar during the night.

The kytoon is attached to the second buoy by a hundred-foot line. And scarcely is the line taut than the whale dives again. The first buoy goes under very quickly. As we watch anxiously from *Calypso*'s deck, it is followed by the second buoy. Then, in consternation, we see the kytoon being dragged down also, until it is level with the surface. Suddenly, it begins to rise into the air again; and rises, and rises, and rises until it disappears from view into the sky, trailing a streamer of broken line behind it.

We Lose Our Whale

The sperm whale has obviously reached, or exceeded, a depth of 2500 feet. Hoping against hope, we add another 1000 feet of line and a third buoy. Then we begin inflating another kytoon. As soon as the whale surfaces, Bebert sinks another harpoon and we attach the new buoy.

The whale dives again; and this time the first two buoys are dragged down with him, but the third one remains on the surface, moving slowly forward.

It is not possible for us to determine precisely what depth the whale has reached on this dive, since he apparently has not gone down vertically. Even so, when he comes to the surface, he is still rather close to the spot at which he dived — which means that, while it may not have been an absolutely vertical dive, it was not far from it. I think we can say that the depth of the dive was more than 2500 feet, but less than 4000 feet.

At nightfall, we begin tracking the cachalot by radar, as we did on May 12 and 13 with our other whale. But the wind soon rises, and the choppy water interferes with reception. We can no longer locate the kytoon on our screen. Hastily, we organize a "Zodiac watch" near the third buoy. Bonnici has the duty first, and he notifies me by radio that the wind has blown the kytoon down onto the surface — no doubt because, when we launched it, we had nothing with which to make a rigid frame for the stabilizer. At any rate, Bonnici unhooks the kytoon from the buoy and attaches it to the Zodiac, where he can keep an eye on it.

In the middle of the evening, Bonnici informs me that the third buoy has suddenly stopped moving. Either the whale has shaken off the harpoon, he says, "or else he has fallen asleep." Taking no chances, we continue the Zodiac watch until dawn.

(Right) A sperm whale passes in front of *Calypso*'s bow in the Indian Ocean.

(Below) The Zodiac heads toward the spouts of two gray whales.

Tuesday, May 23. At daybreak, we begin hauling in our lines and discover that our cachalot has, in fact, freed himself. An examination of the harpoon reveals that the last of the three bards, which we were counting on to hold the harpoon in the whale's blubber, is gone, and the stem is broken. The steel line by means of which the nylon line is attached to the harpoon is about two thirds cut through, but apparently it was still holding. Obviously, it was the harpoon's head, with its three sharp ridges, that cut the surrounding flesh and allowed the harpoon to work itself free.

That the whale should be free was no surprise. What is astonishing is that our flimsy little weapon, with its bits of steel and nylon line, should have held such a Leviathan for so long a time.

In the Trap

Experts on whales have had much discussion on the maximum depth to which a sperm whale can dive. In 1900, a German scholar, Kukenthal, declared that they could go down to 3250 feet.

Kukenthal's opinion was apparently corroborated by a curious incident. In 1932, an American cable layer, the *All America,* was working on a telegraph line in the open sea off British Columbia. The ship's crew was amazed when they raised the defective line — with great effort — to find the carcass of a cachalot tangled in the line. The animal had obviously been trapped by the cable, and had drowned. The interesting fact was that the cachalot's body had not been crushed by the water pressure — even though the cable had been laid at a depth of 3330 feet.

Professor Budker writes: ". . . it now seems to have been proved that sperm whales often swim at depths of around 3000 feet. It seems plausible therefore to conclude that sperm whales when they become entangled in underwater cables are in search of food. That is, they are swimming with their lower jaws hanging open, stirring up the upper layers of sediment on the bottom."*

So far as the length of a line attached to a harpooned whale is concerned, we cannot say that it gives an exact indication of depth, since there is always a certain amount of horizontal slant involved which must be taken into account.

*Kenneth S. Norris, in his *Whales, Dolphins, and Porpoises,* records that, in 1957, another sperm whale was discovered caught in an undersea cable — this one at a depth of 3850 feet. Several other cases of this kind have been discovered since that time.

Some relatively precise experiments have been performed by a group of Norwegian investigators who, in observing humpback whales, used harpoons equipped with pressure gauges. The greatest depth registered in the course of five experiments was 1180 feet. The humpback whale who established that record returned to the surface with such vigor "that he towed the boat for a full half hour and finally had to be slowed down by a second harpoon." *

Our own observations indicate that the depth to which whales dive varies according to species. The large marine mammals dive out of necessity, in order to find food. For that reason, baleen whales do not dive as deep as sperm whales. We will see, for instance, that cetaceans who feed on krill (a crustacean that remains near the surface — sometimes in great abundance — and is never found at depths of more than 325 feet) are the ones who do not dive deep.

Sperm whales, who feed on the giant squid found at depths of 1500 to 2500 feet, are apparently the champion divers of the world. It is also possible, however, that the bottlenose whale is an even more brilliant performer.

It is worth noting that diving ability seems to be to some extent a function of size. The larger the individual whale, the better diver he is. In practice, this means that adult male whales are more proficient at diving than young whales, or females.

Ninety Minutes of Apnea

How long can a sperm whale remain beneath the surface without breathing? There is a considerable amount of data available on this point, and the consensus seems to be that large males can remain in apnea — that is, do without breathing — for between sixty and ninety minutes.

It is true, however, that in almost every case the whale in question was being hunted or chased, and that he was seeking to escape. He therefore remained under water for as long as possible. His dives, therefore, cannot really be regarded as "normal."

The cachalots that *Calypso* has pursued have probably never been really frightened, in the sense that they fortunately have never been fighting for their lives and been compelled to remain without breathing to the limit of their endurance.

---

*These experiments are described by Professor Paul Budker in his *Baleines et baleiniers,* p. 76.

Bonnici and Falco prepare the buoys and the nylon line that are attached to the harpoon.

In my journal, I find the following entry, written at sea off the island of Socotra:

March 14. During the morning, we sight five or six groups of cachalots. Sometimes there is only one group at a time, and sometimes two. Whenever we approach, however, they dive; but several times we are able to follow their

Canoë Kientzy and Bernard Delemotte in the Zodiac with harpoon and buoy.

Two launches attempting to encircle a sperm whale.

trail. This "trail" is a sort of slick, similar to an oil slick. I am more and more convinced that the trail is the result of the movement of the whales' tails.

They are swimming only 15 to 30 feet beneath the surface, but they are capable of infinitely greater depths than that. They often remain twenty minutes without breathing, even when there is no particular reason for them to be wary of coming to the surface.

Obviously, there is no absolute rule in a whale's behavior. The spectacular sight of a sperm whale jackknifing to dive and thrusting the whole of his tail out of the water usually indicates a deep dive. And yet, we have seen on several occasions, cachalots also dive without that foregoing maneuver. In such cases, they seem to go down only to a moderate depth.

In general, baleen whales do not perform deep dives while they are migrating — unless they are disturbed or frightened.

Our observation of gray whales from both *Calypso* and *Polaris III* leads us to believe that these toothless cetaceans remain in a dive for much less time than a sperm whale.

We have an exact record of the length of apnea among gray whales encountered along the Pacific coast, and also of the probable depths of their dives. The record dive lasted 8 minutes and 27 seconds, while the average dive lasted between two and four minutes. The greatest estimated depth was

500 feet. Bernard Mestre was in charge of these records and calculations, and he fulfilled his responsibilities with scrupulous care.

Humpback whales seem somewhat better endowed as divers than gray whales. We have timed their dives at between ten and fifteen minutes.

Apparently, only the finback whale rivals the sperm whale in the durations of its dives, as was demonstrated by the specimen that we marked and tracked in the Indian Ocean.

What amazes me even more than the length of a whale's dive, or its depth, is the fact that, in some mysterious way, a whale under the surface — no matter how great the depth — seems always to know what is happening at the surface and to act accordingly. We had a startling example of this ability with our finback whale near Mahé, who so dexterously gave us the slip (see Chapter One). During his dives, he seemed to know the exact location of *Calypso*, of the Zodiacs, and of the launch — even if their engines were not running.

Myoglobin

Not all mammals are able to hold their breath for the same amount of time. Cats, dogs, and rabbits can remain in apnea for three to four minutes; muskrats, twelve minutes; seals and beavers, fifteen minutes.

It is obvious that the cetaceans' apneic abilities are shared to some extent with their relatives on land. Land mammals have simply developed that ability to a smaller extent. And even this is not always true; for beavers can hold their breath longer than gray whales. To what does the sperm whale owe its undisputed superiority in this respect?

The obvious answer would be: to its lungs. But that is not so. The cachalot's lungs are not especially well developed in proportion to the animal's overall size.

On the other hand, the sperm whale ventilates its lungs, while it is on the surface, much more than other mammals do. When it surfaces, it renews 80 percent or 90 percent of the air in its thoracic cage — compared to 20 percent for man. (One inhalation by a whale is the equivalent of eight for a man.)

Moreover, a cachalot's respiratory rate is extraordinarily slow: six times a minute. But the rate is even less for baleen whales: who inhale at the rate of once every minute.

The skin of the large cetaceans is very dark, almost black. We have mentioned this coloration is peculiar to mammals who are good divers. The reason is that the color is due to the presence of myoglobin in the system, which stabilizes oxygen in the mammal's muscles. And this is one of the most plausible explanations that can be advanced for a whale's ability to go for long periods without breathing.

According to Professor Grassé, the oxygen that a man uses when he dives comes from the following sources: 34 percent from the lungs, 41 percent from the blood, 13 percent from the muscles, and 12 percent from other tissues. For a whale, the breakdown is : 9 percent from the lungs, *41 percent from the blood, 41 percent from the muscles,* and 9 percent from other tissues.

It remains to be explained how cetaceans, who are, after all, lung-breathing mammals like us, seem to be immune to the perils that the human diver runs because of nitrogen in his system. This immunity, which we envy so much and which has haunted my dreams for so many years, seems to be due to a complex of physiological pecularities.

The first of these is the whale's very unusual circulatory system;* a system which one finds also among certain Pinnipedia and among sea otters. This system includes a complex of blood vessels running on both sides of the spine down to the tail. These networks are of two kinds: arterial and venous.

The advantage conferred is that these vessels assure the proper distribution of blood to the brain and the heart during a dive. It is possible, too, that it serves as a temperature regulator. It has also been said that the whale's aptitude for diving is due to the size of his venous sinuses. And it has been pointed out that cetaceans' thick layer of blubber may contribute to the absorption of nitrogen during apnea. (This same function may be filled by the oily emulsion that we have noted in the whale's lungs, and which would also be the cause of the whale's visible "spout.")

A possible clue: the heartbeat of cetaceans is as slow as that of the aquatic reptiles — snakes, or the marine iguanas of Galapagos — who also remain in apnea for long periods.

There is nothing certain about any of these explanations. They are all hypotheses. What is missing is true experimental knowledge. But are experiments possible with animals of this size?

The Spout

After Philippe had spent some time reconnoitering the lagoons of Baja California in search of gray whales, he returned to San Diego by air and flew over the interior coast of the Gulf of Cortes. He was accompanied by Ted

---

*The scientific name of this system reflects its quality. It is called *reta mirabilia* — "wondrous networks."

Walker and Wally Green.

Along the Mexican coast, they flew over the Canal de las Ballenas (Whale Canal) which lies between the shore and the island of Angel de la Guarda. From the air, they saw a school of finback whales which, if they were not permanent residents of the canal, seemed at least very much at home there.

Philippe, Ted, and Wally immediately landed near a fishing village and rented a boat. Here is Philippe's account of the day:

"It was a beautiful day, and we set out early to find the school. The scenery alone was well worth the trouble. Along the coast there were high cliffs, reddish in color, majestic, but completely denuded of any sort of vegetation. There was not a tree or a blade of grass. It was an untouched desert; but a desert of rock. The cliffs descended vertically to the sea that lay 150 feet below.

"The sea was like a lake, and our motorboat was surprisingly quiet — as quiet as only Americans can make a motor. We had no trouble in finding the whales, and, when we drew near, we cut our engine. In the almost total silence that followed, an enormous spout shot up from a finback not ten feet from our prow. It seemed for a moment that the universe was filled by that geyser. I am certain that it was a finback. We were in the Gulf of Cortes, and there are no gray whales there.

"Ted began shouting and pointing, and we quickly saw why. We were completely surrounded by finbacks, one on each side of the boat. We started the engine and advanced slowly. Our whale escort stayed alongside of us, moving at the same speed, remaining at a distance of 15 or 20 feet from us. From time to time, they sank gently below the surface, and then rose again. We continued moving forward, and we noticed that the water in front of us was filled with bubbles, like soda water. They came from a school of tiny fish that kept diving and then coming to the surface to empty the gas from their swimming bladders.

"Then I understood what was happening. The finbacks around us were using our boat, and the sound of our engine, to round up the little fish. And, for the first time, I experienced, and saw in operation, the intelligence of these animals. Moreover, it had not taken them long to devise this plan. We were not there for more than twenty minutes before they arrived and stationed themselves aound the boat.

"The water was cloudy, and I was unable to dive to shoot some film, but I

(Left) Cameramen trying to film a sperm whale that is already out of range.

Gray whales spouting in Scammon Lagoon.

did not really regret it. I don't see how I could have found anything beneath the surface to equal the scene that we witnessed from our boat. What an extraordinary sensation it is, in the silence of a desert, to see a whale — to say nothing of several whales — swimming alongside more slowly than a man walks. One of these giants, the one on our starboard, was three times the size of our boat. Ted estimated its length at 85 feet. The one to port was smaller.

"This was my first real contact with a whale at close quarters. Of course, I have seen whales since I was a child aboard *Calypso*. But that particular day, I could see and hear the spouting, and the whale was very close. It was very different from anything that I had experienced before. The noise, especially, amazed me. It was as though we were in a cave, listening to the repeated echoes of a mysterious sound.

"All in all, it was one of the most unforgettable days of my life. I was

In Bermuda, the divers explore the island's coral waters when they are not chasing humpback whales.

able to understand how so many legends are told about whales, and to understand how they began.

"Up to that time, I had not known very much about whales. I had heard more or less romanticized stories, seen drawings, read books. But to see a whale in real life, and especially to *hear* a whale — that is beyond imagining. And to think that, in the midst of that monstrous sound there is a life form even greater. . . .

"One of the most memorable things about that afternoon was that I actually *breathed* the whale's breath. Its spout rained down on us like a gentle drizzle, and a fog covered my face and hands and the boat itself. Surprisingly, there was no unpleasant odor, but a slightly musky smell; one which only the sovereign authority of a nearby giant could impose on us whether we were willing or not."

Halitosis?

A very widespread opinion has it that the spout of cetaceans has an unpleasant odor. However, our divers have often been sprinkled by this spray,
and they have rarely complained of its smell. It should be noted that, in their
contacts with whales, their minds were usually occupied with matters other
than whether or not the whale had halitosis. Even so, there was no trace of an
unpleasant smell on their diving gear, or on their bodies, on such occasions.

It is possible that the spout of a sperm whale has a more disagreeable
smell than that of a baleen whale, since the cachalot's diet is very different.

As far as gray whales and finbacks are concerned, it may be recalled that
Philippe was abundantly sprinkled by their spout, and he denies absolutely
that there was any disagreeable smell whatever. According to Philippe, whalers are responsible for the story that cetaceans have halitosis; and he points
out that the only whales that whalers have contact with are those who are
either exhausted by a long chase, or wounded.

An Asthmatic Whale

"Thar she blows!" is the ritual cry by means of which the sighting of a
whale is announced. It was also the alarm given aboard *Calypso* when we
were whale chasing in the Indian and Pacific oceans. (That is, we used the
French version: *Elle souffle* — which means exactly the same thing.)

When a whale surfaces after a dive, his blowholes are the first thing to
break water. Out of them (or it, as the case may be), comes the spout, a white
column of vapor that resembles a steam geyser and which is perfectly visible
above the water. That it is necessary for a whale to spout is an unfortunate
arrangement of Nature, for the spout makes it possible for the whale to be
sighted from a good distance away. And the spout is accompanied by a rush
of air the sound of which can be heard at 800 feet. This was the "repeated
echoes of a mysterious sound" that, heard from close up, made such an impression on Philippe.

The *Curlew*'s* team, during their expedition in the waters around Bermuda in pursuit of humpback whales, had the opportunity to record this
sound on many occasions. Our sound engineer, Eugène Lagorio, noted that,
so far as sound itself is concerned, there is a considerable amount of difference between the spouts of different whales.

*The *Curlew* was the boat that we rented for our Bermudian adventure.

On one occasion, conditions were particularly favorable for this kind of observation. The day had been spent in exterior shots, and, toward evening, the *Curlew* was at anchor, with its engines cut. Seven or eight whales had remained in the ship's vicinity, apparently unworried by the presence of the hull in their waters. Even when divers went down, the whales seemed hardly to notice them. This was in relatively shallow water, and it is likely that the whales were quietly, and even somewhat lazily, feeding. They remained on the surface a good deal of the time, diving occasionally and always reappearing near the *Curlew*. Lagorio was therefore able to tape-record their spouts individually. There was one whale among them whose spout was noticeably different, harsher and louder.

Lagorio, who is *Calypso*'s reigning deadpan, remarked: "An asthmatic, I presume."

A Fifty-Foot Spout

Cetaceans are able to dive only after they have inhaled and exhaled a certain number of times on the surface; and the number depends upon the species. Dr. Budker says that "the blue whale breathes only three to five times; the finback, five or six times; the Sei, ten to fifteen times. The sperm whale, during its ten to eleven minutes on the surface, breathes sixty to seventy times, which shows a respiratory rate much faster than that of baleen whales."

The spout of a whale emerges from its blowholes under considerable pressure and sometimes rises 50 feet into the air. The longer and deeper the dive, the higher the spout that follows it. Experts have devised the following rule of thumb: a sperm whale sixty feet long, weighing 60 tons and remaining in a dive for 60 minutes, will breathe sixty times.*

Experienced whalers are able to tell, from a whale's spout, the species, age, and even the size, of the whale.† The finback whale, for example, has two blowholes, both of which spout; but since the two blowholes are very close together, the spout becomes a single jet of vapor. The spout of the right whale, on the other hand, is actually two distinct jets, and is aimed forward. And the spout of the humpback whale is a single straight column that spreads at the top, like the spout of a fountain.

---

* Cited by Kenneth S. Norris, *Whales, Dolphins, and Porpoises*, p. 698

†See the word "Spout" in the Glossary.

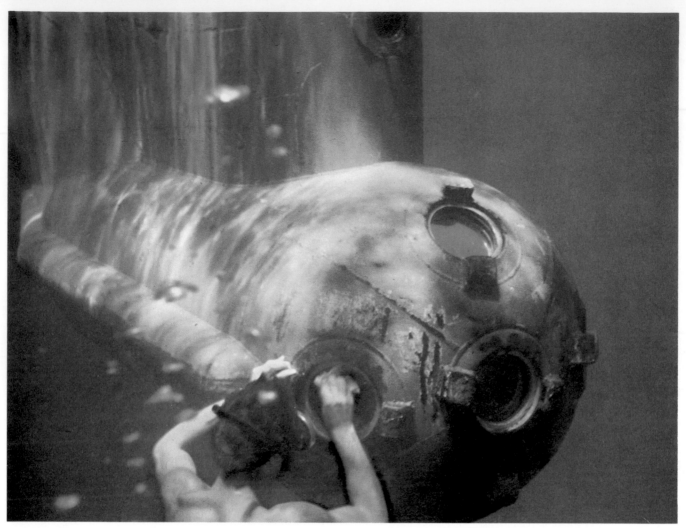

A shipboard chore: cleaning the portholes of *Calypso*'s observation chamber.

Another Riddle

Contrary to what is commonly believed, the whale's spout is not simply a jet of water. Professor Budker places great emphasis on this point. "Anatomically," he writes, "it is impossible for a whale to eject water through the blowhole, for among marine mammals there is no connection between the respiratory and digestive tracts. Breathing and digestion take place independently of one another, and water absorbed through the mouth has no way of being ejected through the blowhole."

What gives the spout its appearance of white steam? The most feasible explanation is that air, compressed in the whale's thorax by his dive, expands at the moment of exhalation. The air's temperature is thus lowered, and it condenses into water vapor.

Bernard Delemotte is our resident tooth-collector. Here, he has just put a killer whale's jawbone out to dry.

Among the smaller cetaceans — dolphins and killer whales, for example — the spout is invisible.

The Misadventures of a Cardiologist

There is a connection, it seems, between the spout and the rate of a whale's heartbeat — as there is between that rate and the amount of time spent in apnea. An American cardiologist, Dr. Paul Dudley White (among whose heart patients was President Eisenhower), has actually succeeded in running an electrocardiogram of a whale. Dr. White, who is a friend of Ted Walker's, had already taken electrocardiograms of an elephant (30 beats per minute), and of a bird (1000 per minute). Apparently, the larger the animal the slower the heartbeat.

Ted Walker explained to us that Dr. White had chosen gray whales for his experiment because he considered that species more accessible than others. He got together a team, organized an expedition, and equipped a boat. Once in the water, however, his team, which had little familiarity with the customs of gray whales, attempted to install their electrodes on a mother whale accompanied by her calf; and mother whales are always touchy. This one reacted violently to their impertinence. She charged the boat, smashed the rudder, bent the propeller, and left a gaping hole in the hull. It was all the crew could do to pump out the water fast enough to keep the boat afloat until help could arrive.

Dr. White finally found a 30-ton subject in Scammon Lagoon, installed his electrodes without mishap, and took a reading of 27 per minute. The fact that the whale was grounded at the time obviously had some effect upon the reading, for the normal rate has been established at nine beats per minute.

FIVE

They Talk, They Sing—and They Listen

The fact that certain cetaceans "speak" is not a recent discovery. Aristotle knew it, and wrote about it. His record, however, was ignored and passed off as a legend until the day, during World War II, that the American navy began using underwater microphones (called sofar — sound fixing and ranging) to detect the presence of enemy submarines. The device immediately picked up a series of grinding sounds, clicks, and mewings along the American coast. And thus were discovered the voices of the World of Silence: the noises of the crustaceans, the groaning sounds of the fish, the whistles of the porpoises, the squeaking of the dolphins, the calls of the sperm whales, and the trills of the baleen whales.

Certainly not all the sounds made by cetaceans are part of a "language." Some of them are not a means of expression, but a method of orientation and detection.

Man was not the first mammal to use sonic and ultrasonic guides in the depths of the sea. Cetaceans have a natural sonar device.

The sonar system of marine mammals, by means of which they detect

The head of a humpback whale. One can almost make out the expression on its face.

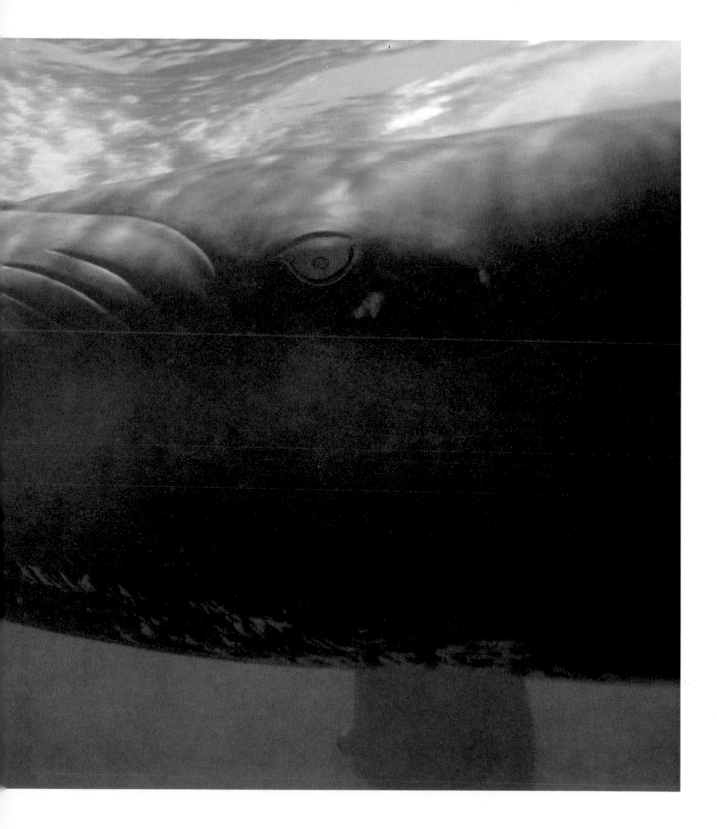

obstacles and locate their food and their enemies, is more complex than one may think. Today, it is believed that this system functions at two levels. The lowest frequencies, for example, seem to be used by cachelots to locate squid in very deep water, or by dolphins to locate prey or obstacles from afar, while the high frequencies seem to serve as a means of communication among individuals of the same species.

A New World of Sound

Sight, which is so important to land mammals, is not the sense upon which cetaceans rely most. Hearing is most important for them. Baleen whales and cachalots live, and organize their lives around, a world of sound. And, even though they have no vocal chords, they speak, and they sing. They also listen; and they send out sonic signals that, by their echoes, give information on the cetaceans' surroundings.

Cachalots *grunt* in order to communicate with one another, and they emit a series of rhythmic *cracking* noises, at a very high sonic level, to explore the area around them. They hear one another, and are able to locate one another, at distances of over three (marine) miles.

This explains why one occasionally finds a whale calf alone, far from its parents. For the parents know perfectly well where their offspring is at any given moment; and the calf also knows where its mother and father are located.

This ability to locate, this sonar device, is not automatic, and not merely passive. Whales broadcast and receive, in my opinion, directionally; and it seems probable that they must rotate, like a radar antenna, when they are exploring their surroundings. This would explain why *Calypso* is able to approach whales from the rear without disturbing them.

On the other hand, when whales want to know what is going on around them, they assume a vertical position with their heads protruding above the surface. This is not in order to be able to watch *Calypso*, as we once thought. The angle of transmission (and perhaps of reception also) is perpendicular to the whale's cylindrical body; and, no doubt, there is a special "ear" which is kept turned toward the ocean bottom.

On the surface, sperm whales are constantly attuned by sonar to the depths. If their constant crack-crack-crack discloses the presence of one or more sizable squid at 2000 or 2500 or 3000 feet directly underneath, then they dive vertically and go straight to their prey. The hypothesis that they transmit vertically seems to me to explain the *vertical* dives of cachalots and pilot whales.

Whales apparently find the noise of outboard motors especially annoying. This is probably a question of frequencies. And it is also probably because of overlapping frequencies that our tactic of the virazeou, using outboard motors, seems to work.

In the center of the circle of noise, the sperm whale's sonar reception may be garbled; and he would therefore have to remain stationary (and furious) on the surface. And, since he relies upon his sonar for diving, he would not be able to dive. (It would very likely be improper to suggest that a cachalot would dive "by reflex," since he is sufficiently well developed to have a choice of alternatives in his behavior.)

Before we began to understand the effectiveness of their auditory equipment, we foolishly accused cachalots of disloyalty, and we were completely wrong. When a cachalot is in trouble, the head male orders the school to withdraw. But the school then remains within sonar range — a range that may extend for several miles. If the whale in question is unable to get away, the school sends one or two members to investigate — the mother, if the whale is a calf, or another adult if it is a full-grown whale. On several occasions, the school disappeared about a mile to the east of the captive, and then reappeared a mile to the west of him thirty or forty minutes later. To travel that distance, it ordinarily takes a whale less than twenty minutes. Which means that the school apparently spent some time within sonar range of the whale on the surface, calling him and telling him that they were waiting for him to rejoin them.

Bermuda

Philippe spent two months observing and recording the most loquacious, and the noisiest, of all cetaceans: the humpback whale.

Bermuda seemed the ideal place for such an undertaking, because Bermuda is one of the regular stopovers of humpbacks in the spring, when they are en route to the Arctic for their summer feast of small crustaceans. During this particular year, however, the weather was very disagreeable, and working conditions were proportionately unfavorable.

The largest boat that we were able to rent was an old sailer, the *Curlew*, whose ballast had been removed so that it could travel in shallow water. It therefore rolled so violently that it was impossible for anyone to stay at sea on the *Curlew* for more than one or two days at a time.

On the first day, everyone was enthusiastic. The *Curlew* began by crossing the lagoon, where the water was very calm. Then it got out into the open sea, where there were waves six to nine feet high. Almost everyone aboard

The humpback whale is recognizable by its large white flippers.

was instantly seized with *mal de mer*. And, of course, whales began popping up all around the ship. Despite their discomfort, the divers began to prepare to go down. As soon as the *Curlew* was in the proper position, however, the rudder broke. Fortunately the *Curlew* was able to hold the course on its own, with one engine running at reduced speed. Otherwise, she would inevitably have smashed into one or more of the submerged coral reefs in the area and sunk.

Bernard Delemotte and Philippe took turns working in the hole, trying to repair the rudder pulley, with the help of the ship's captain, Philippe Sirot. Finally, the *Curlew* was able to limp back into port.

Several days later, the *Curlew*'s rudder was as good as new, and she put out again with Philippe and his friends. Alongside a level reef, they encountered a group of seven whales who began swimming and playing around the boat, rubbing against one another and emitting a series of extraordinary

(Right) Humpback whales are specialists in underwater acrobatics. Note the shape of the mouth as seen from above.

sounds: modulated, and very audible sounds.

Philippe, who had already suited up, dived immediately into the middle of the school. The water was cloudy, and all that he could see were "large wings" passing, waving. The flippers of humpback whales are white, and very large, measuring one third the length of the whale's body. (The body itself is black.) They do, in fact, look like wings — or, as they pass in a cloudy sea, like ghosts in white sheets.

A Concert

The weather finally improved, and the sea became calm. It was now possible to tape-record the "songs" of the whales. It was decided to do so at night, for humpback whales are much more communicative after dark than in the daylight hours. Apparently, they are able to transmit more strongly then; and indeed they speak to one another over considerable distances.

As their recording site, the team chose an underwater canyon. The *Curlew* was moved to that location, and microphones were placed 60 to 75 feet from the surface.

On certain nights, Eugène Lagorio, our sound engineer, was able to record what amounted to a veritable concert. There must have been, he says, a hundred whales over a more or less extended area, all "talking." Early in the evening, there were only a few sounds, scattered, uncertain; as though the musicians were tuning their instruments.

Then one whale began to sing; and a second; and a third. Soon, the mewings, creaks, and whoops filled the water. Some of the performers were close, and some were far away. And, because of the underwater canyon, the sounds echoed two or three times at intervals of five or six seconds. It seemed almost that one was in a cathedral, and that the faithful were alternating the verses of a psalm. . . .

Lagorio's recordings show beyond a doubt that whales communicate with one another. The whale nearest to the *Curlew* would make a series of sounds, and others, farther away, would answer. The sounds alternated, just as in a conversation; but it was a mysterious conversation, and an untranslatable one.

A Thousand Different Sounds

The sounds made by humpback whales are different from those of any other animals. They extend over a much wider range and have a variety of expression greater even than that of birds.

I think that we could probably distinguish a thousand different sounds, each one individually audible to the human ear. The timbre, the volume, and the frequencies present an almost infinite variety. There are trills, creaks, janglings, and very short mouselike squeaks. Sometimes we heard a bellowing, like the belling of a deer. Occasionally, these bellowings overlapped; but almost always they seemed addressed to another whale. They were weird, alien sounds, exchanged — it seemed to us — on secret wave lengths.

Lagorio, who has been part of our team for many years, had found the job of his life. Sitting in the darkness, twirling his dials and flicking his switches, he was like a wizard summoning monsters who, from the bottom of the sea, were answering with moans, sighs, and clanging chains. No sound engineer has ever undertaken a more modern project, or one more evocative of ancient myths.

On certain unusually calm nights, the songs of the humpback whales blended into what Lagorio called "choirs." These sounds, which were very near the *Curlew*, were truly polyphonic, an "ensemble" of voices. And the bass section always was taken by a sound like the creaking of rusty hinges.

A few of the men aboard the *Curlew* were of the opinion that the whales might be making noise for the sheer joy of making noise. And yet, not even the birds sing entirely without reason.

There have been cases in which it seemed possible to attach a particular meaning to a whale sound. One night, when they were talking more than usual, and they could be heard very clearly over the microphones, they surfaced near Lagorio's boat and began looking him over. Lagorio was sitting there, in the open, earphones on his head, surrounded by his wires and lights and dials and all the paraphanelia of his trade, and they seemed quite interested. They came very close, and began making little squeaking noises, like mice. Lagorio was convinced (and still is) that they were talking about him. And that they were saying flattering things.

"I could feel somehow that they were discussing what they saw in the Zodiac," he says. "Maybe they were wondering whether I was dangerous or not, and if they should run away."

Conversations

Lagorio is very proud of the fact that the whales finally decided to stay. They must have concluded that he was a friend.

(Following page) A diver has been allowed to latch onto a humpback whale's tail — but only for a moment.

Even though one may know intellectually that it would be foolish to give too human an interpretation to the acts and sounds of another species, it is nonetheless difficult to ignore one's immediate impressions. When one hears whales "talking" in the night, it seems quite obvious that they are able to communicate with one another; that they are not simply indulging in a series of sounds without meaning, but that they are actually exchanging thoughts and opinions.

My friends and I have perhaps spent too much time with whales; we may be the victims of an illusion. But how can we explain those alternating voices, and such a diversity of modulation, except by concluding that it is actually conversation? In any event, it cannot be denied that there are signals of some kind being exchanged — perhaps signals that are acknowledged from a distance by the cetacean equivalent of "roger"; or even that one whale "speaks" and that another answers.

The most startling transmissions are those, like Lagorio's choirs, that are group manifestations or forms of collective sound. Sometimes they sound like a rumbling, or buzzing, which varies in intensity. The overall effect is the same as a group of children reciting their lessons aloud.

Is it possible to define any of those sounds? Can we say that such and such a noise is an obvious cry of surprise? This, of course, is entirely subjective. The sounds of "surprise" that Lagorio heard one night were heard again on other occasions; and there is no doubt that, when the whales discovered the presence of the *Curlew*, or of a Zodiac, they gave little cries that may well have been expressions of curiosity. And they did not run away. They swam slowly around the craft, while squeaking softly. It was obvious that they were interested in us; and it is possible that was the meaning of the noise they were making.

It does not seem that whales have a special sound for alarm, as the birds do — the crow, for example. In any case, we have never recorded any whale sound that was followed by a withdrawal of the school.

A Bellowing Male

One night, while the *Curlew* was at anchor, Philippe and Lagorio were able to spend an hour — from 11 P.M. to midnight — in an extraordinary recording session. I say "extraordinary" because they were able to get an excellent recording of the sounds of a school of whales that was "talking" as its members swam slowly on their way. Occasionally, a loud bellowing would drown out the other sounds. We cannot say for sure that it was actually the bellowing of a male. And yet, that seems the most plausible explanation, for, on another occasion, it was possible to record a nearby bellow, and then one far off, as though the second was answering the first. Was it a mating call? A challenge? We know too little to be able to tell.

So far as humpback whales are concerned, it should be noted that, at the time that we were in Bermuda, it was not the mating season. Humpbacks mate at the end of winter and in the spring; and they do so around the Bahamas and the Antilles. Bermuda is merely a port of call for this species; they come to feed and to rest before resuming their northward trek. It does not seem likely, therefore, that the bellows we heard were addressed by a male to a female.

Bermuda has an abundance of the kind of food that humpback whales favor; and this, of course, is why they stop there. Through our earphones, we could hear perfectly well the crackling of the crustaceans that they were eating. Sometimes it was so loud that it garbled the sounds of the whales themselves.

These recordings, in fact, presented a number of problems. Underwater microphones give faithful reproduction only when the water is at a dead calm. If there is a swell, we get a lot of interference, in the form of the swell's noise, on the tape. And Bermuda seems to have more than its share of bad weather.

When the sea was not calm, Lagorio's Zodiac, obviously, rose and fell with the swell. And, just as obviously, the microphones rose and fell with Lagorio's Zodiac. . . and that section of tape was garbled. Lagorio tried everything that his not inconsiderable ingenuity could devise to compensate for this surface motion: buoys, floaters, springs, and, finally — which gave the best results — a Rube Goldberg arrangement of springs and pipes that, somehow, worked.

The chief disappointment of the *Curlew*'s team during their stay at Bermuda was their failure to record the sounds exchanged between a whale mother and her calf. It was impossible to get close to any of the mothers and to keep them in one spot. They could have used the virazeou on the calf; but then the Zodiac's noise would have prevented them from recording, because the sound of its motor would have drowned out any exchange between the mother and its calf.

Among the recordings made of humpback whales at Bermuda, there is nothing that goes beyond the range of the unaided human ear. The highest frequencies used by the whales were 8000 or 9000 cycles per second. Lagorio was prepared to record up to 35 kilocycles, but there was nothing taped that went into the ultrasonic range.

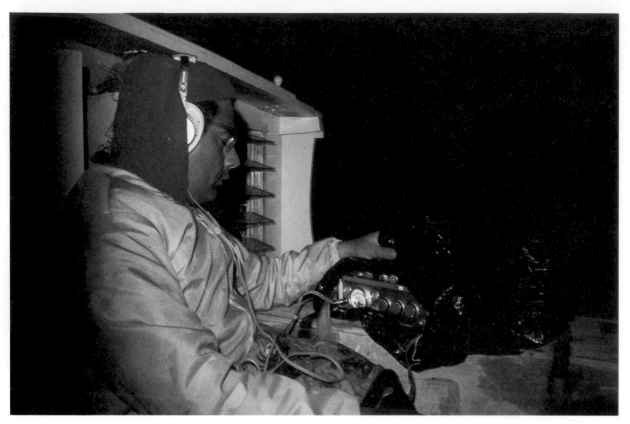

Eugène Lagorio, called "Gegène," with all his gear for recording the sounds of whales.

(Right) *Calypso*'s team listening to the whale "talk" recorded by Lagorio, who is to the right and wearing earphones.

Gray Whales

In the lagoons of Baja California, the water was extremely dirty; so much so that at the entrance to the lagoons we could scarcely see the whales. But we compensated for this by being able to hear them very well indeed.

It was again Lagorio who taped their voices. Usually, he stationed himself in one of the launches at a certain point, and lowered his microphones. Then, earphones in place, he would wait. He could locate the whales by sound as they approached his boat, and he could see the waves that they made on the surface. But the water was so cloudy that he could scarcely see what they were doing. Indeed, visibility was so poor that he often had the frightening

impression that the animals were heading straight for him and would ram the boat.

Then, at a given moment, the frequency of the whales' sounds increased perceptibly. They had sensed the boat in the water and were establishing its location and its shape by their echo-location system. The sonic waves they sent out sounded like ta-ta-ta-ta. . . . Then the transmission ended by a continuous trilling sound: trrrrr.

The animals increased their sounds in order to obtain more precise information on the object in their path. And, finally, Lagorio, without being able to see the school, could hear them turning away and swimming in another direction as their sounds decreased to a normal rhythm.

Lagorio and his team ordinarily went out in their launch very early in the morning, before dawn, because we had noticed that this was often the time that the gray whales entered the lagoon. (At night, they went out into the open sea, and returned to the lagoon at daybreak.)

It was therefore the best time to listen to them. But, again, there were problems in recording. The microphones drifted in the current, while the launch was blown in the opposite direction by the wind. Moreover, the choppy water striking the boat's hull garbled the sounds of the whales on the tape.

Despite these obstacles, Lagorio succeeded, on one occasion, in recording the sonar exchange between a mother whale and her calf. Their two trills are clearly recognizable. The mother's "clicks" are louder than those of the baby whale. And Lagorio saw their two dark silhouettes gliding alongside the hull of his boat.

These sonar messages were not the only sounds picked up by the microphones. Gray whales also emit the short mouselike squeaks that we had heard among the humpback whales of Bermuda. But gray whales are less talkative than their humpback cousins, and their voices are less strong.

A Time for Silence

An observation of Philippe's on gray whales deserves to be reproduced here:

"In the Matancitas lagoon," he says, "we would lower a Zodiac into the water, and then put down a microphone. If we listened for a while, we would hear a large number of very diverse sounds. The whales were there, all around us, but invisible. They had increased their sonar transmissions, however, because they were in such dirty water.

Eugène Lagorio, our sound engineer, records "the song of the whales".

"We dived with aqua-lung equipment, and the whales located us from far off. They passed under us; but visibility was so bad that we could hardly make them out, and they quickly disappeared into the gloom.

"What was strangest about the whole thing was that, as soon as they had located us, it seemed that all whale sounds in the lagoon ceased instantly. All that we could hear through the earphones was the noise from the bottom — especially from the crustaceans. Obviously, there was a rule of silence; a rule that one of the whales had invoked. And it worked, for there was instant and general silence. The tapes are a record of this phenomenon. At a given moment, there was not a sound to be heard from a whale on any track.

"Very likely, the 'silent treatment' was a security measure that the gray whales had developed as protection against marine animals whose hearing is as keen as their own; against killer whales, for example."

A Long-Distance Conversation

It has been said that the cry of a humpback whale in the Arctic Sea can be heard by another whale at the equator; but this, of course, has never been demonstrated. Whatever the case, we know for a fact that the sonic range of whales is fantastic.

How far do their sounds really carry? It all depends on the species, and perhaps on other circumstances: migration, the mating season, and so forth. There are certain empirical data that may begin to answer the question. We know, for example, that gray whales swim at an average speed of 5 to 6 knots.

Now, we hear gray whales one hour before we see them, and we can hear their sounds one hour after they have passed our position. It should be added that the cries of gray whales are far from being as loud as those of humpback whales.

Dr. Payne, an eminent American authority on humpback whales, is of the opinion that this species uses sound corridors — "deep sound channels," they are called — to communicate with one another over long distances. Moreover, water is a better conductor of sound than air, and it is an excellent transmitter for the sonic emissions of whales. It seems likely that humpback whales choose the place, and the depth, that is especially favorable to the dissemination of their sounds. It is also possible that a particular sound may be relayed from one group of whales to another throughout the course of a migration.

Another Mystery

What organ produces the sounds that a whale makes? How are the sounds made? No one knows for sure, and the experts are still studying the problem. One complicating factor is the fact that cetaceans, noisy as they are, have no vocal chords. They do have, however, a larynx, and a respiratory tract, and a blowhole — all of which may be used to produce sounds. But these are very complicated organs and systems which we have hardly begun to understand.

The problem has been studied especially with dolphins in captivity, and researchers have been able to distinguish two basic kinds of sound: "cracks" and whistles. The cracks are produced regardless of whether the blowhole is open or closed, but their frequency is different in each case. But high-frequency sounds apparently can be produced only when the blowhole is closed. From this, one can conclude that cetacean sounds are produced by a

A sight familiar to *Calypso*'s men: sea fans and coral—this time on the level reef that surrounds the main island of Bermuda.

complex of anatomical factors, of which the blowhole is only a part.

We could hardly hope to resolve this mystery of sound merely by observing sperm whales and baleen whales in the open sea. Nonetheless, I remember Philippe's excitement during a dive when he saw a stream of modulated bubbles emerging from a humpback whale's blowhole — which meant that the whale was there, in front of Philippe, talking. Perhaps it was even talking to *him* — a dialogue of the deaf.

The Invisible Ear

Cetaceans, even though they have no visible external ear, have a great advantage over fish: they have a middle ear, and an internal ear. Fish, on the other hand, have only an internal ear, and they cannot locate the origin of a sound that they hear. Cetaceans, however, do have an external ear — one which we cannot see because it is buried in the animal's skin.

The middle ear and the internal ear have properties that no doubt assure very keen hearing. The middle ear is partially surrounded by a substance that resembles beaten egg whites; and the internal ear has sensory cells that are especially well developed — like those of animals who hear ultrasonic noises (bats, mice, cats).

Another very important peculiarity is the unusual size of the auditory nerve in cetaceans. In the human brain, the centers of vision and hearing are of the same size. Among cetaceans (and bats), however, the acoustical centers are larger than those of sight. It should be noted that both cetaceans and bats at one point in their evolution abandoned life on land and adapted to another way of life: bats, to a nocturnal life in the air; and cetaceans to a life in the water which reduced visibility.

Cetaceans and Language

We know that society and language are related. We know also that whales are social animals, and that they communicate with one another. It is our ambition not only to listen to, but also to understand, the conversation of these social animals among themselves.

With land animals, the human voice has a function: it warns, it quiets, and, sometimes, it commands. What can it do, however, with cetaceans? One day, we will know. Man is trying — *we* have tried — to enter into verbal communication with these animals. But these have been clumsy efforts and vague attempts. Nonetheless, the cetaceans do not run away when we try. They stay; and we might even say that, in certain instances, they seem to be willing to co-operate. All of man's experiences with dolphins and killer whales in captivity indicate this. We have recorded their voices and sounds on miles of tape. It is not likely that we will learn to interpret their language very soon; but we are at least in a position to begin studying it.

It seems likely that, when man and cetacean communicate, it will be by means of sound, by voice. But communication does not consist in the mutual production of sound. Dr. Lilly has tried, in vain, to teach English to dolphins. But dolphins speak only dolphinese. If anyone is going to learn a new language, then it must be man. And there is no obvious reason why man cannot learn the language of the dolphins.

Nearsighted Whales

Baleen whales and sperm whales guide themselves by their sonar equipment, and hearing is the sense that is most important for them. Sight also plays a part in their sensory system.

The eyes of most cetaceans are blue, and slightly clouded. But they are eyes, as divers will tell you, that are full of life. Seen from close, they are quite beautiful — blue-black orbs that shine like crystal. But the eyes are small, and have the appearance of nearsightedness. This is true at least of baleen whales and cachalots. Killer whales seem to have excellent vision.

The size of a whale's eye in proportion to the body is almost unbelievable. One would say that everything grew except the eye. Man's eyes constitute one seventieth of his body; those of a mole — traditionally a nearsighted animal — are one eightieth of its body. But the eyes of a whale are only one six-hundredth of its overall mass. Perhaps he does not need more; for even when a whale is swimming on the surface, his eyes remain in the water.

Some divers claim that whales — especially humpback whales — seem careful not to disturb a man in the water. It is not known for sure whether or not that characteristic has anything to do with a whale's vision. And, for that matter, humpback whales, when they take action to avoid running into a man in the water, do so by raising their flippers. This means that they are probably aware of the man's presence in front of them through sonar, and not by sight; for their eyes are on the sides of their head and they do not have front vision.

None of this means that the whale's eyes are useless. His vision may be different from ours, or it may be bad; but a whale sees nonetheless. We have taken photographs of whales from as little as three feet away. And the eye that we see is not that of a blind creature.

"In the water," Canoë says, "there can be little doubt that a whale sees you, and that he is looking at you. Sometimes you even feel that it is *not* a kindly look; but that may be because there are several folds of skin under its eyes that make it *look* mean.

"Whenever I met a whale in the water, I always had the feeling that he saw me. And the look that a whale gives you is very different from that of a shark. A shark only glances at you. It passes with the appearance of not having seen you at all. But a whale's look is quite open. He doesn't look at you out of the corner of his eye."

Canoë is a man who has not only encountered cachalots, humpbacks, and gray whales in the water, but who has touched them, and even been towed by them.

Michel Deloire, who has filmed whales — sometimes in rather acrobatic circumstances — says this:

"Several times, I have caught the eye of a whale. I mean that there was no doubt at all in my mind that the whale *saw* me. Of course, that is a purely personal and subjective impression.

"So far as the cachalot is concerned, what gives him such a strange look is that his eyes are so inconspicuous and so hard to locate. They are far back in his head, and very low, almost at the corners of his mouth. Because of their location, these eyes cannot have binocular vision. Do the zones of vision of each eye overlap in front of the whale? For baleen whales, perhaps they do. But I doubt that this is the case for the sperm whale. Because of his enormous head, he must have a blind area in front of him.

"It would seem easy enough to find out about this by a simple experiment. In other words, when a diver is fifty feet in front of a sperm whale, does the whale see him? But it is not that simple. There is always a time when the diver is a bit to the right or to the left — and therefore within the range of those eyes."

A Sensitive Skin

The sense of touch, it seems to me, is third in the order of importance among cetaceans. Actually, I am not talking about "touch" in the same sense that man has that sense, but rather of a special sensitivity that extends over the whole body. The skin of cetaceans is different from that of land mammals: the epidermisis and the dermis are both thinner. Even among the largest whales, they are only about two and one-half inches thick. On the other hand, the layer of blubber which covers the entire body is exceptionally thick. The thinness of the skin probably entails great tactile sensitivity and thus sensations which it is difficult for land creatures to imagine. . .

We have, on several occasions, seen whales rubbing against one another. This action is almost always the preliminary to mating. Whale calves also seem to thrive on physical contact with their mothers; and they seem to enjoy rubbing against the hull of *Calypso*.

Lagorio was a witness to the following scene: in Scammon Lagoon, a baby whale left its mother's side to rub against *Polaris III*. The mother immediately went after the calf, pushed it far away from the ship — and then struck it several times with her flippers. The blows had every appearance of being slaps, and they were obviously administered in order to teach the baby not to confuse a ship's hull with a mother's stomach.

There is no doubt in my mind that cetaceans, like land animals, love to be petted and stroked. Dolphins, pilot whales, and killer whales in captivity seem to enjoy physical contact with humans. According to trainers and keep-

(Right) Between whales, our divers enjoy the splendid coral waters.

ers in aquatic zoos, the best way to domesticate one of these animals is by touching it, or brushing it.

There are other aspects of cetaceans' tactile sense that we know almost nothing about. Finback whales, for instance, have small bumps at the end of their snout; and several species have very sensitive "whiskers" on their cheeks. And the cells that are found in different organs may indicate the presence of another sense, one related to the perception of variations in water pressure or turbulence.*

So far as we can tell, cetaceans are not especially well endowed with respect to the other senses. At the base of their tongues, as in the case of man's tongue, they have "buds" — taste buds. We may therefore believe that whales are capable of appreciating the taste of krill, or squid. But we cannot say that cetaceans are difficult to please when it comes to food. They are not equipped to be gourmets; for the "taste nerve" which runs from the tongue is very small, and probably does not convey very intense taste sensations.

The sense of smell, which is well developed among fish, is very weak, or nonexistent, among marine mammals. It is completely absent in toothed cetaceans, and only rudimentary among baleen whales. In their blowholes — which are their nostrils — cachalots do not have the equivalent of the nerve cells that humans have. Baleen whales, however, have retained a certain number of olfactory cells.

Them and Us

The little that we know certainly does not allow us to form an adequate idea of the sensory life of cetaceans. We can say, however, that life is very complex, and occupies an important place within the framework of animal psychology. (Let us remember, for example, that the cachalot's brain is the largest of any animal in existence, and that its skull also contains an extraordinary and mysterious organ: the "tank," in which the spermaceti is enclosed.)

We have no way of knowing what the emotional life of these giants may be. We can hardly even imagine what it must be like to live in the water, and guide oneself by sonar, to depend more on sound than on sight. We can only resign ourselves to the fact that we will never be able to feel what a whale "feels."

---

*The "whiskers" seem to be the only capillary growth on the whale's body. The embryo does, however, have some hair growth.

A Whale's-Eye View of Man

Naturalists, as well as novelists, have always been concerned with what man knows and thinks about whales. But no one has ever wondered what whales think about man. This question has been much discussed aboard *Calypso* and everyone has his own opinion.

Philippe says that "when you latch onto a whale's back, it is like performing a trick on the trapeze or going up in a balloon. It is exciting for man. But I doubt that it does anything at all for the whale. They simply continue on their way. We probably annoy them somewhat, like a fly buzzing around a man. I doubt that they find us amusing. But they are so powerful that they do not even find it necessary to react, or to show any resentment or aggressiveness."

It would be interesting to know what whales think about us, what kind of creatures they believe we are, what sort of mental image they have drawn of us through their nearsighted view and their sonar equipment.

In the sea, they go out of their way to watch divers. They are, obviously, curious. A veteran diver in Bermuda assures us that a whale used to pay him regular visits while he was working on a particular job. I believe him. Whales, like dolphins, seem to seek out human company. We, unfortunately, are not in the same position. We cannot disappear when we wish. But whales can lose a diver in ten seconds by one swish of its tail, or dive straight down and vanish. So long as we are not able to go where they go and to stay by their side, we will never bridge the gap that separates us.

A piece of tail fin from a giant squid, which we found floating in the sea, is an object of great curiosity. It is being held by our chef—who plans to serve it for lunch.

SIX

The World's Greatest Flesh Eaters

It is May 20. We are in the Indian Ocean, and the weather is almost beautiful. Dawn is just breaking — and Didi Dumas reports a whale spouting off *Calypso*'s stern. Soon, we see others, many others, ahead of us on the horizon.

At eight o'clock, Dominique Sumian, who is on watch in the crow's-nest, calls out:

"Captain, there is something white floating to port."

Instantly, everyone is alert. On the sea, the most ordinary object may be a clue to what we do not see, or do not understand; to something that is happening, or has happened, beneath the surface. Any seaman worthy of the name must have in him the soul of what we call in French a *badaud* — that is, an unhurried browser in the marketplace of life, curious, eager for the unexpected, on the alert for something that will dissipate (or create) a mystery.

I take the binoculars and look. Dominique was right. There is something, a large white object. But what is it? It never occurs to us not to find out. Bebert takes one of the Zodiacs and brings back the object, holding it at arm's length. It is a large, heavy piece of flesh, white and flaccid — a piece of a giant squid's tail. The front part of it is torn, and it is covered with punctures similar to those inflicted by the teeth of a cachalot or a pilot whale.

Everyone is excited. We are no doubt close to a school of sperm whales. Apparently, there has just been a battle at the bottom of the sea, for the piece of squid is still fresh. In fact, it is so fresh that our chef announces that we are going to have it for lunch. It doesn't seem to bother anyone that we will eat the crumbs from a cachalot's table.

Bebert has also brought back a piece of flesh shaped like a saucer, or rather like a plate. It is one of the squid's suction cups. Dr. François measures it, and announces that its diameter is 24 inches. This, obviously, was a "small" giant squid. Its body probably measured between 8 and 10 feet — in addition to the large arms, of course. A handsome specimen, no doubt, and a worthy opponent.

As it turned out, it was also inedible, except by a cachalot. Our chef cooked the piece of the tail with garlic, but it was so tough that we could not cut it. And as for the suction cup, it was too horrible for us to describe. It was as though we had tried to make a meal out of a hunk of soft rubber.

Sperm whales apparently have no objection to this kind of diet. In fact, being devoted flesh eaters, they prefer squid to anything else. They find this delicacy in very deep water — between 2000 and 3500 feet — where the squid sometimes reach a length of forty feet. But cachalots will eat not only squid and octopus, but also just about anything else. So far as diet goes, they are easy to please, and consume quantities of giant crustaceans, seals, rays, and even sharks 10 or 12 feet long. Even so, they show a marked preference for cephalopods. We can therefore conclude that sperm whales, which are capable of remaining below the surface for as much as two hours, dive down to the bottom and swim for several miles there in search of anything edible. Their natural radar undoubtedly plays a great part in this hunt in the darkness of the deep.

The "monster squid" of the depths, the fantastic "Karken," is not a creature of legend. It exists in reality, but it is little known because it is almost impossible to capture since it comes to the surface only rarely, and then only at night. This is above all the case with the *Architeuthis,* the largest of the giant squids. No man has ever seen an *Architeuthis* except as food not yet digested in the stomach of a sperm whale. In the stomach of a whale killed near the Azores, a squid was found whole and intact, with its tentacles. It was 35 feet long and weighted 397 pounds. The sperm whale itself measured 47 feet in length.

The giant squid is by no means an easy prey for a cachalot. It has a well-developed nervous system, excellent eyes, and salivary glands that secrete a poison. We can surmise that a sperm whale's attack depends upon surprise. It tries to rush in and swallow the squid before the latter has time to resist. From the remains that we found today, it is evident that he does not always succeed. And when this is the case, the battle between these two giants, with such different weapons, must be on a scale beyond our power to conceive. The squid attempts to position his tentacles on the eyes and the blowhole of the cachalot, and rips at his attacker with his beak; and the whale, in the meantime, is trying to regain the surface while holding the squid's enormous weight on its head. One can imagine the whale tearing at the squid's soft body with those terrible teeth, as pieces of the victim float to the surface. But the battle continues still, for the squid's vital organs are not easy to reach, even for a cachalot.

We can only imagine what these battles must be like in the blackness of the great depths. Both the squid and the cachalot must use wit as well as force; for they are both magnificently (though differently) armed; and it is likely that their intelligences, though also different, are comparable. To the terrible jaw of the cachalot, the squid opposes its tentacles, suction cups, and beak. And, because of their highly developed nervous systems and senses, cephalopods are able to move as quickly, and with as much precision, as vertebrates. Moreover, given their undoubted intelligence, in combination with these weapons, they are adversaries worthy of the great sperm whales.

A Collector of Teeth

Calypso's divers, whenever they meet a cachalot in the open water, are always struck most by the animal's enormous square head, in which the eyes are situated far to the rear. The mouth also is strangely placed. It is far down from the whale's rounded muzzle, and, indeed, might almost be described as being on the whale's underside. The lower jaw is comparatively narrow and thin, and it carries the whale's teeth: sixty of them, in two parallel rows. Some of these teeth weigh six or seven pounds and are eight inches long — which, given the size and weight of the cachalot, are rather modest dimensions. These teeth fit into sockets in the upper jaw, where there are only tiny vestigial teeth.

The cachalot's teeth are all alike. That is, there are no incisors or molars, and they are used only for seizing the whale's prey. For this great animal, who to all appearances is so well armed and a flesh eater, does not have the teeth of a carnivore. The cachalot does not pulverize his food, nor does he chew. He does not even really bite. Instead, he swallows his food whole, in a gulp.

Aboard *Calypso*, everyone has more or less specialized in a particular area of marine life, and this specialization often has little to do with one's assigned job on the ship. The consuming passion of Marcellin, our electrician, is coral; and Laban, the engineer, dives to paint underwater landscapes. Delemotte has a special calling as a collector of teeth. He has brought back walrus teeth from the islands of the Pacific, and killer-whale teeth from Alaska. To these treasures he now adds cachalot teeth from the Maldives. His collection is actually quite instructive, and even beautiful. It is a pleasant pastime to look at these handsome bits of polished ivory — so long as they are not attached to a monstrous jaw.

We spend much of our limited leisure time discussing these various specialties and avocations among ourselves, and there is much sagacious nodding and much stroking of beards. For, in the ancient maritime tradition, *Calypso*'s men have always distinguished themselves by their personal adornment as well as by their accomplishments. There was the era of turn-of-the-century mustaches. Now, we are at the stage of beards and long hair. And everyone, of course, is perfectly free to experiment as much as he likes, since there is no one to witness either failure or success in this line except seals and cormorants and whales.

Bernard Delemotte's beard, which serves as a resting place for his curved pipe, is reddish blond, and Philippe's is brown and curly. Some of the divers sport the royal beard of King Louis XIII; and others, a more modern style of short, square beard. There are even some who favor the elaborate sideburns and mustaches of the Emperor Franz Joseph. It is something of a shock to see these time-honored decorations protruding from a diving mask. . . Only Laban has remained faithful to hairlessness of face and skull (and one is as unnatural as the other, for he shaves his head every day).

What would Jonah think of all this, I wonder. The truth is that his own story is not entirely a myth, and that for Jonah, certainly, it was a miracle. It has actually happened that a man who fell into the sea was swallowed by a whale. And, like Jonah, he was not chewed or ground up. He did not, however, emerge alive after three days. His chest was crushed, and by the time his body was recovered, the whale's gastric juices had begun to work on the corpse. This modern-day-Jonah story was recorded by the man who performed the autopsy on both the man and the whale, Dr. Egerton Y. Davis of Boston, in the 1947 issue of *Natural History* magazine. Shortly afterward, Dr. Davis, his scientific curiosity piqued, found a man who was willing to play Jonah experimentally. The man crawled, feet first, into the mouth of a sixty-five foot (dead) sperm whale. The throat, however, was so narrow that he was able to get through it only with difficulty. According to Davis, a man would be

The massive, indescribable form of a sperm whale, seen diving.

dead before reaching the whale's stomach. And as for spending three days alive in a whale, that would be absolutely impossible.

The "Teeth" of Toothless Whales

All cetaceans are carnivorous and consume an enormous quantity of living flesh. It would be impossible for them to feed their giant bodies if they lived on dry land. (And, in fact, even in the age of the dinosaurs, there never existed creatures of comparable size.) Whales can survive, and find the incredible amount of nourishment that they require, only in the living wealth of the sea; for a whale's mouthful of food can weigh more than a ton.

In order to feed itself, a baleen whale, while continuing to swim along, opens its gigantic mouth. The under-jaw is lowered; and the pleated crop—which is half the length of the whale's body—swells up as it takes in several tons of water, along with whatever food is in the water. The mouth then closes. The baleen in the upper jaw acts as a sort of strainer and, as the crop contracts, the water is forced through the baleen. The whale then swallows the solids that have remained in its mouth: crustaceans, jellyfish, small fish. But, even knowing this, to see a finback whale feeding, with its gigantic mouth open, is one of the most astonishing and awesome spectacles that a diver can witness. Bonnici saw it once, in the Indian Ocean. Our handsome finback whale — the one on whose dorsal fin Bonnici had hitched a ride — was the animal in question. When its mouth was closed, one could see only the lips, and a rather elongated and almost flat muzzle. On a single occasion, when Bonnici was present, that mouth opened. He could see the baleen grill, laid out in a circle of black and white, like something out of a nightmare. Then, the cavelike orifice closed without a sound, without a ripple. The head was flat once more, and the baleen was once more a secret. But the whale had not eaten, and we have no idea why it chose that particular occasion to exhibit its oral equipment. Was it a yawn? Or was it a sign of irritation — of resentment against Bonnici's antics? That is not important. What is important is that we succeeded in seeing and in photographing the toothless whale's baleen.

These whalebone fixtures are one of the strangest attributes of the *Mysticeti,* or toothless whales. They sometimes measure nine or ten feet in length, and seem to be closer in composition to fingernails than to teeth. (This was the "whalebone" of whalebone-corset fame.) They are tough, but flexible, and are found only in the upper jaw. Moreover, they are edged with a fringe , the spacing of which depends upon the size of the crustacean that the particular species of whale eats. Thus, the finback, who eats very small lifeforms, has a filter as fine as wool. And the blue (or sulphur-bottomed) whale, who subsists on larger crustaceans and on small fish, has a more widely spaced fringe.

Regardless of what whales eat, the fact remains that they require tons of food every day. And their primary task is to find this food. In summertime, they seek it in the highest latitudes, in the Arctic and Antarctic where the extended daylight of the long days causes the development of a photoplankton that entails the production of a zooplankton which whales devour.

At this time of year, whales gorge themselves twenty-four hours a day in the polar regions. They will need this nutrition when they begin their polar migration, in the course of which they do not eat at all. The subcutaneous layer of blubber which is formed is a reserve food supply for this trek; but it is also an indispensable form of insulation for these warm-blooded animals. (Indeed, whales are so well insulated that their bodies remain warm as long as thirty-six hours after their death.) Moreover, this layer is composed of tissues that are lighter than water, and which therefore offset the weight of the whale's body. In combination with the air in the whale's lungs, the layer makes it possible for the whale to float.

To give one an idea of the amount of nourishment that is involved when whales feed, let me mention that a young finback whale, while he is growing, eats about three and one half tons of plankton a day. An adult finback consumes between a ton and a ton and one half — which means that he takes into his mouth, and filters out, approximately one million cubic meters of water every single day.

An Orgy of Krill

The basic food of the baleen whale is krill *(Euphausia superba)*, a crustacean that is never more than two to two and a half inches long. Krill are found in greatest abundance at about depths of between 35 feet and 350 feet, even though they exist as far down as 3000 feet. In the waters of the Arctic and Antarctic, during the summer months, veritable blankets of krill cover hundreds of square miles of surface — so much so that the water takes on a reddish-brown color from the carotene (rich in Vitamin A) in their bodies. For the whales, of course, this is a feast without limit. They are surrounded by food, and have only to open their mouths in order to eat their fill.

Their menu is not limited to krill. In addition to this unique dish and the plankton, the whales sometimes swallow fish — and occasionally even a penguin, perhaps in the course of a yawn. In the stomachs of our humpback whales, for example, naturalists have found mackerel, herring, whiting, cuttlefish, and even a cormorant.

"Even though there are at least eight species of toothless whales," Ted Walker remarks, "each species seems to prefer a kind of crustacean that is not found everywhere in the oceans. Thus, the various kinds of whales do not conflict in their search for food."

Front view of a sperm whale. This is what our cameramen and photographers see coming toward them in the water.

The Nightmare of the Toothless Whale

Our friend the gray whale is very eclectic when it comes to food. During the summer, along the coasts of Siberia, it eats crustaceans from the bottom: amphipods. During the winter, in the lagoons of Baja California (where we observed it), it eats shellfish, clams.

When Philippe was diving in the lagoon of Matancitas he saw how the whales "fished" for their favorite mollusks. They always did so at low tide, and when the tide was slack, they slept. When the tide was either going out or coming in, the whales could be seen grouping and then swimming in or out against the current. They found food by holding themselves toward the side at a 90° angle and digging trenches on the bottom with their bodies. They would take sand and water into their mouths along with shellfish, and then rise to the surface and, with their heads sticking straight above the surface, filter out the liquid through their baleen by using their tongues as pistons. The sand was expelled with the water, and the shellfish were swallowed — partly by the force of gravity, and partly, no doubt, by the action of the esophageal muscles.

Observers have long wondered why gray whales thrust their heads up above the surface as though they were inspecting their surroundings. They are able to maintain this position for about a minute at a time — a position that is called "spyhopping." Old-time whalers believed that the whales were watching them. It is more likely, however, judging by what we have seen, that they do this for convenience in eating. Gray whales are able to swallow while in a horizontal position, but a vertical position allows them to filter the debris out of their mouths and to swallow rapidly whatever remains.

It is not entirely safe to watch a whale clam-fishing from too close. This Delemotte, Philippe, and Chauvelin learned the hard way. They had rowed one of the Zodiacs to a position directly over a whale busily engaged in rooting around the bottom. The whale suddenly decided it was time to come up for air, and when she did so the Zodiac was overturned and the three curious inspectors thrown into the water. We all agreed that it was unintentional on the whale's part; an accident. But I suspect that there may be times when a whale, like any other intelligent being, wants privacy. If so, this one made her point.

February 19. We are in Scammon Lagoon. The sky is relatively clear, and so is the water. The weather seems to have put our whales in a good humor, and there is a lot of leaping and playing all around *Calypso.* Is it the same whale who is doing all the jumping, or do they all have spring fever?
Our cameraman, Jacques Renoir, sets his camera up on deck and suc-

ceeds in filming a sequence that we have attempted many times before without success: a whale leaping completely out of the water, not once but twice in succession. It is likely that when they jump in this way they begin by supporting themselves on the bottom with their tails, and then thrust upward. But this is not absolutely necessary. Blue whales have been seen to leap out of the water in spots where the bottom was 250 feet below them. (This was off the coast of Gabon in Africa.) This sort of "spyhopping," therefore, is not necessarily linked to the whales' feeding habits.

One can imagine what it is like to see a great whale leaping out of the water to become silhouetted against the sky for a moment, and then to fall back with a cataclysmic splash and a noise like a thunderclap. It is no wonder that everyone aboard *Calypso* is intrigued and excited by these gymnastics, and that Ted Walker is bombarded with questions: Is it a game? Or a sexual rite of some kind?

Ted, stroking his gray beard, answers: "Perhaps, perhaps." He himself inclines to a less romantic explanation and believes that these leaps have something to do with the whales' digestive process. They jump, in other words, to help the food go down into their stomachs. This would be true particularly of mollusk shells which whales cannot break because they lack teeth. Moreover, as Ted points out, they have such disproportionately small throats that "sometimes what they eat cannot go down by itself."

Three Stomachs

The whole digestive apparatus of whales is, by human standards, very strange. As I have already mentioned, whales do not chew. Cachalots cannot do so because they have no molars; and baleen whales because they have no teeth at all. Since they all swallow their food whole, whales must necessarily have strong stomachs. And, in fact, many of them have three separate stomachs, or gastric pouches. The first one, or forestomach, produces no gastric juices, but serves to pulverize the food by means of a very sturdy muscular wall (which among finback whales attains a thickness of two and one half inches). This stomach also contains sand and pebbles, which helps in crushing the food.

The forestomach and the stomach are sufficiently large to hold a ton of krill — about a cubic meter of food. An inventory of an 80-foot finback whale's stomach revealed that it contained five million shrimp weighing two tons.

The head of a gray whale submerged in Matancitas lagoon.

The third stomach, which secretes digestive juices, is called the "pyloric stomach." It opens into the intestine by means of a circular aperture (the pylorus) — an arrangement which the whale has in common with man.

Sperm whales have only two stomachs. They may swallow a squid in one gulp; but squid have soft flesh that does not require mastication. There is only one hard part to a squid: the beak.

Our chef's experiment with squid meat taught us a lesson that every

Gray whales seem to raise themselves out of the water to look around. This is known as "spy-hopping."

cachalot probably knows from birth: one does not attempt to chew a squid, but swallows it whole. The trouble was that, having swallowed it, we needed two stomachs to digest it, like a sperm whale; and, unfortunately, we had only one apiece.

If we had succeeded in swallowing the squid's beak along with the rest of the animal, it is possible that we might have turned into producers of ambergris, that precious substance indispensable in the manufacture of expensive perfumes. Ambergris is found only in the intestines of sperm whales, and it very likely is formed from the beaks of squid that have been digested. The largest block of ambergris ever found in a cachalot's intestine weighed close to a thousand pounds and was worth a fortune.

The chances are that cachalots would have fared better at the hands of the whalers if it had not been for ambergris; for their flesh is mediocre and their oil inferior to that of baleen whales. Ambergris ("gray amber"), however, has always been highly regarded, first for the medicinal qualities imputed to it, and, now, for the strange quality that it has of causing a scent to linger. In addition, sperm whales offer another treasure: an exceptionally pure wax, called spermaceti.

A whale's digestive tract terminates in the intestine — and what an intestine it is, being much longer, proportionately, than that of man or of any land animal. The human intestine is five or six times the length of a man's body. That of a cachalot is twenty-four times the whale's length.* In a whale 55 feet long, the intestine measures over a thousand feet. That of a dolphin is less developed; it is only twelve times the length of the dolphin's body.

A Visit to the Pantry

However familiar we may be with whales — and no team has approached as many whales as we have in the waters of every sea of the world — our astonishment never lessens at their size, their strength, their gentleness, and their appetites.

Whales are the only creatures truly created on a scale worthy of the seas themselves. But are the nutritional resources of the seas equal to the task of feeding whales? Do whales struggle to find the necessary food, or is it easily available in sufficient quantity for them?

In the Arctic and Antarctic, as we have seen, whales find their tables already set, and groaning under an indescribable load of food. When they leave the polar regions to mate in the tropical zones, however, they eat hardly at all, and perhaps not at all. This is generally true — although we have noticed that gray whales and humpback whales do not turn up their noses at an occasional mollusk or crustacean.

Sperm whales, those mortal enemies of the giant squid, are another matter. Their principal habitat seems to be between 40°north and 40°south; and

*According to Sarah R. Riedman and Elton T. Gustafson, in *Home is the Sea for Whales.*

these are the farthest limits of their migrations. Unlike baleen whales, they cannot simply open their mouths and swallow a few million tiny crustaceans whenever they wish. They must seek out their prey, and sometimes they must fight in order to eat. They are not only meat eaters, but flesh eaters.

From this, two questions arise: Do sperm whales find enough victims in the sea? And do they find them in the comparatively restricted area in which they live?

It is my impression, from what I have seen in the Red Sea and the Indian Ocean, that cachalots move about with their sonar systems tuned toward the bottom, apparently in search of prey. This is probably also true of other cetaceans: dolphins, grampuses, and pilot whales. We can use *Calypso*'s sonar device in much the same way, in order to discover the layer below us that is richest in life forms. And it is my ambition not only to find the pantry of the whales, but to visit it, and if possible to make an inventory of it.

Plankton Soup

During our expedition in the Indian Ocean, I noticed that there were certain places, at about the level of the equator, where we were almost certain to come across killer whales, sperm whales, pilot whales, dolphins, and sharks, all in the same area. It seemed to me that these large marine animals all gathered there because of the abundance of food, and I wanted to investigate the truth of this supposition. For this sort of undertaking, we have aboard the SP-350 — the minisub — which would be ideal in determining the density of life at various levels of the sea.

Here are my journal notes:

April 8. Our first day on the high seas after leaving the Maldives.

In order to make sure that we will not miss anything, I have the automatic camera in the observation chamber checked in the morning and again in the evening. This camera records every living being passing within range of the *Calypso*'s prow, beginning at 6:30 A.M.

Saturday, April 9. We are traveling practically along the equator. Right now, my intention of running an inventory of the biological resources in these waters seems almost ridiculous. The job is simply too great to be undertaken. From the surface, one would think that the sea is empty; but we do not know what is going on 200, 300, or 3000 feet beneath the surface. It is my old dream — to see beneath the surface, to see and understand what no man has yet been able to see and understand.

After dinner we have our first minisub dive in the open sea. We have

A gray whale, accompanied by her calf, in Matancitas lagoon.

often talked about doing this, but we have never done it before. We lower the minisub into the water and attach it to our launch by a nylon line 1200 feet long. Bebert is in the minisub, and Maurice Leandri in the launch. Aboard *Calypso*, I am in touch with the minisub by sonar, and with the launch by walkie-talkie. What we intend to do is to allow the minisub to go down to about 1000 feet, and then to climb. (The purpose of the nylon line is to make sure that we do not lose the minisub.)

There are times — and this is one of them — when I feel that I am wasting

Aboard *Polaris III:* Philippe Cousteau (center) and (right) Eugène Lagorio, our sound engineer.

my time on something absurd. It is almost certain that we will see nothing. The ocean is vast, and the chances are against there being anything to see. Even from our observation chamber, it is very rare that we see anything. To send down the minisub is like looking for the proverbial needle in a haystack, unless — unless the layers of water below *Calypso* are richer than we think. And, of course, at night, when there is a general migration upward toward the surface, we may discover something interesting.

I set the sonar for 12 KC and note two DSL, two layers registering at 100 fathoms and 150 fathoms. At 34 KC, there is only one layer, at 150 fathoms. We shall see what we shall see.

Here is what we find:

75 feet: a plankton soup clouding the water. Little silvery fish from the deep. Tiny shrimp and crustaceans.

150 feet: an even thicker plankton soup. Two small squid who are very curious about Bebert. There are some fish with luminous organs, but it is hard to see them clearly because the water is so cloudy.

300 feet: still plankton soup. A seven-foot shark is circling the minisub and gives it a push.

450 feet: the water is clearing, but there is less life here.

525 feet: shrimp, with very long antennae.

850 feet: nothing. Clear water.

1200 feet: released ballast, and the minisub begins slowly to rise.

700 feet: a very large cephalopod, absolutely immobile about 30 feet from the minisub, is staring fixedly at Bebert. This is sperm-whale bait. Is it sleeping? Dreaming? If a whale comes along, the monster will be swallowed whole.

625 feet: released the second ballast. As the minisub rises, it is escorted by two sharks.

The minisub vertical reconaissance, lasting about one hour, has been very helpful. We now have information on several points:

The registering layer that rises to the surface at night is a cloud of plankton, crustaceans, and small fish from deep water. This cloud rises and falls at a speed of from 2 1/2 to 4 1/2 inches per second.

The water is more cloudy and more filled with small life forms at 150 feet than at 75 feet. And this confirms what we learned during Operation Lumen in the Mediterranean.

Large animals: three sharks, two squids, and an enormous cephalopod. Its great eye is perhaps luminous.

All in all, the dive was successful, and we will have to make more use of the minisubs in this fashion. Unfortunately, the SP-350 cannot go down far enough, and, in the future, we will use the SP-500 and the SP-3000.

One curious thing: the deeper layer, at 150 fathoms, seemed to vanish as the minisub approached it. I saw the same thing happen in the Indian Ocean in 1954 when we used the first automatic cameras with an Edgerton flash. On that occasion, we could see the layer dissipating on the depth finder. Perhaps our huge cephalopod is a part of that mobile layer characterized by negative phototropism.

Squid in Layers

April 11. Everyone in the deck and saucer teams is up at 4 A.M. By 5 A.M., the SP-350 is in the water for a dive that we will call "S-15." Dawn has not yet broken.

Here are our tentative conclusions. Last night's dive (S-14) was made a bit too late in the day. The various layers had probably finished rising. Dive S-15, however, produces results that are more typical: there is a layer at 125 feet, another at 400 feet (which has already sunk). The minisub catches up with the third layer at 725 feet, and finds that it is made up of shrimp and siphonophores swimming toward the bottom as fast as they can.

If we were going about this in a strictly scientific manner, we would have to make hundreds of dives of this kind; and then I would collate all the data as elements toward a study of DSL. But we are here in order to work with film; and, from this standpoint, dives early at night — say, one hour after sunset — seem to be those that find the most life forms (and the strangest) within range of the minisub.

There are two things that we must do better with. First, we must tow the minisub more slowly during its descent and ascent so that its pilot can observe as much as possible. Second, the kind of thing we are going to film will require that we improve our lighting drastically. We will have to work something out.

After dinner, there is another minisub dive, but this time the nylon line is attached to *Calypso* rather than to the launch. In order to assure that the line will not be too slack in the equatorial current, we double the minisub's ballast; and we also fasten the line to the forward bumper, so that the minisub will move front-forward.

The minisub is put in the water at 9:35 P.M., about two hours after sunset. At 10:25 P.M. it is at its maximum depth of 900 feet. At 11:15 it is back on the surface.

This dive is interesting, but disappointing so far as filming is concerned. I hoped to find zones of life corresponding with those expanded and deep layers. Everywhere there were one or two layers of squid. And often there were sharks. And yet, the minisub goes down at random, and its range of visibility is very limited. The tens of thousands of squid are probably the destined prey of the large animals, dolphins, cetaceans. For food to float downward from

A diver manages to come close to a gray whale.

(Facing page) Launching of the SP350 in the Indian Ocean in order to study the various quantities of food available at different depths.

Canoë and Captain Cousteau are pleased after a good day's work.

those fields of microscopic algae that comprise the upper layer, the yield (in weight) that is passed from one echelon to the next echelon in the nutritive chain must be greater under water than on dry land.

This, apparently, is so, for almost all the animals are cold-blooded — which means that they do not have to expend calories to maintain their body temperatures (unlike men, cattle, or dolphins). Weight does not exist; and therefore no calories have to be used to keep one upright. Calories are used only to move (and the bodies are designed to make movement as easy as possible) and to *grow*.

Is the whole thing an illusion? These minisub dives have given us unexpected results and have given me a new and broader outlook on marine life. It also seems to me to be a more logical outlook, because we have seen and photographed the huge cephalopod and the schools of squid on which the cachalots feed — which explains the squid's presence here. It is as though someone had given us the key to the pantry that I have been looking for, for so long.

SEVEN

The Art of Love

Love, it is said, makes the world go round. Certainly, it makes the whales go round. Love, or at least sex, is the reason why whales leave the glacial waters of the Arctic for the warm lagoons of Baja California. For, once they have completed the migration, they mate.

The age of sexual maturity among cetaceans varies according to species. For the blue whale, it is five years; for the porpoise, seven years. For most baleen whales, the age at which they are able to reproduce is between two and three years. Sexual maturity, however, does not mark the end of growth among these giants. Having attained puberty, they continue to grow.

In the school of gray whales that Philippe and his team followed southward aboard the *Polaris III,* in addition to the whales who were looking forward to mating, there were also expectant mothers who would give birth to their young in the tranquil waters of the Mexican lagoons. Having carried their calves for almost a year, they sensed their time was near,* and, accord-

---

*The length of the period of gestation among whales depends upon the species in question. For the gray whales, it is twelve months; for sperm whales, it is sixteen months.

Bernard Delemotte succeeds in establishing contact with a gray whale.

ingly, they seemed in great haste to reach their destination. It would have been unthinkable for them to give birth in the open sea. They required shallow water, a protected lagoon, warm waters. And they knew where there was such a place. The pregnant whales formed the advance party of the migrating school. They would be, as they always were, the first to reach Baja California. The others traveled more slowly; they were not expecting, and they could afford a more casual pace.

It was the latter group that the *Polaris III* followed, with our friend Ted Walker aboard. All along the California coast, the team was busy trying to mark and to film individual specimens of the school. And it was with these, the last to arrive, that Philippe and his companions reached the Mexican shores and the Gulf of California.

The coast of Baja California is studded with gray dunes on which no vegetation grows. It forms a complicated network of channels and passes and presents an appearance of strangely beautiful but savage isolation. Al-

Full-face view of a gray whale's head. This photograph was taken in Scammon Lagoon.

together, it is an ideal place for whales in search of privacy, for there is little chance of intrusion by strangers. The marked preference of gray whales for this kind of locale, for sand and solitude, has caused them to be nicknamed "desert whales."

It seemed to Philippe, who was on hand when the whales reached their destination, that they were perfectly familiar with the place. For many of the school, this was not their first visit. They had been here every year over a long period of time, and they remembered the "secret passage" — the inlet — that led to the lagoon; or, if this was their first trip, they followed the older and more experienced members of the school. In any event, they all seemed to know, beyond a doubt, that, just beyond that narrow neck of water, there lay a personal paradise ideal for giving birth, or for practicing the art of love.

These places are so well hidden that, until the middle of the nineteenth century, they were unknown even to the most avid whalers. They were finally discovered in 1852, by Captain Charles Melville Scammon, commanding the brig *Mary Helen.* Scammon had been attracted by a series of spouts seen from afar, and, in his search for their origin, it occurred to him to enter the lagoon. There, he discovered a concentration of whales such as he had never dreamed existed.

Over a period of nine years, Scammon and his harpooners slaughtered whales in the hundreds and filled thousands of barrels with whale oil. Naturally, they kept strictly to themselves the secret of this windfall — the fact that Scammon had happened upon the pass leading into the most populated of the lagoons of Baja California, into what today is known as Scammon Lagoon.

In the tenth year, Scammon's competitors, consumed with envy and determined to share in this good fortune, had spies set upon Scammon's ship. In a short time, his secret was in their hands. Thereafter, the slaughter of gray whales reached such proportions that, by the beginning of the twentieth century, the species was on the verge of extinction. It was saved only by a series of international agreements — agreements which the government of Mexico enforced with commendable severity. Even so, it took almost fifty years for the species to recover from the havoc wrought by Captain Scammon and his fellow whalers; and it was not until the middle of the twentieth century that the gray whale began to be found again in appreciable numbers.

Today, most members of the school are less than thirty-five years old, and they average 50 feet in length. If they are left alone, they will live for another half century or more, and will reach lengths of 55 to 60 feet.

Captain Scammon differed from his associates to the extent that he combined an ardor for whale hunting with a taste for zoological curiosities and a certain talent for writing. He was the author of a book on the subject that he knew better than any of his contemporaries: *Marine Mammals of the Northwest Coast of North America.*

Scammon recorded that, when the female whales were about to give birth, they withdrew to the farthest reaches of the lagoon, which lay about thirty miles inland from the coast. My own observations indicate that expectant mothers seek out isolated spots where the water's greater salinity offers increased floatability, and where the abundance of food enables them to produce adequate amounts of milk. Nonetheless, many of these whales remain near the pass while giving birth.

When I first entered the lagoon, I suspect that my astonishment was at least as great as Captain Scammon's. There were spouts in every direction, almost as far as I could see, rising toward the gray sky. Everywhere, whales were floating on the surface, immobile, apparently asleep. There were at least a hundred of them in sight at that moment.

The Bay of Solitude

After one passes through the channel, Scammon Lagoon comes into view in all its immensity. It is not easy to explore, for channels branch out in every direction. Sandspits, which are exposed at low tide, make navigation difficult. Philippe, when he first reconnoitered the Baja California coast by airplane and boat, selected for us a lagoon other than Scammon: Matancitas, which appeared to be better suited to our work. Matancitas is a narrow strip of water separated from the sea by sand dunes. Entry into Matancitas is feasible only through Boca de la Soledad: the passageway of solitude. There is another channel, but it leads into Magdalena Bay and is very long and winding.

The whales themselves use only Boca de la Soledad, and the *Polaris* chose to follow their lead. In its explorations, it wandered up tiny channels, followed the line of mangroves that border the beaches, and investigated Magdalena Bay. The *Polaris* has a draft of five or six feet, and it often touched bottom in the course of its wanderings. Fortunately on such occasions, the bottom was always of sand or mud, and no damage was done; but the ship's local crew, unaccustomed to this sort of touch-and-go navigation, spent their days in a state of near panic.

As isolated as the region appears, there is a small town in the vicinity, Matancitas, which gave its name to the area. The town comprises nothing more than a canning factory, some fishermen's houses, and a landing field. And, over the whole, there reigns an incredible odor; an odor so strong that those who tried to sleep there for the first time — the *Polaris* was too small for everyone to be able to sleep aboard — found it virtually impossible to do so. The stench is due to the canning factory, whose main product is anchovies, and whose waste is dumped into the lagoon.

The First Dive

The first time that our divers went down into the Matancitas lagoon, they received an unpleasant surprise: the visibility was practically zero. The presence of sand and mud in the shallow water makes it perpetually cloudy.

There was one advantage at Matancitas, however, that made the *Polaris'* team willing to put up with the cloudy water. The fact that the lagoon, lying as it did between two dunes, and comprising the maze of waterways that it

(Following page) A gray whale diving in a lagoon of Baja California.

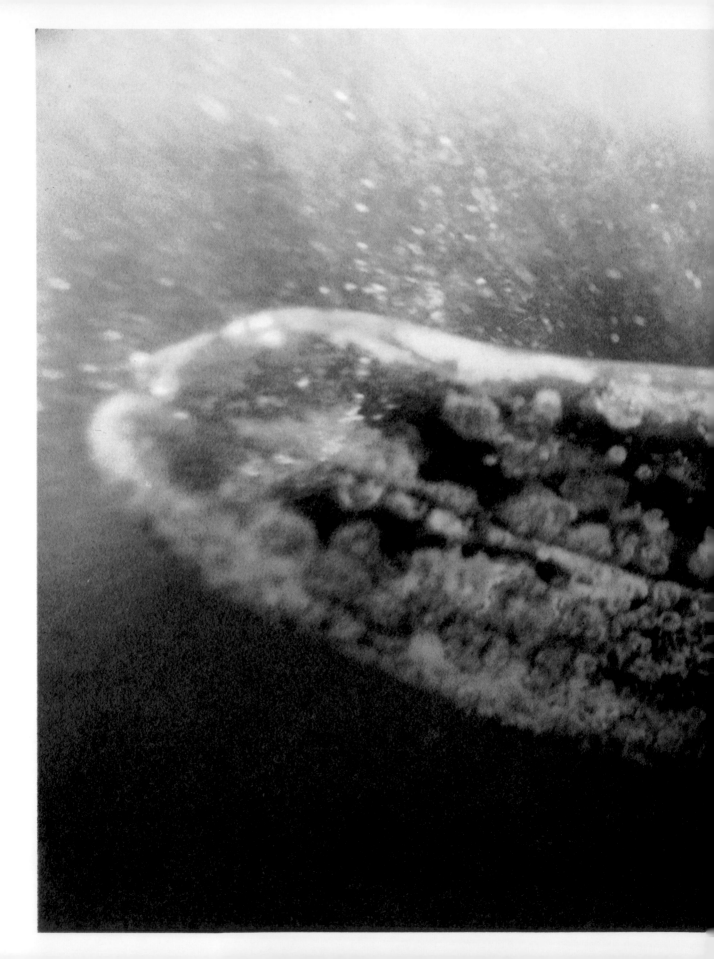

Our team—trying not to disturb a finback whale at night.

The balloon is of the traditional type — a classic Montgolfière, no less — and the hot air is provided by a fuel-oil burner. The chief problem is that it is difficult to handle because of its thermic inertia. It tends to rise and descend at a rapidly accelerating rate, and it requires considerable dexterity on the part of the pilot to keep it at the desired altitude. Moreover, its effective operation requires that there be no wind to speak of.

Philippe took advantage of an exceptionally fine day to go up in his balloon with a battery of cameras — and with his wife, Jan, who insisted on accompanying him.

"In my mind's eye," Philippe reports, "I can still see the balloon's shadow on the lagoon. The air was unusually calm, and it was a spectacular day. I could see the whales below me as they rose to the water's surface. And, from my vantage point, I could also make out some rays and sand sharks on the bottom. It would have been impossible to see them from the Zodiac.

"It was an absolutely magnificent experience. I got many shots that we could never have gotten even from an airplane, because a plane travels too fast and because its noise panics the animals.

"Of course, the balloon makes noise too, but only when it is being launched. The flame from the fuel-oil burner — it's about three feet high — roars like a lion. But, once the balloon is stabilized, we need only a small flame to keep it going. So, we are able to remain over one spot in the water for as long as we want without disturbing the animals. To them, we probably look like part of the landscape."

After Philippe had been in the air for a period of time, however, the wind rose and began pushing the balloon out to sea. He then dropped a line to a waiting Zodiac, and the balloon was towed back to the *Polaris*

Philippe's balloon ascent uncovered several important things, among them the locations where there were the largest concentration of whales, and also the sheltered spots to which they went to give birth to their young.

From the air, he was able to observe the technique of a young male who quite obviously had designs on the virtue of a female accompanied by a calf. The female would have none of it, and kept pushing away the male with her head while his tail thrashed violently in the water. The male, however, was difficult to discourage, and his advances continued.

"It was quite a spectacle," Philippe said. "The male would literally hurl

Aerial view of a group of gray whales during the mating season in Scammon Lagoon.

himself upon the female at a high speed. It was like watching two ships collide. The calf, who was unlucky enough to be between the two when the male charged, was actually lifted out of the water by the force of the charge.

"The matter was finally settled when the female, her patience apparently exhausted, gave the male a great swat with her tail, and sailed away with her calf in tow."

An Amorous Trio

Ted Walker had already described to us the gray whales' technique for coupling. The two animals lie side by side on the surface on their backs. Then, they turn over on their sides and there is the first attempt at penetration. (This position, awkward as it sounds, is at least more comfortable than that of other species of whales, who couple standing vertically on their tails.) The male's organ, which is curved like the handle of a cane, is proportionate to the whale's size — generally, one tenth the length of its body — and it is placed far back on its body.

Ted has had a vast amount of experience with the behavior of whales; and he has an extraordinary instinct for recognizing the significance of a particular act, gesture, or position. He keeps special watch, for example, over the tail and the flippers; and he is hardly ever wrong in his interpretations.

One day, toward noon, Ted was watching the lagoon from *Polaris'* rear deck. "Look! Look!" he yelled. "Hurry up, everyone. They're mating!"

Bernard Mestre, one of the cameramen, and a diver jumped into a Zodiac, very excited, and shot out to the spot that Ted had indicated. There, they found not two, but three whales, all rolling around together and stirring up a sea of foam.

It took a while to understand what was actually happening. It seemed at first that the two males* were competing for the female's favors. Each one apparently was trying to displace the other — a situation that did not seem designed to facilitate mating. But Ted explained that, in the sexual encounters of whales, there are almost always two males. The second male has a specific function: he lies across the male and female who are coupling, in order to help them maintain their position in the water.

---

*Ted Walker is very competent at distinguishing males from females by the shapes of their heads. The males' heads are narrower. It is true, however, that, in the present instance, there were other ways of telling one from the other.

Philippe Cousteau as director of "Project Gray Whale."

Be that as it may, by the time the Zodiac arrived at the scene, the second male's function seemed to be limited to swimming in great agitation around the other two whales, who were making a great deal of noise.

The Zodiac team could see that the female was using her flippers to hold the male in an embrace. It was a strangely touching sight.

It is probable that the team arrived at the very beginning of the mating process. The preliminaries, and the initial attempts at penetration, went on for a long period of time. Finally, the whales coupled, or attempted to do so, perhaps ten times.

Meanwhile, the Zodiac was only a short distance away, and our team was fascinated by the sight. The overall impression conveyed was one of an alien sexuality, a sort of erotic nightmare. It was an act of love on such a gigantic scale, and so difficult, as to be almost pathetic. There was an element of pain, almost tragedy, in the repeated attempts of these leviathans to

Philippe and two other men carrying his balloon's nacelle.

Philippe has become particularly adept in handling his hot-air balloon.

The balloon enabled us to observe and film the gray whales without frightening them.

The balloon is deflated and folded aboard the *Polaris*.

achieve penetration — an element reflected in the frenzied gyrations of the third whale around the mating pair.

The team in the Zodiac — the cameraman and the diver — had intended to get into the water, but the scene was so violent that they thought it better to go no closer than they already were. The action of the whales, however, was so complicated and confused that they were unable to shoot any good footage. And, of course, the movements of the whales made the water even cloudier than it already was.

What would have happened if the men had decided to dive into the water for a closer look at the whales? There is no way of knowing for sure. What is certain is that the three whales were in the grip of violent emotions and no longer conscious of what was going on in the water around them. Gray whales are not particularly aggressive, except when it is a matter of defending their young; but, in this instance, there would have been a serious danger of being struck, unintentionally, by a flipper or a tail — a blow capable of crushing a man.

After a while, Ted Walker noticed a large spot of froth on the surface, covering an area about a hundred feet long. In his opinion, it was probably the sperm of the male whale; or perhaps a substance secreted by the female. Another possibility is that the water of the lagoon, containing as much organic matter as it does, had been simply whipped into a foam by the movements of the whales.

It is certainly possible that the mating had not been successful, and that the male's sperm had been lost in the water. According to all the experts, it is relatively rare that the male succeeds in penetrating the female. And this, no doubt, is the reason why the attempt is repeated at such brief intervals and lasts such a short time.*

The main obstacle in the mating of whales is the fact that it is necessary for them to rise to the surface in order to breathe. Sexual contact takes place in the water, when the two whales are partially submerged; and the pair must co-ordinate their breathing in such a way as to be able to rise and sink together.

It seems that when whales dive deliberately, they are able to remain submerged longer than when, half asleep, they merely sink back beneath the surface, or when they do so in the process of mating. Before a dive, in order to

---

*According to K. S. Norris, the sexual act lasts for only ten to thirty seconds, and may be repeated every eight minutes for an hour and a half. There are numerous contacts between the male organ and the stomach of the female before penetration is finally achieved.

Maintenance of the balloon is time-consuming and complicated.

be able to remain as long as possible beneath the surface, a whale prepares itself by hyperventilating its lungs. However, when it sinks beneath the surface, either while it is sleeping or when it is excited, it does not hyperventilate, and it must necessarily breathe again in a short time.

For males, the act of coupling is a rare and important phenomenon. According to Ted Walker, a successful penetration is the exception rather than the rule in the love life of the whale. Success requires the simultaneous realization of several conditions: the proper time of year, a suitable place, a female in heat, victory over one or more rivals, and, of course, the consent of the female. Under the circumstances, mating is impossible during the migratory trek from the Bering Sea. All the energies of the school must be devoted to swimming, for the time available for the voyage to Baja California is relatively brief.

Not all cetaceans mate in the same way, and the behavior of gray whales is somewhat exceptional. It happens frequently that the female rather than the male is the initial aggressor, in that she shows the male that she is in season. Since whales have virtually no sense of smell, the male must rely upon his sight.

Humpback whales mate facing one another, chest to chest, and the climax occurs as they rise together, at considerable speed, to the surface. A technique as acrobatic as this one can only be effective when sexual contact is very

A humpback whale. Its mating habits are particularly arduous.

brief, lasting no more than a few seconds.

During the *Curlew*'s observation of humpbacks in the waters around Bermuda, there was no opportunity to witness this technique in action. But our friends did see humpback whales making fantastic leaps out of the water, and these may have been part of the mating ritual; or they may even have been the last phase of an unsuccessful attempt at copulation.

Humpbacks are the acknowledged champions of this sort of high jumping. Their bodies leave the water completely, and then they fall back, onto their backs, with a loud noise and an enormous splash. Altogether, it is an impressive demonstration of the power of these 40- or 50-ton giants.

At Bermuda, Philippe witnessed another episode of love-making among whales, and this one did not involve humpbacks.

"One especially fine day, we had just taken the *Curlew* outside the lagoon when we saw one spout, and then two, in the distance. When we got closer, we put the Zodiac into the water, and Bernard Delemotte, Dominique Sumian, and I set out to investigate.

"We saw two whales. At first, we thought that they were gray whales. They were not quite as dark as the humpbacks that we were used to, and they had no dorsal fins.

(Right) Gray whales are champion acrobats. In order to make such leaps, they must attain a speed of 25 miles per hour.

The habits of the sperm whale are quite different from those of the baleen whale. Their love-making is much more violent, and the males are devoted polygamists. It is not unusual for a large male to have gathered around him a combination harem-household comprising twenty to fifty other whales — females and offspring.

The lord and master of this family unit may, sooner or later, find himself dispossessed. There seems to exist among cachalots the same sort of rivalry for females that one finds among sea elephants and seals; and there are always young males around the fringes of the reigning male's household.

A dethroned male is left alone in the sea and, to escape his shame, he takes refuge in the waters of the Arctic and Antarctic. It was in polar waters that whalers used to find those immense and very old solitary males whom they called "Emperors."

"We stopped the Zodiac about 200 yards away so as not to frighten them, and Delemotte and I swam the rest of the way. Unfortunately, the water was cloudy. Nonetheless, we saw clearly enough what was happening. There were two whales — right whales — mating. There was no mistaking it. They were rolling one on top of the other, caressing each other the length of their bodies.

"It all happened very quickly. They were not so caught up in each other as not to be aware of our presence. As soon as they discovered us, they disappeared. I was able to shoot only about thirty-five feet of film.

"There is no doubt that these were actually right whales. They had short, well-defined triangular flippers, and no dorsal fins. Their mouths were enormous; and their stomachs were spotted. Their appearance was very different from that of any other species of baleen whale that we had ever seen. They looked like great cows, swollen and heavy."

Whales generally are monogamous to the extent that a male will remain with the same female for at least one season. In any case, during the mating season one meets whales in couples or in trios. It is possible that gray whales, who are the "liberals" of the cetacean world, practice polyandry. We saw some indications of this in Scammon Lagoon. So far as the other baleen whales are concerned — the finbacks, humpbacks, etc. — they seem to play in couples what Professor Budker describes as "games designed to assure the continuation of the species."

EIGHT

The Nursery of the Leviathans

After the excellent work done by Philippe and his team in Baja California's Matancitas Lagoon aboard the *Polaris III,* I decided to wind up our observation of gray whales with a visit to the bay of Scammon. Philippe had decided that this lagoon was too large to be studied with the equipment that he had on hand on the *Polaris.* With *Calypso,* however, and our launches, Zodiacs and other equipment — to say nothing of our twenty-nine men, including divers — I thought that we would well be able to undertake the observation of the gray whales that, we were told, were everywhere at the bay of Scammon.

One of our fondest wishes was to be present at the birth of a whale calf. The *Polaris* team had been able to watch whale mothers nursing their young, and even to film the scene. But no one had yet witnessed the birth of a whale or of a cachalot, although dolphins in their tanks had been observed, and filmed at length, bearing their young. It seemed to us that whale maternity would be a marvelous subject.

Generally, baleen whales have a calf every two years, and they nurse the calf for nine months. Among cachalots, however, gestation lasts sixteen

A camera team, in the Zodiac, follows in the wake of a whale.

months rather than a year, and there is a birth only every three years.

We know that almost all cetaceans are born tailfirst from the belly of their mothers. This is a rather striking trait, for all other species of viviparous mammals* bear their young headfirst. Among cetaceans, being born tailfirst prevents the calf from drowning during birth; and then, as soon as the process of birth is complete, the mother very quickly takes the calf to the surface for its first breath of air. She is aided throughout by one or more females — midwives, or, as they are called in California, "aunts" — who continue, after the calf's birth, to act as "mothers' helpers." There is every indication that these surrogate mothers are bound to the calf by emotional as well as practical ties.

Bringing *Calypso* into Scammon Lagoon was not an easy operation, nor an entirely safe one. The only entrance is quite narrow and shoaled. The

*The only other exception are the *Chiroptera* (bats).

Two gray whales in Matancitas Bay.

channel is a series of twists and contains a number of sandspits, and its con-figuration varies from tide to tide. Moreover, the first part of the lagoon is filled with salt marshes and would be totally impossible if buoys had not been placed, in a zigzag pattern, to mark a channel.

Calypso touched bottom twice; but, fortunately, the bottom was muddy in both places, and she was able to extricate herself without difficulty.

After we had found good anchorage within the lagoon, the two Zodiacs and two launches went out every day to reconnoiter the area. There were gray whales everywhere, and the small craft had to maneuver among them con-stantly and as quietly and inoffensively as possible.

Many of the whales seemed to be asleep, with their calves lying along-side of them. Some of the calves were even resting their heads against the mothers' chests near their mammary glands. But they were not nursing. Sometimes, mother and child seemed to play by rubbing against one another.

Like all infants, whale calves seem to be unaware of danger and to have confidence in the goodness of all creatures. They are also very curious.

(Above) In a Zodiac piloted by Canoë, Bernard Delemotte has rescued a wounded pelican and is bringing it back to *Calypso*.

(Right) This particular pelican has developed a great affection for Bernard Delemotte who is holding him.

(Facing page above) Pelicans always gather at the same time and on the same sandbanks.

(Facing page below) Pelicans are excellent underwater fishermen.

to their young ones. When they were awake and we came near, they were immediately ready to charge. And, in every instance, they would immediately place themselves between the Zodiac and their calves.

On one occasion, Bonnici and Delemotte unwittingly caused a great uproar in the nursery. Several mothers were sleeping, while their calves were playing in the water near them. As soon as the Zodiac appeared, two of the calves swam over for a better look at this strange apparition. But, at that moment, the mothers awoke; and all that Bonnici and Delemotte could see were indignant spoutings emerging from a minor hurricane in the cove. By the time the water was calm again, the calves had been forcibly returned to their mothers.

Everything had happened so quickly that the men in the Zodiac had not even had time to react. The cameraman, on instinct, had waved his camera around — but the film, when developed, showed nothing more than an enormous splash of water.

In earlier times, whalers often took advantage of whales' maternal instincts in order to meet their quota. Captain Scammon, for example, for whom this bay is named, used to begin by firing upon the calves, which inevitably led the mother whales to charge the whaling boat; his men could then throw their harpoons at close range. It was a dangerous game, however, for it is not always easy to evade the charge of a furious 40-ton animal; and, in fact, Captain Scammon had many boats crushed by mother whales mad with rage. But he also succeeded in killing a great number of gray whales.

The Cradle

After a while, we became more and more adept at approaching whales without disturbing or frightening them. Our teams would maintain absolute silence, and would always approach a whale from the rear. This tactic allowed the teams, on several occasions, to see mothers nursing their calves — an extraordinary spectacle, and a moving one. Even among giants, the act of nursing one's young has an air of tender familial intimacy about it.

While the calf is nursing, the mother whale's flippers play such a large role that they almost seem to be arms cradling the young one. The whale lies on her side and holds the baby with her flippers while he nurses. As long as she is not disturbed, she rises and descends slowly in the water, carrying the young one with her. At the same time, she keeps the baby's head above the surface, and he nurses a few seconds at a time.

The breasts of the mother whale are in proportion to her body and, al-

Delemotte force-feeding his pelican.

(Following page) A mother humpback whale supporting her calf.

The grateful pelican cannot tear himself away from Delemotte.

though located in a fold of skin, they are very large. A muscle squeezes the breast and sends out a jet of milk under a pressure sufficient to carry it straight up for six or seven feet.

We have had the opportunity to see this milk on the surface, and even to taste it. It is yellow rather than white, with a strong taste and an oily flavor. It is extremely rich in fat — 35 percent, as contrasted with 3.5 percent for cow's milk.

A baby whale grows at a rate that is almost incredible: about 230 pounds a day, or almost 10 pounds every hour. A ton every nine days. No other animal in the world grows at a comparable rate. (We are of course talking about the infantile rate of growth.) A blue whale calf reaches a length of about 50 feet in three years; and its "youth" breaks down as follows: infancy lasts 7 months; adolescence, 17 months; and another year passes before he reaches sexual maturity.

A Rubber Doll

In spite of our best efforts, it was impossible for us to witness a birth. It was not because the whales were particularly shy, but because we never managed to be in the right place at the right time in that gigantic maze which is Scammon Lagoon. The actual birth is probably very brief in duration. The calf must be free of the mother's body very quickly, otherwise it will die. Infant mortality, indeed, is high, if one may judge by the number of bodies of baby whales that we have seen along the banks of the lagoon.

Ted Walker tells us that gray whales give birth in shallow water, lying on their backs, and that they push their offspring to the surface so that they may breathe immediately after they are born.

The new-born calves that we have seen have all been in very shallow water with their mothers. When they are that young, their bodies are very soft — like foam rubber — and they cannot swim. Even when they move their tails, they remain in the same spot. Nor do they float. Their density is too great at that age for them to do so, and their thoracic cages are not yet sufficiently developed for the air from their lungs to keep them afloat. Their mothers must therefore hold them on the surface. I have often seen, from the Zodiac, a mother whale carrying her baby with her flippers, either against her chest or below her head. The baby rolls in the water like a barrel, and spends more time on his side or back than on his stomach; but the mother always sets him right side up again and keeps his head above the surface.

The fact that baby whales can neither swim nor float explains why the gray whales of California travel four or five thousand miles to Baja California's shallow waters in order to give birth. If their offspring were born in the open sea, they would almost surely drown.

February 17. The whole day has been spent getting ready for a dive tonight. The diving suits have been painted phosphorescent red, and strips of the same color have been attached to the Zodiacs and launches. The reason for making this dive at night is that Ted Walker believes gray whales may give birth only after dark.

We begin at two o'clock in the morning. The Zodiacs and launches set out into a night so dark that it is almost opaque. Everyone watches for disturbances in the water, and for spouts. The cameramen are in the water, and the divers have lighted their floods. Ahead of them, we see silhouetted the motionless bodies of whales asleep. Nothing moves. The divers remain at a slight distance. It would be pointless to disturb the animals — especially since we do not know how they might react.

We look over the sleeping whales very carefully, but, so far as we can see, no female is giving birth.

We shoot some film and then return to *Calypso.* By now, dawn is breaking, and the dunes are pink in the morning light.

The Pelicans

We learned gradually to understand and love this "desert" of Baja California, in which a secret animal kingdom flourishes in the dry sand, at the foot of the cliffs with its mangroves whose roots twist like serpents into the water.

Our primary purpose in going to Scammon and Matancitas was to study gray whales. But, once there, we discovered the pelicans, and found them only slightly less interesting than the whales. We could hardly miss them, and it was a revelation to discover how intelligent they are, and how beautiful in flight. They resemble bombers in formation. When they land, they put their feet out in front and water-ski a bit before settling into the water, sometimes for as much as thirty feet.

The pelicans were with us every day. Every morning and every evening, at the same time, when the light was reddish pink, they would fly in single file over the pink and gray dunes as though this was a planned maneuver which they were obliged to perform.

They had a particular place during the day, and one for the night, and they assembled in those spots in numbers that must occasionally have

Ted Walker talking with Bernard Delemotte and Dr. François aboard *Calypso*.

reached a thousand. Sometimes, as though on a whim, they flew in a straight line only a bit above the surface of the water.

When the pelicans fished, each one of them was accompanied by a sea gull. The sea gull followed his host pelican closely, eating whatever the pelican would not eat or what he let fall. When the pelican dived, the sea gull dived also.

We found a pelican with a broken wing and took him aboard *Calypso*; but the next day he escaped over the side and fell into the water, crying pitifully, unable to fly. Serge Foulon jumped overboard and rescued him, and brought him back to us. Up to that time, the pelican had shown no enmity to any of us; on the contrary, he seemed friendly and easy to train. But, from the moment that Serge brought him back aboard, the bird could not bear the

(Left) A humpback whale and her calf seen from beneath.

sight of his rescuer. Everyone else could pet the pelican except Serge. If Serge went near him, there was an uproar, screams, and a great clacking of the pelican's beak. A pelican's beak is a rather dangerous weapon, ending as it does in a pointed and very sharp spur.

It was Delemotte's job to feed the pelican. He named it Alfred (in honor of Alfred de Musset), and Alfred returned the favor by eating, very gently, out of Delemotte's hand.

As soon as Alfred could fly again, of course, we released him.

A Sewing Job

No sooner was Alfred out of sight than we had another resident pelican aboard. This one we found on the beach, weak and thin, and very sad-looking. Philippe caught him and brought him aboard, where we examined him and discovered that his pouch had been ripped from top to bottom.* He could no longer eat, since all of his food would fall through the tear. The bird's condition was not the result of an accident. We learned that the children of Matancitas, when they catch a pelican, slit open its pouch with a pocketknife.

Dr. François, our ship's doctor, selected a spool of heavy thread and a large needle. After sterilizing them in alcohol, he sewed up the pouch. The next day, the animal was able to eat. A few days later, Dr. François pronounced him fit to travel, and he was released.

In a surprisingly short time, we had all developed an attachment for our two pelican patients. The pelican's combination of natural dignity and natural humor is hard to resist.

After living for weeks in close quarters with the birds, after seeing them flying and hearing their cries daily, we looked upon them as an inseparable part of the locale, along with the spouting whales and the sand and mangroves. They became a symbol of this place that is at once so desolate and so full of living things. The entire atmosphere of the place makes one think that this is the way it must have been at the dawn of time.

Pelicans and whales live here cheek by jowl, as it were, but without interfering with one another. The pelicans do not touch the bodies of dead baby whales. That is left to our local carrion-eaters, the turkey vultures *(Cathartes aura)*.

*The lower half of a pelican's beak is very long and contains a flexible pouch which can be distended to accommodate a large amount of food.

A Devoted Aunt

Calypso left Baja California when the gray whales began to emerge from the lagoon and enter the waters of the Pacific for their northward migration. The older specimens, who knew the way, went first, and the rest of the school followed them. They were headed for the Arctic Ocean, 4000 miles beyond the horizon. They were leaving their desert for the marine fields of plankton that flourish in the cold polar waters. Even the young whales, those who survived the perils of infancy, undertake the voyage, with the help of their mothers and their "aunts."

It was at this time that we noticed the sharks — large white sharks, some of which must have been thirteen feet long — lying in ambush at the mouth of the channel. They were waiting for any young whales who might be more or less in trouble. On their own, they would not dare have attacked. They are much less aggressive than killer whales, and less intelligent.

We sent down our anti-shark cages and, despite a strong current, our divers and cameramen prepared to film the passage of the whales — hoping in their hearts that they would also be able to film a battle among giants. But they were disappointed. Nothing happened; and, in any event, the water was very cloudy.

We therefore began following the school of whales who, at a slow pace, had begun their migration to the arctic regions. Their moderate speed was due, of course, to the presence of the calves, of whom the adult whales were extremely solicitous.

The family unit is the basis of a school of whales, and maternal love is at the root of the family. We know for certain that a new-born whale, from his birth until several years later, needs constant protection. But the mother by herself cannot defend him against all dangers and teach him everything that he must know. Apparently it is another female, and not the father, who helps her in this task. This second female is called the aunt.

There is a physiological foundation for the phenomenon of the aunt. Whales cannot give birth every year, since the gestation period lasts twelve months. During the year that follows the period of nursing and the time when the calf is more or less "on his own," the female is at loose ends, and her maternal instinct drives her to care for the calves of other females. This is a peculiarity common to all the great marine mammals, and also to certain large land animals.

Elephants, too, have "aunts." And there are other points of similarity between whales and elephants, perhaps because both species have such long gestation periods and because their young mature so slowly.

A diver getting ready to pass a line around a young sperm whale's tail.

We have had occasion to see for ourselves how effective the aunt's protection can be. We once found two large female whales standing guard, one on either side of a calf. When we tried to maneuver in such a way as to isolate the young whale, one of the two whales always succeeded in getting between our Zodiac and the calf. (The calf was too young to be able to dive.) One of the two females kept spouting, turning, and seemed very excited. Curious about her reactions, we tried to get close enough to her for a good look, but she always succeeded in staying just out of range.

It was not until we looked around and saw that the mother and calf had disappeared from our sight that we realized that the whole thing had been a trick to get us away from the calf — a trick that had succeeded very well indeed. At that moment, the aunt dived, and she too disappeared. We had been outsmarted.

The sperm whale has been lassoed.

Humpback whales, like gray whales, also have aunts, who fulfill the same functions. Philippe Sirot, who was captain of the *Curlew* during our expedition to Bermuda, noted that when a school of humpback whales is chased, the entire school will flee if there are no calves in the school. But, if there is even a single young one who cannot swim at the same speed as the adults, the school waits in the vicinity while one adult whale — perhaps the aunt — takes on the job of leading the pursuers away.

Something similar occurred on one occasion when the Zodiac team had almost succeeded in cutting off a young whale. The calf was obviously exhausted from the chase and on the point of allowing himself to be captured. The mother seemed unable to help him. It was the aunt who charged the Zodiac, and kept the men occupied while the mother led her offspring to safety.

Sperm whales

The family ties of cachalots or sperm whales seem even stronger than those of baleen whales. The reason is that a school of cachalots may be composed of a hundred individuals, all of whom belong to the same family. And the family is presided over by one large male.

Here are my notes describing our encounter with cachalots in the Indian Ocean:

Monday, May 15. At 8:35, a number of whales are sighted, and the Zodiac goes out immediately. They are sperm whales, swimming in small groups. Whenever the Zodiac approaches a group, they dive and remain under for twenty or twenty-five minutes, and then come up some distance away. The Zodiac rushes from one group to another without being able to put its Virazeou technique into operation. Now Bebert tries another group of whales, and these begin jumping first to the right, and then to the left, quite near *Calypso.* If I didn't know better, I would think that they are playing with us.

At 11:21 A.M., one of the groups dives and comes up after nine minutes. Ahead of *Calypso,* to both port and starboard, two other groups are spouting. How funny. Bebert is rushing from one group to another without being able to catch any of them. And here the whales are, surfacing all around us and swimming calmly alongside our ship.

At 1:53, Bebert gives up.

A superb coryphaena swims through the clear water at our feet.

Tuesday, May 16. During the afternoon, Didi goes down to his bunk for a nap and, through the porthole, sights a school of sperm whales. (I wonder what those who were awake on deck were doing at that moment.)

It is 2:05 P.M. We try to approach several different groups of the cachalots in our Zodiacs, but without success. *Calypso* tries now; but the whales are too wary to allow her to draw near.

The Zodiacs try once more; and twice they are almost capsized by a giant tail striking the water directly in front of their bows.

A Young Whale Escapes

Finally, Falco spots a "young" whale weighing only about three tons, and his Zodiac manages to overtake it, circle around it, and establish the Virazeou ring of noise and water. The whale seems confused. He remains on the surface, turning first in one direction then in another. Soon, confusion gives way to irritation, and, mouth open, he attempts to seize the Zodiac on every pass and close his jaws on it. At first, he attempts to do this from the normal surface position, with his mouth downward; but then he turns onto his side and exposes his mouth. Twice, Falco fires his special marking harpoon at the angry whale, and twice the spear bounces off the whale's skin.

Maurice and René come to the rescue in a launch and, while Falco loads his harpoon again, they distract the now thoroughly disoriented animal.

Then, gathering his strength (and his wits) for a final charge, the whale throws himself at the launch and strikes it with a great crash.

The outboard motor falls off into the water and remains hanging behind the boat. Maurice Leandri is also thrown overboard by the impact; but, propelled by terror, he is back in the launch in an instant. And the whale, now free and apparently satisfied, dives peacefully and disappears.

But Falco and Maurice do not give up so easily. As soon as the outboard is back in place, the two craft are once more in hot pursuit — so hot that they find the whale about a mile away. Once again, the circling begins; and, once again, the whale becomes a prisoner on the surface, as though by magic.

Calypso is only a few meters away from the marine battleground, and Barsky is filming away. We can hear Falco's shouts, and excitement grips everyone aboard. Everyone grabs a camera and rushes to the prow.

The whale once more tries to attack the launch and the Zodiac with his jaws. And everyone holds his breath when Maurice falls overboard a second time. The whale rushes, weaving to the right and then to the left — and bites an iron bar that is protruding from the launch's stern. Then he veers off while Maurice scrambles aboard.

Twice, Falco's Zodiac was struck by the whale tail; and both times it was lifted out of the water but, fortunately, came down right side up.

Falco now fires a short, harmless harpoon by gunpowder; and the spear bounces off of the whale's side as though it were made of rubber. He fires again, aiming at the blubber of the whale's stomach. This time, the harpoon penetrates the whale's skin.

The whale remains motionless for a moment, then he begins to swim westward at eight knots. By 5:05 P.M., the buoy at the end of 1500 feet of polypropylene line is leaving a long serpentine wake on the surface, and we begin preparing a kytoon for tonight.

The whale's breathing is now normal: once every fifteen minutes. And he is still heading directly west. Soon, we see two spouts rising in the distance, undoubtedly from the whale's parents. By sunset, the young whale has rejoined his family. The kytoon has been attached, and we are looking forward to an interesting evening.

But, suddenly, the buoy stops moving, and the kytoon floats quietly over the water. Bernard and Falco rush out to the buoy and pull in the line. It has not broken, and, at the end of it, they find the harpoon intact.

"These are remarkably intelligent animals," Bebert declares. "Unless someone proves otherwise, I will always believe that the adult whales pulled the harpoon out of that young whale's stomach."

This is not impossible. There are stories of whales helping one another; and one hears of cases where whales who had been harpooned were freed by their companions.

And, as though to overcome any doubt that we still might have, we catch sight of the three whales, swimming quietly away into the twilight.

The Baby Whale Who Lost His Head

We had one more adventure with a baby whale whose group was determined to protect him.

Calypso was heading toward Djibouti for supplies. We were all very enthusiastic about our encounters with whales so far, especially since we had just seen the films recording these encounters.

Tuesday, May 24. Sperm whales have been sighted. *Calypso* has tried four times to get close to them. The first three attempts were filmed by Li from the observation chamber. But we were not close enough at any time for Falco to be able to shoot his harpoon from *Calypso*'s prow.

We have put two Zodiacs into the water, and they are beginning to close the circle around a young animal. For an hour and a half, the Zodiacs keep him there while Bebert is feverishly preparing his weapon. At 10:30, the young sperm whale is harpooned. At 11:00, the launch pulls away from *Calypso* carrying the equipment for underwater filming.

In a short time, the young whale is joined by two adult cachalots (perhaps his parents) and then by an entire school. We can now count eleven sperm whales around *Calypso*, some of which seem to be enormous. Very impressive.

From 11:25 to 12:30, there is a constant coming and going between *Calypso* and the whale as we take exterior shots, underwater shots, sound recordings, and underwater photographs.

Lagorio, our sound man, wires hanging down from every part of him, his head covered with earphones and a tape recorder dangling over his stomach, is jumping from one launch into the other, shouting "Silence!" in his deep singer's voice, and making more noise than anyone else.

Nineteenth-century whalers used to engrave pictures of what they loved most on sperm whales' teeth—usually their girl friends or their ships. On the one to the right, we see the American flag, the lance used to give the death-blow to sperm whales, and a whaling scene in which a boat has been overturned. *Collection Jean-Horace Chambon.*

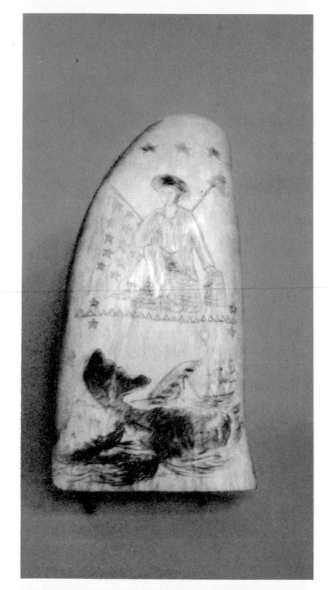

Finally, the young whale succeeds in escaping.

We examine the harpoon's point and conclude that we are very poorly equipped for this kind of work.

From *Calypso*'s deck we can see that there is great excitement in the school of whales. Three cachalots leap into the air — a sign of joy, no doubt, because the young whale, either alone or with the help of adults, has rejoined his family.

They are celebrating too soon, we think. The Zodiac once more cuts off the young whale and immobilizes it. And, at 2:40, Falco once more harpoons the animal. But it turns out that we have made a mistake. This is not the same whale. It is slightly larger than the other, and there is no trace of an earlier harpoon wound. But the fact is we have little time to discuss our mistake. For five minutes later, the harpoon is dislodged and the whale dives and is swimming away.

By 3:15 we have caught up with him again, and Falco sinks a harpoon into the middle of his back, where it sticks up like a small mast. And this time it holds. We set about the same routine as before: a buoy, 1500 feet of nylon line, a kytoon. Filming and sound-recording.

Meanwhile, the young whale's relatives are swimming forward of *Calypso*, to starboard, waiting and, at regular intervals, emitting sounds as though to encourage the captive, or to show him the way to them. Another cachalot, close by, seems to answer the cries of the young whale.

Through our underwater microphones we are picking up three distinct levels of sound from the whales: the young, captive animal; then the young whale's mother; and, finally — and perhaps — the chief male of the school.

This time we will have no trouble following the kytoon by radar. The weather is beautiful.

Tuesday, May 25. At dawn, the school of whales is still with us. They followed *Calypso* for twenty miles to the north during the night.

We are picking up a radar echo from Aden, 56 miles at 313.

We are going to try to lasso our young captive's tail so that we can remove the harpoon and release him. This is easier said than done. Bonnici and Alan try again and again, but fail, and they are exhausted. Then the whale himself takes over and, by twisting and turning continually, manages to wrap the line around his tail. He has succeeded where we failed.

But how will we be able to get the line off of him?

Bebert, in his Zodiac, tries next to remove the harpoon, but the handle breaks and it falls into the water where it, too, becomes entangled in the line.

Lagorio, meanwhile, is near the launch, taping everything that is being said in the water. There seem to be many whales "talking" nearby. The entire school apparently is waiting to see how we are going to get out of this.

Finally, Bebert and Alan, who have now rested a bit, try to cut the line around the whale with a knife so as to free him. But the whale squirms so much that they cannot get hold of the flipper to cut the line, and they are afraid of cutting him by mistake.

At 4 P.M., there is a very solemn moment when Deloire films, under water, two divers who hack away the snarls and knots of the line and release the animal. It is all over.

We see the young whale swim away toward his school; and Gaston, from the crow's-nest, watches through his field glasses the joyful demonstration with which the whale family greets the return of their prodigal son.

Ted Walker has gone to find water in an effort to save the grounded baby whale.

The wounded calf is sprinkled with water.

With the greatest care, the animal is placed in a net.

NINE

The Baby Whale Who Wanted to Live

February 24. Before leaving, I want to take a last look at Scammon Lagoon which, by now, has become so familiar to me, with its nursery, its love chambers, and also its cemetery. Philippe takes me up in the Cessna for a ride over the whole lagoon.

Just before leaving, I ask the *Polaris* and *Calypso* to take a census of the whale population in the various lagoons. I would also like to know how many bodies there are of baby whales, so as to be able to estimate the rate of infant mortality.

At birth, a gray whale calf is about eleven feet long and weighs nearly a ton. Three months later, it is strong enough to undertake its first northward voyage, and now measures about twenty feet. That is, if it survives.

Whale calves are subject to a number of diseases, and they also have natural enemies — grampuses and sharks. And, in fact, from the air we can see about ten dead whale calves lying in the lagoon. Among the mangroves bordering the beach, we can see whale skeletons. The roots of the mangroves have grown and, sometimes, disturbed these bones.

Not all of these cadavers are the result of disease or sharks. Whales, unlike man, follow an inexorable law of nature. If a whale calf seems, at birth, to suffer the slightest defect, it is immediately abandoned by the mother and, of course, dies. Heartless? Perhaps, but only by human standards. In nature, death goes hand in hand with life, and it might be more cruel to prolong a defective calf's life than to allow it to end as soon as possible after birth. The calf's presence in the school would expose all the members to attack by enemies and slow its migrations. And it would be all for nothing, for, even if cared for by the mother, a defective calf's chances of survival would be negligible. In the sea as in the jungle, nature's law is still in force, and only the fittest of each species survive adolescence.

Baby Whale in Distress

On February 28, the pilot of our reconaissance plane signals us by radio that a whale calf has run aground at the entrance to the lagoon. Dr. Walker, Philippe, and Michel Deloire set out immediately in the launch to examine the whale.

The weather around the lagoon is, as usual, leaden and a bit foggy. Then, suddenly, the sun breaks through the low-lying clouds and fog. Philippe sees in the distance, on a finger of sand, a dark shape. The launch heads for it. It is undoubtedly the baby whale. But is the whale still alive?

Ted Walker and Philippe begin the examination as soon as they arrive, while Michel handles the camera. There are still signs of life, but they are weak. Dr. Walker, who has managed to look into the calf's eye, reports that there is a glimmer of life — and of intelligence. Frantically, Walker ransacks the launch for cloth or canvas — anything that can be dampened and used to cover the calf's body.

Out of the water, a beached whale succumbs very rapidly to the heat. It dehydrates, and the sun burns its skin. It can also happen that, once it is weakened, it will drown in the rising tide.

Seen from close up, with its long flat muzzle stretched out on the sand, its rubbery skin slightly tinged with blue, its eyes closed, the calf looks for all the world as though he were already dead. Lying there, trapped by its own weight, crushed against the spit of sand only a few yards from the blue water that it needs to live, this son of giants can do nothing but wait helplessly for the end to come. Unless we are able to do something to save it, its fate is sealed, and it will shortly become nothing more than food for birds.

The calf seem to get a certain amount of relief from the water that is poured over it. Ted Walker, sweating and out of breath, his beard dripping, carries buckets of water from the sea to the sand spit, pours them over the suffering whale, and then goes back for more, his wet sneakers squishing audibly. And the calf stirs a bit.

An Orphan?

Philippe has alread notified *Calypso* by radio of the situation, and has asked them to send out a team immediately with a net and lines.

The whale, meanwhile, is again still, its eyes closed to protect them from the sun. It seems that he is already dangerously dehydrated. And on his head there is a large open wound, bleeding, inflicted by birds — probably sandpipers, who are voracious little animals.

From the size of this wound, Ted concludes that the calf has very likely been ashore for several hours, perhaps since last night. We really have no idea of exactly what happened to him. It is hardly likely that he would have been taken off guard by the tide. At his age, the mother whale is usually able to extricate her baby from any such difficulty — even from being trapped by a retreating tide.

It is not impossible that this baby is an orphan. Or that it is unhealthy and has been abandoned by its mother. In any case, it is thin and obviously undernourished. Later on, we discovered bits of clam in his excrement, which leads us to surmise that perhaps he was trying to feed himself; or that, even though he was nursing, he tried to eat clams. It is not possible to know for sure.

Ted Walker is almost beside himself with impatience, waiting for the rescue team to arrive. In his nervousness he is not unlike a father in a panic over his sick son.

First Aid

The rescue team arrives at full speed in the Zodiac: Delemotte, Bonnici, Delcoutère. They have brought a large net and some line; and now the struggle begins. The baby whale must weigh over two tons. He is extremely difficult to handle, and the job is not made easier by Ted's absolute insistence that this 4000-pound baby must be handled very gently, and also by Philippe's frequent orders to "Hurry! Hurry! We have to get him back into the water immediately!"

Slowly, painfully, the six men roll the inert mass onto the net, and then drag the net a few yards to the life-giving waters of the lagoon. At the moment when the whale feels the coolness of the water, he breathes a sigh that causes his whole body to shudder. But he is not yet safe. He is again in his natural element, but he is too weak to stay afloat. His blowhole is under water, and he is in imminent danger of drowning.

Working frantically, the team rigs up a litterlike contraption alongside the launch by suspending the ends of the net, which is still around the whale, from a spar. The calf is now alongside the launch, held by the net at surface level, with his blowhole above water. By the time the job is completed the broiling sun is high in the sky; but the whale is alive, and breathing normally. Ted Walker, standing above the whale in the launch, is petting him and talking to him in a soft voice.

Slowly, very slowly, the launch begins the trip back to *Calypso*, with Ted insisting, every few yards, that Philippe reduce his speed even more. Everyone now feels that there is a fair chance of saving the whale. It all depends on how severely he was dehydrated before we were able to reach him.

A Moral Obligation

This incident with the whale calf has become a psychological and philosophical adventure for everyone aboard *Calypso*; and for me it has also taken on the dimensions of a personal challenge.

The whale's presence here is a measure of our sensitivity, and it is fascinating to see how each of us reacts. Some of us pretend a hardhearted indifference — but sneak over to the side every once in a while to make sure that the baby is still breathing. And some of us are overly emotional about the whole thing; but this is rare. *Calypso*, after all, is a hard school. The most interesting reactions, however, are those that are the coolest, that produce the most ingenious and effective ideas for handling the situation. And it is from that aspect that I have been able to realize how difficult it is for a man to keep his sense of proportion in dealing with animals.

Certainly, we — thirty humans and a ship — are not there for the purpose of attempting to repair nature's accidents by saving dying animals, or by trying to reverse infant mortality — which is one of nature's methods of conservation. Still, whether or not it seems reasonable, the fact remains that this whale is, somehow, our responsibility. It was on the verge of dying, and we took it and, we hope, saved it. That act represents a sort of commitment on

The team succeeds in getting the victim back into the water.

our part. We now have an obligation to do everything that we can to make sure that it survives.

For the three days that the baby whale is with us, an unprecedented sense of well-being reigns aboard *Calypso*. Everyone volunteers to stand extra watches at night. And everyone is aware of the smallest change in the whale's breathing, and of its slightest movement.

The day that the whale was found and brought to *Calypso* it seemed best to me for it to remain suspended in the water in its net alongside the ship. In that way, I reasoned, it would slowly regain its strength. And I hoped, above all, basing myself upon experience, that his mother would come looking for him and, no doubt, hear his cries. This would have been the ideal solution from our standpoint. We could then have turned him loose, restored to his mother.

Until then, however, it seems best to have a full-time guard assigned to our ward, for he would be an easy prey for the many sharks in the lagoon. The guard, who is armed with a loaded rifle, will be relieved every two hours, throughout the night. He is also instructed periodically to check the baby, and to notify me immediately if the mother should show up.

The first night passes without incident. In the morning, the calf is still alive, but there is still no sign of the mother.

Jonah

In the wardroom we decide on a name for the baby: Jonah. It is a logical choice, for we know for certain that this creature at least has emerged alive from the belly of a whale.

Jonah now seems better. His eyes are open, and they are no longer glazed, but clear; and he watches us as we watch him. He shows signs of becoming more lively.

The first thing we must do is to feed him. And now I understand how great is the responsibility that we have assumed from the moment that we lifted Jonah from the sandspit and brought him to *Calypso*. What, and how, does one feed a baby that weighs two tons? Ted Walker is at work whipping up a sort of puree made of all our condensed milk, of flour, and of vitamins. When it is ready, he carries it over to Jonah.

The whale, showing no sign of surprise, watches Ted approach him, and politely opens his mouth when Ted thrusts some of the puree toward him. But the food will not go down Jonah's throat, and it spills into the water.

Next, we rig up a giant baby's bottle, made of a barrel and a length of hose. When Ted has transformed the puree into a more liquid form, we put the nipple end of the hose into Jonah's mouth, hoping that he will instinctively draw the food into his mouth. He does — but is still unable to swallow it.

He Loves Me!

Ted has now concluded that Jonah is very likely old enough to require solid food, and, with a group of volunteers, he has made up a mixture of clams and squid. This, Jonah swallows; and he shows every sign of enjoying it. Ted continues until all the food is gone, putting it, handful by handful, onto Jonah's enormous tongue, which, for the occasion, the whale rolled into a cylinder-shaped trough. Jonah, when he has finished eating, holds onto Ted's hand, refusing to let it go. And Ted Walker, who has tears in his eyes, begins to shout:

"He understands that we want to feed him. He understands . . . he loves me!"

Ted, having spent his life studying animals and loving them from afar, has been deeply touched by Jonah's gesture, by his appeal for help.

I order the camera and sound to be cut off. It seems somehow wrong to record the great emotion of this lover of animals.

It has taken a day's work to feed our baby whale 25 pounds of mollusks, for four men had to gather up the clams and squid from the bottom of the lagoon. And 25 pounds is not much food for even a baby whale.

Obviously we will have to continue.

Calypso's daily routine is now a thing of the past, and life aboard her revolves around Jonah. Meals are no longer served at regular hours, and our work schedule is completely disrupted. Everyone gathers around Ted Walker, who knows so much about whales, offering to do whatever they can to help him save Jonah. And everyone, according to his temperament and background, is searching his mind for a way to keep Jonah alive.

I must confess that we are poorly equipped for this kind of thing. Even the food we have, except for mollusks, is intended for men rather than for whales. And this will be a serious problem. Nonetheless, for the moment Jonah seems to be growing stronger. I seriously believe that he is trying to help us help him.

What we need above all if Jonah is really to recover is a large pool where we can look after him. And, of course, we need medicines and a veterinary expert. We have none of these things, and no way of getting them. On im-

pulse, I telephone the Marine Zoo of San Diego. The director of that institution assures me that they would be delighted to take care of Jonah, until he is well enough to be turned loose again. This really seems to be the best, and perhaps the only, solution. It would be difficult for us to part with our baby whale, to turn him over to strangers. Yet, it would be inexcusably selfish for us to keep him, knowing that we may very likely not be able to save him. Besides, we know that at the San Diego zoo he would receive the best of care from expert hands, and that what could be learned about whales from observation of Jonah, by scientists with the latest equipment at their disposal, would benefit not only Jonah himself, but other whales in the same predicament. And so, we have no choice.

But now another problem presents itself: how do we get Jonah to San Diego? He would never survive being towed that distance, even at slow speeds; and it is essential that we get him there as quickly as possible.

A Whale Harness

For the moment, however, our immediate problem is to care for Jonah's head wounds, which are showing signs of becoming infected. Maurice and Henri have had the idea of making a sort of webbing for Jonah so that he may ride alongside *Calypso* more comfortably than in his net. And when — or if — he regains his strength, he will have greater freedom of movement. So, it is decided to hoist Jonah aboard *Calypso*'s rear deck so that simultaneously we may install this harness, and Ted may care for Jonah's wounds.

Lifting a whale out of the water is a delicate undertaking. A whale, even a baby, can "break" under his own weight unless he is evenly supported at all points. By the time we are ready to begin hoisting, a stretcher has been built. We attach this to our pneumatic hoist, very painstakingly move it under Jonah's body; and then, as slowly and gently as possible, the whale is lifted from the water and deposited on *Calypso*'s deck.

Ted gets to work at once. He determines that the sensitive lips that protect the baleen have been lacerated by birds; and there are other wounds around the blowhole as well. He keeps a close watch on Jonah's breathing, and also tries to listen to his heartbeat with a stethoscope; but the layer of blubber is too thick for anything to be heard. Next, he applies a paste of antibiotics and silicone to Jonah's wounds.

Jonah's presence aboard *Calypso* has a strange effect upon us all. We can see him there, hear him breathing; and we sense the existence of life under that dark mass of flesh. We even feel the heat radiating from his body. He is as warm-blooded as we. It matters little that, out of water, Jonah seems nothing more than a rubbery sack of bones. We have seen whales in the water, and we know what marvels of grace and suppleness they are in their own element.

Far from being an alien, anonymous being, Jonah appears to us to be a familiar animal, and we feel toward him as one does toward a beloved pet who has been struck by an automobile. But with this difference, that it was by the merest stroke of luck that we happened along in time to save Jonah; without us, he would surely have died.

The Blowhole

At this moment, no one thinks to wonder whether or not it is possible for men and whales to communicate with one another, whether or not there is an unbridgeable gap between us. We are aware only of the necessity of saving Jonah's life. And we might say that Jonah himself is trying to make us aware of that necessity. He is pathetic; and most pathetic of all is the blowhole through which he breathes, its lips trembling as it draws in the vital air. A whale's breathing is hardly more than a man's breathing amplified, and that similarity is at once more striking and more moving than any other reaction of marine life.

Once Jonah's wounds have been dressed, he is placed gently in his harness and lowered over the side into the water. Never has our hoist been handled with such loving care.

In the water, Jonah stirs and, as though he wants to tell us that he is all right, and to show his gratitude, he gives a few strokes with his tail. The harness apparently is much more to his liking than the net.

By the end of the day, Ted Walker seems convinced that we will be able to save Jonah. But the question still remains of getting him to San Diego. Perhaps we can get a seaplane. Watching Jonah, it appears that he is improving. But I can see that he has trouble keeping his balance even in the light current of the tide.

Never has the landscape appeared more inhospitable than at this moment. Everything is still, deserted, bearing the stamp of desolation as though it were part of another world. It is an appropriate setting for Jonah, whom we have adopted, but for whom we can do no more than we have already done.

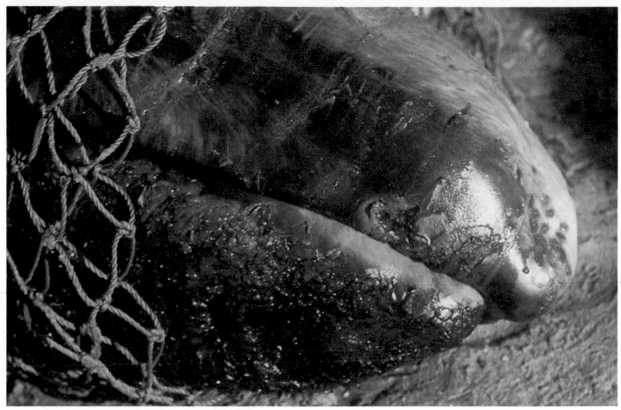

The baby whale seems to give no sign of life.

(Facing page) Ted Walker administers first aid.

Ted Walker opens the whale's mouth to try to feed it.

A Night of Watching

The young orphan whale is fighting as well as he can for his life. We have now done all in our power for him, and I want at least to continue protecting him from the killers who roam the water at night. Therefore we again set up a relay of armed guards.

At three o'clock in the morning, I am awake and go on deck to see Jonah. He seems comfortable. The water is calm.

At five o'clock, Canoë, who is on duty, awakens Caillart, our ship's captain, who rushes to the rear deck. He sees Jonah rolling over on his back, and notices that he is breathing only with difficulty.

Canoë then comes to awaken me. I go up immediately. And I find that Jonah is dead. We had not found him in time. He had been too badly burned, too dehydrated for us, with our primitive means, to be able to save him.

I look up at the light of dawn. The pelicans are awake now, wheeling in the sky.

Everyone aboard, as though awakened by a mysterious alarm, gathers

Ted takes the whale's measurements.

on the rear deck. Jonah has already found himself a place in the history of *Calypso*. For these men, most of them very young, Jonah embodies the great mystery of life and death. He was one of the marvelous works of nature that nature, with a callousness that man finds shocking, destroys on a whim. We have seen great animals of the sea die before; but nothing has moved us as we have been moved by the slow agony of the baby whale who did not want to die, and to whom we had wished to give life. And yet, our reaction is that of creatures of land. In the sea, there is no room for pity or for sorrow.

As in the case of human suffering and death, Jonah's demise released us from our trancelike state of fascination. *Calypso* has resumed the daily routine that was so dramatically, and so tragically, interrupted.

Our first job is to dispose of the calf's body. It is towed out by the launch, weighted, and then sunk in deep water. We have not removed the harness that we made for him. And we do not want to see what will happen to Jonah when the sharks find his body.

Coming out of our dream, we find that the exodus of whales for which

The patient is treated with affectionate care, but its eyes remain shut.

Ted Walker, hanging from the crane, will try to feed the animal, which has been put back into the water.

A funnel and a rubber hose serve as a baby bottle.

(Facing page above) Ted Walker forces open the calf's jaws.

(Facing page below) Jonah now refuses to let go of Ted's hand.

Jean-Clair Riant uses almost all of *Calypso*'s supplies to devise a formula for Jonah.

(Left) A futile attempt to listen to the whale's heartbeat with a stethoscope.

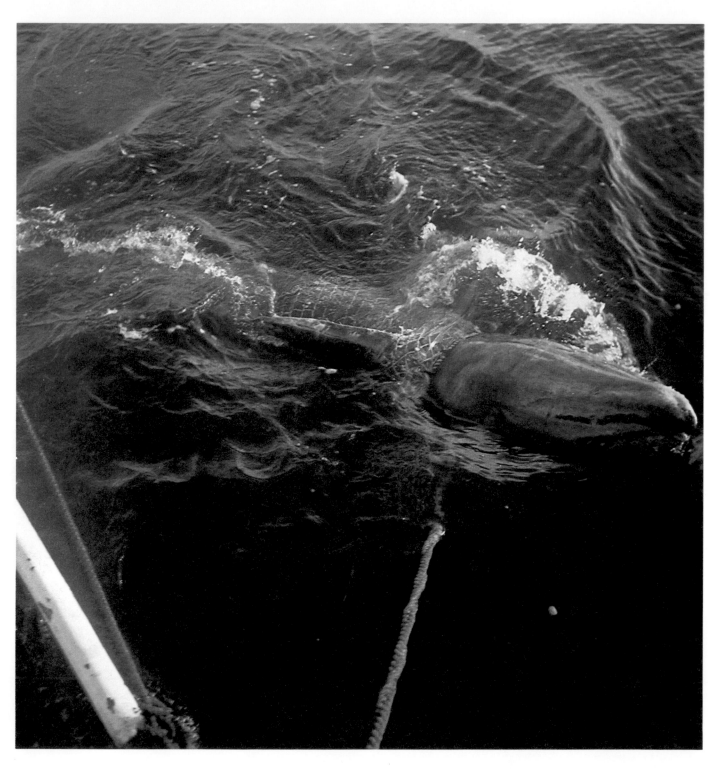

The baby whale has just died, and Ted Walker and Jacques Renoir are deeply affected.

we have been waiting has already begun, and indeed is well underway, without our even having been aware of it.

No matter. They will return every year for centuries to come, to spend here the most important hours of their lives — the hours of love, of birth, and of death.

We have been the respectful, and often astonished, witnesses to all of this. The cycle of life and death is especially impressive when embodied in these giants of the deep. These creatures, with their fifty-foot bodies and their forty or fifty tons of flesh, are not built to a human scale; and yet, they breathe, they love, and they suffer as we do. Our lives and theirs, though different, are not finally distinct.

Will the great adventure of the gray whales continue for long in the modern world? These animals are now protected by law, and they will not be subjected to the massacres that were common in the nineteenth century. But will their refuge in Baja California always be a deserted area? Will their bay forever deserve its name: the Bay of Solitude — a solitude peopled by contented whales?

TEN

The Strongest and Most Intelligent of All: The Killer Whale

Between the enormity of the cachalot and the blue whale, and the sleek grace of the dolphin, there is a whole range of animals of intermediate size who are also marine mammals, and who are intelligent and physiologically similar to man. They all make sounds which, it seems, convey meaning. There are the blackfish (or pilot whales), killer whales (orcs or prampuses), and bottlenose (also called beaked whale) — all of whom are toothed whales.

The relatively small size of these animals makes them rather easy to approach so far as man is concerned. For sperm whales and baleen whales, however gentle they may be, occasionally show signs of not knowing their own strength.

Until very recently, these medium-sized cetaceans were but poorly understood. We knew almost nothing about their behavior, their intelligence, their social instinct. The stories of whale hunters, and the prejudices of man, attributed terrible reputations to some of them; to the orc or grampus, for example, who became known as the "killer whale." It did not help his reputation that nature had endowed him with a set of from twenty to twenty-eight formidable-looking teeth.

the species, like the cachalot, is polygamous. They attain maturity late: the female at six years, and the male at thirteen.

When migrating, blackfish or pilot whales follow their leader blindly — a characteristic that sometimes leads to catastrophe. It happens occasionally that a leader, frightened by something or the other, goes aground and is immediately followed by the entire school.

Pilot whales eat cuttlefish and squid. The memorable night that we filmed the mating of the squid in the Pacific, off Santa Catalina, pilot whales were constantly circling around that enormous assemblage of cephalopods.* The presence of the divers, however, and the floodlights that we used to film the squid in ecstasy, kept most of the mammals at a respectful distance. Nonetheless, they remained in the vicinity throughout the night; and, occasionally, the bravest of them would rush in, sneak a forbidden mouthful of squid, and then disappear. They are very timid creatures — as distinguished from the sharks, who, ignoring lights and divers alike, threw themselves upon the stars of our film and swallowed them in great mouthfuls.

Public Enemy Number One

In 1967, in the Indian Ocean, we met a school of killer whales. We were frightened of them — more frightened than we should have been, as it turned out. At that time, nothing was known about their behavior in captivity or semicaptivity; and we, along with the rest of the world, considered killer whales to be the most fearsome creatures of the sea, the avowed enemies of all life forms to be found in the water, including divers. So far as we were concerned, the killer whale — even when known by the less ominous names of orc and grampus — was the most dangerous animal we could possibly meet. It was more feared even than the shark; for we knew that it was a very intelligent creature.† Also, its teeth were most impressive, numerous, and enormous.

We knew that killer whales were social animals, and that they traveled and attacked their prey in groups. So, as soon as we saw this school of them, we concluded that the sea around us was being subjected to a reign of terror.

*A television film, called *Night of the Squids* was distributed internationally as part of the series "The Undersea World of Jacques Cousteau." The subject of squid and octopuses will be covered in the next book of the present series.

† The shark's intelligence, on the other hand, is comparable to that of the rat — which is not to be dismissed lightly.

Here are my journal entries from that period:

April 12, 1967. At 5:30 in the afternoon, a school of small dolphins — a species that we know to be almost unapproachable — is reported. Bebert, Bonnici, and Barsky go out immediately in the Zodiac and chase them until sunset, without being able to catch up. The tricks that these dolphins use are fantastic. First of all, they separate into two groups that swim in different directions. The group that is followed then splits up into two more groups. When the team that is being chased tires, they dive — and are replaced by the other team. When a single dolphin is isolated, he begins by feinting according to a pattern: first to the right, then to the left, and back again. As soon as the pursuer becomes accustomed to this rhythm, the dolphin changes it brusquely — by diving, or by swimming away in a new direction.

It is likely that this sort of behavior, which is very different from that of our ordinary friendly dolphins who are always ready to play around *Calypso*, is due to the presence of killer whales in the neighborhood. These tactics, which are so effective that they threw our Zodiac off the track, were no doubt designed to have the same effect on the predators.

I think I can conclude that dolphins and whales are almost always followed closely by groups of sharks who feed off their leavings, and who sooner or later attack the infant, young, or sick dolphins and whales. As far as the killer whales are concerned, however, they no doubt create a circle of destruction around themselves, butchering any creature who dares to claim a share of their food.

Even so, we must make every effort to approach these creatures by using the same method we have used with cachalots: send out a Zodiac with a harpooner and a cameraman who is ready to jump into the water with the killer whale.

April 13. As soon as I awaken Simone, the alert sounds. Everyone rushes up on deck, and the Zodiac is lowered into the water. From *Calypso*, we can see very clearly what is in the water: killer whales.

They are easily recognizable by the white markings behind their eyes and on their stomachs, and also by their triangular dorsal fin.

Everyone is excited by the sight. It is still early, the weather is magnificent, and it promises to be a splendid day.

As usual, our visiting killer whales seem to be very quick-witted, and very wary of us. The school includes a huge male who must weigh several tons. His dorsal fin protrudes above all the others, like a standard of a chieftain. Another dorsal fin, slightly smaller, next to his must be that of an adolescent whale, no doubt the son of this giant. Sooner or later, the young one will do battle with his father to obtain control of the harem. It brings to mind the

A school of killer whales, photographed by Dr. Millet in the Bering Strait.

case of certain Arabian sheikdoms in which succession is often determined by parricide.

There seem to be eight or nine adults, each weighing between 1500 and 2000 pounds, and a half dozen younger whales. Like the school that we chased to the south of Socotra in 1955, this one is trying to get away from us, apparently under orders from their leader. They want no part of man or his machines, and *Calypso* is too slow to be able to catch up with them.

Bebert and Bonnici take a Zodiac with a 33-horsepower motor and go out after them, while *Calypso* follows at a distance. At nine o'clock, after a hell-for-leather chase at 15 or 20 knots that lasted ninety minutes, and after persevering through an elaborate series of feints and tricks, Bonnici sees a massive black-and-white shape surface right next to the Zodiac. He throws his harpoon. Bull's-eye. The killer whale takes off, very fast at first, trailing the red buoy. These mammals are capable of speeds of over thirty knots (35 miles per hour); but, as streamlined as they are, they are built for pure speed and not for towing. Even an object of moderate weight, like the buoy, will cut their speed in half.

(Right) The killer whale has an impressive dorsal fin.

The rest of the school, noticing that one of the members was slowing, also cut their speed for about ten minutes, to give him a chance to catch up.

Then, when the leader decides that they have waited long enough, they disappear in a burst of speed. Bonnici, touched by the predicament of his captive, cuts the harpoon line; and the lightweight harpoon disengages itself from the whale's skin. The killer whale then sets out on the trail of his friends.

A Surprise: No Attack.

April 15. Another alert at eight o'clock this morning, and the Zodiac takes off. It returns shortly. The mammals sighted were more of our very shy little dolphins.

A few minutes later, Simone sights a school of blackfish, or pilot whales. We slow down, but the Zodiac is a long time getting into the water. We chase the school, but without success, for over two hours. For some reason, these blackfish, instead of letting us come near as they usually do, flee with every sign of fright. What is the matter with them? This is the first time that we have seen timid blackfish.

A large shark is following *Calypso* close to her stern, but when we slow down it flees.

After lunch, we try once more to catch up with our unapproachable dolphins, but, again, in vain. Something is wrong here. Everything that we have seen for the past three days seems terrified of something. Are there Japanese whalers at work here, exterminating all the mammals in this area? Upon reflection, however, we reject this idea. There are *many* animals in these waters. They have not been exterminated; they have been terrorized.

We think that this situation has prevailed since our encounter with killer whales on April 12. Is it possible that these animals, usually as rare as they are terrible, are present here in large numbers?

By the end of the afternoon, we sight a school of killer whales. The Zodiac is lowered immediately, and the chase begins, to continue until nightfall.

The school is composed of an enormous male (at least three tons, 25 to 30 feet long, with a dorsal fin four and one half feet high), a femal almost as large as the male but with a smaller fin, seven or eight medium-sized females, and six or eight calves. This is not the same school that we saw a few days ago; in this one, there is no young male. But the number of members is about the same. It is a nomadic school, comprising females and children, and with a single male as lord and master of the group. This presupposes the elimination of male competition in a school, and I expect that other males are either killed by the chief or driven off. The latter alternative is hardly better than being killed outright, because I doubt very much that a killer whale, alone and on his own, can find enough food to keep himself alive.

The Zodiac chases the school for two hours, sometimes guided by radio from *Calypso*. Nothing escapes our men on watch in the crow's-nest.

At the beginning of the chase, the killer whales are very sure of themselves, diving every three or four minutes and reappearing about a half mile away. Ordinarily, this would be enough to lose any marine attacker, and to shake off a whaler. But the Zodiac is doing 20 knots on a sea of glass, and is capable of turning on a dime. A few seconds after the grampuses surface to breathe, they hear the Zodiac's wasplike buzzing coming up from the rear.

After a while, the mammals try a new tactic. They surface every two or three minutes now, and increase their speed. But the Zodiac keeps up with them.

The time has come for evasive tactics: the whales dart to the right at 90°, then to the left and back again; then they make simulated turns at 180°. finally, they play their trump card: the male remains visible, eminently so, swimming along at 15 or 20 knots, and occasionally leaping out of the water. He is accompanied only by the largest female. His purpose, obviously, is to lure the Zodiac into following him — while the rest of the school escapes in the opposite direction.

When the Zodiac is about a mile away from the school, but quite close to the male, the latter dives and disappears in the water. Guided by the voices of his companions, he swims straight toward them. From *Calypso*, we are watching all of this with great interest. We, unlike the Zodiac, have never lost sight of the main body of the school. And suddenly we see the leader surface in their midst, certain, no doubt, of having done his duty and played a good trick on the pursuer. We would be compelled to agree with him — except for the fact that he surfaced practically alongside *Calypso*.

This chase has taught us a great deal about killer whales, and has allowed Barsky to get some marvelous (and rare) footage. Nonetheless, we must regard the whole adventure as a failure. The purpose of the pursuit was to mark the huge male, but the light harpoon twisted in flight and struck sideways. Bebert tried four more times, and the same thing happened each time. So, we will abandon this system.

Here is one important observation: during the chase, the Zodiac, traveling at 15 or 20 knots, happened to pass over the back of one of the whales just as it was surfacing. The craft actually took off, like an airplane. Everyone was thrown to the deck and the camera, still running, shot up into the air and

Laying nets in the Juan de Fuca Strait, near Seattle.

(Facing page above) The albino killer whale of the Juan de Fuca Strait.
(Facing page below) The killer whale's teeth are fearsome weapons.

Two killer whales (one is an albino) in the nets.

then fell back into the Zodiac. That will be an interesting shot. In spite of the irritation that an incident like this must have caused the whale, and in spite of all the other annoyances that the Zodiac undoubtedly caused, the killer whales did not once take any aggressive action. These animals, certainly ferocious, terribly powerful, and very intelligent, and moreover armed with a legitimate complaint against the Zodiac, never attacked the frail little boat that was irritating them so. If they had wished, they could have made a single mouthful of Bebert, Maurice, and Barsky. But they did not.

When the Zodiac returned, Bebert told me: "I don't know why, but I had the feeling that they wouldn't do anything."

Ambush

In the lagoons of Baja California, where we spent three months with gray whales, we saw not a single killer whale. We would have sighted them easily by their large triangular dorsal fins, which project above the surface when they swim. We were surprised at their absence, for they could have wreaked havoc among the gray whales there — as much as a whaling ship. And yet, we did see killer whales lying in ambush just at the entry of the lagoon, at the mouth of the channel. Obviously, they were waiting for the gray whales and their calves to leave the lagoon's protection.

They were difficult to see from the surface when the water was rough, but they could easily be seen from the air. And Philippe also saw them from his hot-air ballon.

Some divers claimed that a male gray whale was stationed in the channel to keep the killer whales out of the lagoon. It seems more probable, however, that the mammals, since they are group animals, are unwilling to risk an encounter in a narrow lagoon, in shallow water, where they would have no place to maneuver. Their superiority over gray whales rests on their skill in group strategy; and that strategy would be seriously hindered in a restricted space blocked by sandbanks.

The killer whale is a fearsome adversary. It is capable of diving to depths of over 1000 feet and is able to remain beneath the surface for as much as twenty minutes. Also, its vision is better than that of the baleen whale (its eyes are larger), and it sees as well in the air as in the water. On the whole, its visual acuity seems about equal to that of the cat.

The killer whale, except for man, is the only enemy of the whale. They always attack in groups and sometimes cover their prey from one end of its body to the other. A single killer whale would have no chance against the

Ron Church, our photographer.

strength and the enormous tail of a full-grown baleen whale. Their attacks are always well co-ordinated and tactically effective. Some of the killer whales bite the victim in the stomach and in the genital area, causing it great pain. Others force the baleen whale to open its mouth and they seize its tongue. It is a pitiless and savage onslaught, and the attackers have numbers on their side. In order to discourage such attacks, baleen whales form a defensive circle, or try to beat off the predators with blows from their tails. Killer whales therefore prefer, as their victim, a whale calf, or a young whale; and, when they find such a victim, they mount a diversionary attack against its mother.

Whales are not their only prey. They also attack squids, sea elephants, seals, narwhals—and even dolphins which although they are able to master predatory sharks, seem comparatively helpless against killer whales. (They will also occasionally attack schools of salmon and tuna.)

There are witnesses who state — though I cannot, from my own experience, support that statement — that they have seen a group of some twenty killer whales encircle a school of a hundred dolphins and then slowly close the circle. Next, a single killer whale threw itself into the midst of the dolphins and killed one of them, while the rest of the whales continued to

A diver feeds one of the killer whales of Juan de Fuca Strait.

maintain the circle. Each of the predators then took its turn in attacking a victim, until the water was red with the blood of the dolphins.*

It is my opinion that almost all stories about killer whales are somewhat exaggerated. These animals are, after all is said and done, somewhat rare; and, despite their intelligence and strength, they have never become the dominant species of the seas.

Today, we know for certain that there is no "man-eating" cetacean. Killer whales, whose legendary ferocity has, for centuries, struck fear into the hearts of seamen, never attack divers. In fact, they have proved to be remarkably easy to tame.

Killer Whales in Captivity

I am always terribly depressed at the sight of an animal in captivity, and especially when it is an animal of the size and intelligence of the killer whale.

Even though the behavior of animals in captivity tells us little or nothing about their behavior in their natural environment, the fact remains that the only way man has at present of familiarizing himself with killer whales is to observe them in the great marine zoos. Captivity, therefore, may be a necessary evil. But it may not always be so.

This having been said, let me go on to assert that an animal in captivity deserves our respect; and he also deserves that we try to make him as comfortable and as happy as possible under the circumstances.

The first killer whale to be exhibited in captivity was named Moby Doll, and was at home in the aquarium of Vancouver, British Columbia.† How it came to the aquarium is an unusual story. A Canadian sculptor had been commissioned, in March 1965, to execute a statue of a killer whale; and, in order to have a model, he intended to kill a specimen. After two months of trying, he succeeded in harpooning a whale; but, when the moment came for the *coup de grâce,* the artist could not bring himself to do it. Instead, he brought his victim to the aquarium, nursed her back to health with penicillin, gave her the name of Moby Doll, and, to everyone's astonishment, won the whale's affectionate friendship. This was in 1965, when the killer whale was still regarded as the most savage of marine animals, the "tiger of the sea."

Moby Doll became a celebrity. The Duke and Duchess of Windsor came

* This account is taken from *Home Is the Sea for Whales,* p. 116.

†The whole story is told in the work by Riedman and Gustafson cited above.

239 THE KILLER WHALE

to see her and to watch her savior and friend scratch her stomach with a stiff-bristled brush. When Moby Doll died, the (London) *Times* devoted two columns to her obituary, and she was mourned throughout the English-speaking world.*

A few months after Moby Doll's death, the Seattle aquarium purchased a killer whale from two Canadian fishermen for $8000. Delivery, however, was not included in the purchase price, and Edward Griffin, director of the aquarium, went to the mouth of the Bella Coola river, near the village of Namu, to supervise the operation. His whale, he found, was twenty-three feet long, and weighed about four tons.

After considering the problem from every angle, he decided to encircle the whale with a floating net and to tow him back to Seattle within the net. Using forty empty oil barrels as floaters, and with the help of 200 volunteers from the village of Namu, the net was completed, and in place, in a few days. And, in recognition of the help given by the villagers, the whale was christened Namu.

A ship now began towing the net and its resident slowly along Queen Charlotte Strait, Johnstone Strait, and Georgia Strait. As the net moved, it was followed by a school of killer whales. It appeared that they wanted to free their companion; but they did not attack. Only one male and two females, who were no doubt members of his family, communicated with him by means of a series of whistles and cries. In response, Namu moved his dorsal fin; but he did not try to escape.

Two weeks later, the whale passed through customs at the American border and was placed in a tank at the Seattle aquarium. There he was treated royally. While he was being moved, he had refused to eat for about a week. At the end of that time, however, he accepted two salmon. He seems to have enjoyed them enormously, for he would never touch any other kind of food as long as he remained in Seattle — an unexpected idiosyncrasy that proved to be expensive for the aquarium.

Namu died after a year, in July 1966. He, like Moby Doll, had evidenced much intelligence and a surprising gentleness. This "tiger of the sea" had turned out to be friendly toward man.

During the past few years, about ten killer whales have been captured and placed in marinelands in Seattle, San Diego, and Vancouver. Edward Griffin, aided by a friend, Gerald Brown, has become a specialist in the techniques of capture. Mr. Brown has spent some time aboard *Calypso* as a

---

*When an autopsy was performed upon Moby Doll, it was discovered that "she" was a full-fledged male.

"We were sure," explained Brown, "that if we could get one of them to eat, the others would follow suit. When a whale bites, its teeth make noise in the water. And as soon as another killer whale hears that noise, he rushes over to eat whatever is left.

"We experimented first with a young whale. We rubbed a herring against his lips, and then we put it into his mouth and began pulling it out immediately. He reacted exactly as a dog would react: he bit on it and held it. The other whales, of course, heard the 'crunch,' and they came right over and began eating."

The killer-whale family is a closely knit unit. Usually, there is only one calf at a time, and the offspring is enveloped in a maternal love that seems highly developed. When a mother whale has reason to be afraid for her young, she comes close and "speaks" to it.

There are many reliable witnesses to the phenomenon of mother love among these mammals. A mother who was mortally wounded spent her last hour, and her last ounce of strength, circling around her calf in order to protect him as long as possible. Another mother wandered for three days off Hat Island, near Puget Sound, after her calf was killed there.

There have been several instances of mating in captivity, at Seattle and Vancouver. The whales copulate, after extended caresses, in a frontal position, chest to chest. The gestation period lasts from thirteen to sixteen months.

The sexual life of killer whales seems particularly intensive, and includes a powerful attraction for human beings. And they are perfectly capable of distinguishing between human male and female. Our friend, Jerry Brown, discovered this in the whale tank at Seattle.

"We had a female in a tank there for about a year, teaching her the usual tricks. One day, when the water was especially clear, I went down to take some underwater pictures. As soon as I was in the water, this female — Shamoo was her name — came over to me, pushed me up against the tank wall, and began rubbing against me. I called to a friend of mine to throw some herring into the water at the other end of the tank, but this didn't work. Shamoo wouldn't let me go, and I stayed there, pinned against the wall, for an hour and a half."

The skin of killer whales is especially soft and smooth. When they are swimming in groups, they remain constantly in physical contact by sliding against one another. This may well be a form of sex play.

A final and important characteristic: According to everyone who has worked with both killer whales and dolphins — including experts from the U. S. Navy — the whale is much more intelligent than the dolphin. They understand, and learn, twice as fast as their smaller cousins.

A team from *Calypso*, made up of our photographer, Ron Church, André Laban, and Louis Prezelin went recently to visit Griffin and Brown's killer whales at Juan de Fuca, near Seattle. The dean of all captive killer whales lives there, and he is now in his fifth year of residence.

Prezelin had brought his guitar, and played a few tunes while standing alongside the whales' enclosure. The animals immediately came over to the side closest to Prezelin and listened attentively, and then showed their satisfaction at the man's performance by spraying him from their blowholes.

Our team next tried to teach the whales to sing, with Prezelin accompanying on the guitar. This was less than successful; but there is no denying that killer whales are sensitive to music, and that one can get their attention, and their appreciation, if one is sufficiently fastidious in the choice of melodies.

In the water, Brown's whales ran through their entire repertoire of turns, loops, and leaps for our divers and cameramen.

Falco, after having chased so many killer whales over the water in his Zodiac, now hoped to be able to establish more peaceful relations with them. He went to visit two females at the Marine World of California.

Falco reported that both of the females were obviously very sensitive to the sounds coming from a loudspeaker over their tank. These sounds were the dialogue that had taken place when they were captured, between them and the other members of their school. This exchange, which was composed of clicks and trills, had been taped at the moment of capture and was now being played back to the female whales. The captives were quite obviously moved by the sounds. They swam quickly around their tank, but always returned to a spot near the loudspeaker and replied to it by a series of various sounds.

Falco swam for a while with a female killer whale named (for some obscure reason) Clyde, and he took the opportunity to try a few experiments. For example, he held out a fish to her, but, when she came to take it, he placed a thin plank between the whale and her food. The whale immediately turned away — apparently warned by her sonar of an obstacle.

The language of killer whales, like that of dolphins, remains incomprehensible to us, despite the best efforts of Dr. Lilly and several other researchers. At least we now know that these cetaceans do have a language of some kind, and that we must attempt to discover the meaning of the sounds that they make. This, perhaps, is one of the most exciting challenges that we have to face. It is not impossible that the killer whale, more intelligent than the dolphin, will one day provide us with the means of establishing communication between animals and man.

ELEVEN

A Time for Respect

It is March 8, and we are in Baja California's Bay of Solitude. The weather yesterday was atrocious, the sky covered with low-lying clouds. And, of course, it rained. It was impossible to shoot a single foot of film. To cap it all, the tape recorder fell out of the Zodiac and into the water when a whale decided to romp nearby. It was in the water only a few seconds; but that was enough to ruin it. We had to send Eugène Lagorio to Los Angeles by plane to have it repaired. Fortunately, yesterday was the day for our regular air liaison plane.

And then, last night, one of our camera batteries exploded. . .

Today, vengeance is ours. It is a glorious day, thanks to Bernard Delemotte.

Bernard spent the morning trying to lasso the tail of a whale calf. He would grab the calf, hold it in his arms, and, at the same time, try to get his lariat over the tail. The water was as muddy as that of the Mississippi, and he

(Left) A sperm whale has been overtaken by the launch.

couldn't see a thing. We all thought that he had succeeded, but he was not fast enough with the rope. By then, the calf had tired of the game. With a shrug and a rear upward that would have done credit to a mustang, it freed itself from Delemotte's embrace and disappeared in a cloud of foam, leaving Delemotte standing there with his lasso. (In all fairness to Bernard, I should mention that his "little" whale was about twenty-feet long.)

Our underwater cowboy was disappointed, but not discouraged. During the afternoon, he presented another spectacle for our entertainment and delight; and this time he was truly sensational.

Having succeeded in grabbing and holding on to a whale calf this morning, he conceived the idea of — stunt-riding on the back of a whale, as on a horse. For his prospective mount he chose an animal that appeared to be sleeping. Wearing his flippers and mask, but not breathing apparatus, Bernard swam slowly toward the whale, every movement a study in graceful efficiency. He was now next to her, and she was still asleep. In a single motion, Bernard hoisted himself onto her back and stood. He was mounted.

Michel Deloire was filming away as though it were the end of the world, and we were all watching in complete fascination. How long could Bernard stay on? And, more important, if he succeeded in staying on, how would he manage to get off?

The outcome was not long in doubt. The whale awoke and shook herself, more in surprise than irritation, and moved her head brusquely. Delemotte was off and lost in the commotion. By the time he regained the surface, his whale was far away.

From that moment on, the most vital question aboard *Polaris* has become: who will be the first to be towed by a bucking whale-bronco? Bonnici and Serge Foulon both succeed by using what they learned from Bernard's experience. Gradually, they perfect their technique, and they learn to ride with apparent facility, and even elegance. Each one of the riders approaches his whale and mounts in a manner consonant with his temperament. Delemotte is stern, resolute, his muscles tense, his brow furrowed, and he approaches the whale as though he were going to wrestle with it. Bonnici is intuitive, alert, agile; he observes the situation for a moment, then leaps upon his mount gracefully and rides with the professional smile of a circus bareback performer.

Moby Dick Revisited

Such, briefly, is the new relationship between men and whales. I cannot state categorically that whales have an entirely happy memory of our contact

A whale harpooned during a dive. Nineteenth-century engraving. *Bibliothèque Nationale.*

with them, or even a very lively recollection of it. But I can say that Delemotte's exploit marks a new departure in our relationships with whales. It has an almost historical character, and one that will have many repercussions. Once people see, on television, *Calypso*'s men riding on the back of a whale, they will no longer be able to preserve the old point of view with respect to whales. Man will no longer be able to be as limited, as utilitarian, and uncomprehending as our grandparents were in the nineteenth century. They will no longer believe in the "ferocity" and "malevolence" of "underwater monsters."

It bothers me enormously to read the traditional accounts of whaling in the era of sailing ships. These are recitals of deeds of bravery, and even of heroism; but they are also monuments to human incomprehension and misunderstanding. There, one reads only of the "ferocity" of sperm whales — of living, intelligent beings transfixed by eight or ten harpoons, their flesh torn, their eyes gouged out, mad with pain, flailing about in agony.

Thanks to Delemotte's experiences with the gray whales, to those of Raymond Coll with cachalots, to those of Philippe with humpback whales and of Bonnici with finbacks, misunderstanding may give way to admiration and comprehension. In my opinion, man will honor himself finally in being able to feel respect for the largest creature on the face of the earth, in being able to touch it, in being able to understand that it is an innocuous being.

When we drew near to a humpback whale in the water, we imagined that he gave us a friendly look.

A shark's look is more steady, and more misleading, than that of a whale.

Cetaceans may now no longer be relegated to that area of the human psyche which causes human beings to feel obliged to react, out of fear, with violence and death.

Until the twentieth century, the relationship between man and whale was that of killer to victim. When limits were finally established to the massacre of whales, they were limits dictated neither by pity nor by a feeling of respect for these "marvels of nature." What happened was that whale hunters realized at one point that they were finding fewer and fewer whales. And, in fact, there *were* fewer and fewer. The constant and continuing improvement of weapons for hunting, the use of fast boats and of "factory ships," was taking a toll far greater than anyone realized. The whalers now saw that if they continued slaughtering whales at the same rate, soon there

Bernard Delemotte manages to stand up on the back of a gray whale.

would be no whales left to slaughter. They therefore decided, or felt compelled, to exercise moderation so as to conserve their whale "capital" in the oceans. They had already seen what unrestricted whale hunting could, and would do: the whale population of the Bay of Biscay had already disappeared — either through extinction or flight.

It was the twentieth century, however, and not the nineteenth, that produced the greatest slaughter of whales. At the beginning of the century, whale hunting was extended to antarctic waters, and the butchery of these great mammals was intensified until it resulted in the virtual extinction of the right whale *(Eubalaena glacialis)*. Our century, as it turned out, was much more destructive with respect to whales than the period of the great romantic hunts as described in the work of Herman Melville. A hundred years ago, a whaler's three-year expedition netted him thirty-seven whales. Today, a whaler's modern weapons and fast boats give him one whale a day; and sometimes three or four.

At the present time, whale hunting is a regulated industry, and in principle, all species are protected by international agreements arrived at by the International Whaling Commission.*

A Continuing Threat

The fact of regulation does not mean that whales are now safe from extinction. Regulation has come much too late for that.

Right whales, unless they are spared completely, will probably become extinct because of the way they were hunted early in this century.

Blue whales, the largest animals ever to live on the planet, also constitute an endangered species. The hunting season on them is now limited, and, in certain areas, they are completely protected. But conservation experts tell us that it will take fifty years of such protection for blue whales to be out of danger as a species.

The finback whale, or common rorqual, even though it is now hunted on a reduced scale, will also have to be more adequately protected if it is to survive.

From year to year, a different species of whale becomes the principal victim of the whalers. In 1964-65, for example, it was the Sei whale — a very migratory whale of relatively small size — that was butchered. The total count for this period was 24,453 Sei whales, or double the total for the preceding season. For the Sei whale, this was the beginning of the end.

Humpback whales have been an endangered species for a considerable period. They are smaller than Sei whales but, unfortunately for them, their bodies produce twice as much oil. Humpbacks have been hunted with such intensity by Soviet and Japanese whalers that it was necessary to grant them absolute immunity for a two-year period. Even so, it will take half a century before the species is able to re-establish itself.

The International Whaling Commission, in the interest of a more effective protection of each species, has now decided to abandon the quota system based on the famous "BWU" — Blue Whale Unit — and to establish a quota for each separate species during each individual hunting season.

*See Appendix II, "Whale hunting."

Front view of a gray whale.

Converts and Missionaries

What is true of coral and of all other forms of marine life is also true of whales. We are no sooner able to approach them, to learn to admire them, to observe them in the water, than we realize that they are in danger of becoming extinct.

Calypso's men are perhaps more aware of this, and more struck by it, than anyone else. We have seen the eye of the whale. We have admired the delicate muzzle of the finback and the white flippers of the humpback. And we have been converted. We are now on the side of the whales.

Like all converts, we wish to convert others. Will we succeed in changing public opinion? Will we be able to reverse the trend, to assure a place on the earth, in the seas, for whales?

We must try.

Surely whales have more to offer us than "seafood" for our dogs, or oil (which we now get in abundance from other sources), or stays for corsets and ribs for umbrellas. We can learn much from their extraordinary diving ability, and about the depths that they reach, and from their ability to suspend breathing for comparatively long periods of time. Instead of being man's victims, whales should be his guides and teachers in the exploration of the marine world that has just been opened up to human investigation.

A diver holding onto the dorsal fin of a finback whale.

We now know that there exists a certain link among mammals. This mysterious sense of unity, and solidarity once it has been acquired, can never be lost. Something has changed in the sea. Cruelty and indifference to marine life will henceforth be regarded as intolerable by the vast majority of men.

It is evident that people everywhere are disturbed by what has happened to whales, and that whaling has come to be regarded as a foolish anachronism. Californians, for example, have the opportunity to see migrating whales near their shores, and they have developed a decided affection for these creatures.

Reaching an Understanding

The sympathy that is developing between man and the cetaceans still has an element of distance, of the abstract, about it. It is based more on common sense than on true understanding and affection. But we can hope that things will continue to change for the better; and that they will change especially when man and the whale meet under the surface of the water. Man must learn to know the cetaceans in their own element, in the water; and then the survival of the whale will be seen in its proper emotional and moral context. Right now, public opinion regards the killing of a dolphin as a crime.

Very soon, the same thing will hold true for the killing of a whale.

There is a great difference between seeing a gray whale on the surface of the water and seeing her beneath the surface, constantly maneuvering to keep herself between her offspring and a diver. Right now, we may deplore the massacre of humpback whales that took place at the turn of the century; but from now on we will react with sadness and anger, once we have had a chance to hear a humpback whale "talk"* or glide through the water or turn on its great flippers.

Can we go even further? Is it possible that one day there will be a true "understanding" between men and whales?

Our encounter with the great marine mammals was hampered from the outset by the fact that we knew absolutely nothing about the behavior of whales with respect to man. Little by little, however, we learned. We made overtures, we tried to approach these animals. And, once we discovered that contact was indeed possible, we became more daring and increased our efforts. *Calypso*'s divers eventually were able to confront these mountains of flesh without fear. They had learned to behave in such a way as to be tolerated by creatures whose weight was a thousand times their own.

Man took into the sea with him his desire to impose his will, to make himself understood, to make other animals obey him. During our expeditions in the Red Sea, we demonstrated that we were able, if not to assert our authority, then at least to awaken the respect of an animal such as the shark.

With whales, however, the situation was different. There is no longer any reason for us to feel fear. All that separates us now is a difference in scale. I mean that a man in the water is too small to assume much importance in the eyes of a whale, while, for an average-sized shark, he is big enough to be worthy of the shark's attention.

Despite all the problems of understanding and interpretation, the divers of *Calypso* were able to discern nuances in the whale's attitude toward them. We are beginning to open up, and to explore, a psychological domain in which direct observation is no longer out of the question.

But where will this lead?

That is the essential question. If we are successful in limiting, or even abolishing the practice of whaling, we will have to do the same thing for dolphins and blackfish and grampuses. Will we then put all animals in cages, under the pretext of "saving" them? Will we end up with nothing more than a succession of zoos and marinelands?

---

* Dr. Payne has put together a commercially available phonograph record, which reproduces the "speech" of humpback whales.

In California, biologists are already worried about the large number of cetaceans in captivity, not all of whom survive. Dr. Scheffer has asked the crucial question: is it not only legal, but is it moral and "human" to hunt grampuses? Since 1965, just in Seattle, six grampuses, or killer whales, died as a result of attempts to capture them. And many others have been mortally wounded by harpoons, by bullets containing narcotics, or by nets. In Dr. Scheffer's opinion, however, killer whales, because of their high degree of social evolution and their intelligence, may learn to avoid the areas where they are in danger. If this is true, then the shores of California will no longer have these animals which people have learned to enjoy, and which have become friendly because they knew that they had nothing to fear in those waters. Then, it will no longer be possible to see these magnificent mammals in their free state, or to approach them. As a solution, Dr. Scheffer suggests that a special permit be required to capture a grampus, and that the permit be given very rarely and only for good reason.

There are other, and specifically modern, dangers that threaten the whale. The gray whale, for example — who is a relic from another age, a true fossil, the oldest of all the species of whale — has had its habitat limited more and more every year. At the present time, there are only three or four lagoons in which it can spend the winter.

The lagoons of Matancitas and Scammon are, for gray whales, a miraculously preserved universe, with their deep waters and their beaches bordered by mangrove plants. But this is the last refuge of the whales. So far, these lagoons are intact; but, already they are threatened by the insidious danger that has already affected so much of the world: pollution. The waters of northern California are already infected, but the pollution has not yet reached Matancitas or Scammon. The latter is visited only by a few fishermen and, except for a small number of salt marshes, has retained its primitive purity. But any amount of pollution would exclude the gray whales from this paradise where they come to mate and bear their young.

But that is not the worst of it. The worst is that recently the various navies of the world have begun to take an interest in whales. Their interest is not purely scientific. It is their intention to "recruit" whales, to use them as underwater detectors, as spies and liaison agents. No sooner has man discovered that whales are intelligent creatures than he tries to involve them in his own stupidity, in his wars and battles. As long ago as 1963, L. Harrison Matthews, an English authority on cetacean life, was writing: "As intelligent as these animals are, they are not intelligent enough to refuse to co-operate, or to address to their trainers some of those underwater clickings which, translated into human language, might convey their profound contempt."

Two divers on the back of a finback whale.

Perhaps the time has come to formulate a moral code which would govern our relations with the great creatures of the sea as well as with those on dry land. That this will come to pass is our dearest wish.

If human civilization is going to invade the waters of the earth, then let it be first of all to carry a message of respect — respect for all life.

Acknowledgments

We owe a special word of thanks to M. Charles Roux, Deputy Director of the Laboratoire des Reptiles et Poissons at the Musée National d'Histoire Naturelle of Paris, who was kind enough to read the manuscript of this book and to offer some very constructive criticism.

Professor Paul Budker, Director of the Laboratoire de Biologie des Cétacés et autres mammiferes marins, at the Ecole Pratique des Hautes Etudes in Paris, once again gave us the benefit of his incomparable experience and advice in the preparation of this book.

The migration of gray whales from the Arctic to Baja California.

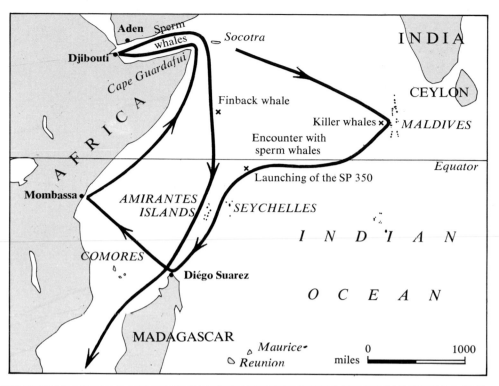

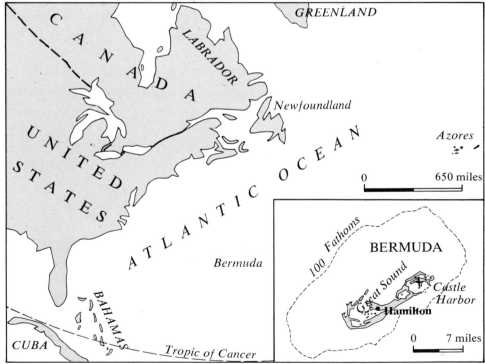

(Above) Encounters with cetaceans in the Indian Ocean.

(Below) Bermuda, where we undertook "Project Humpback Whale."

APPENDIX I

The Cetaceans

The Cetaceans

Cetaceans are marine mammals whose ancestors were probably land animals.* They are warm-blooded creatures; and, as Aristotle noted more than two thousand years ago, they breathe by means of lungs. Fertilization of the egg and gestation are internal, and they nurse their offspring.

* This appendix is based upon the works of Kenneth S. Norris, Dr. Harrison Matthews, Dr. F. C. Fraser, Ernest P. Walker, and upon the classification of the International Whaling Commission.

All cetaceans are characterized by tails that spread horizontally rather than, as in the case of fish, vertically. Also, they all have a blowhole or vent at the top of their heads, through which they breathe. The position and shape of this blowhole varies according to the species.

The cetaceans include approximately one hundred species and are divided into two orders: the *Mystacoceti* or toothless (or baleen or whalebone) cetaceans; and the *Odontoceti,* or toothed cetaceans.

The Mystacoceti

The *Mystacoceti,* or baleen whales, are characterized by the presence in the mouth of plates of whalebone (baleen), whose fringed edges act as a sieve through which water is strained to remove the small animals on which the whale feeds. The spacing of the fringe depends upon the size of the animals upon which a particular species normally preys. There are three families of Mystacoceti:

1.   The *Balaenidae,* which, in turn, is composed of three genera:

(a)   *Balaena,* which includes only one species *Balaena mysticetus,* or the right whale.

The right whale grows to a length of 50 to 60 feet and has black skin, except for the throat and chin which are cream-colored. One third of its body length is taken up by the enormous mouth. It has no back or dorsal fin, and no ventral furrows. The right whale is able to suspend breathing for from ten to thirty minutes. Its gestation period lasts nine or ten months. Its principal food is krill.

Right whales were still abundant in arctic waters at the beginning of the nineteenth century. By the twentieth century, however, the species was almost extinct. At present, right whales are no longer found between Greenland and the Barents Sea. There are perhaps a thousand surviving specimen in the neighborhood of the Bering Straits, and these are protected by international agreement.

(b)   *Eubalaena,* whose external characteristics are the same as those of the right whale, except for the mouth which is smaller and accounts for only one quarter of the total body length. *Eubalaena* includes the following species:

Eubalaena glacialis, which inhabits the North Atlantic and which, because of its modest size (40 to 55 feet) was hunted by the Basques as

(Right) The *Mystacoceti.*

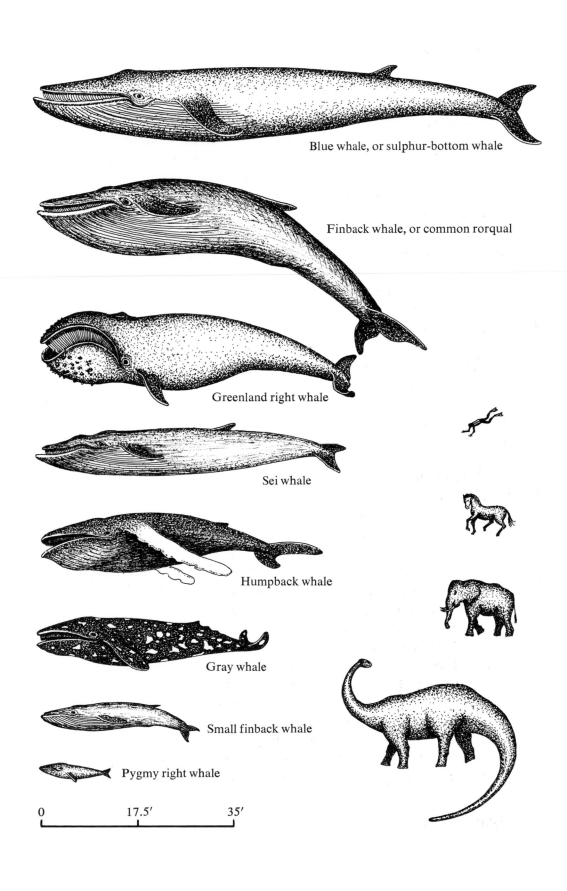

Blue whale, or sulphur-bottom whale

Finback whale, or common rorqual

Greenland right whale

Sei whale

Humpback whale

Gray whale

Small finback whale

Pygmy right whale

0   17.5′   35′

early as the ninth century. Specimens are extremely rare, and the species has been protected for the past thirty-five years.

Eubalaena australis, which lives in the waters of the Antarctic. Fifty years ago, this species counted its members in the hundreds of thousands. Whalers almost destroyed the species, however, and, at the present time, after thirty-five years of absolute protection, there are once again a few schools in the South Atlantic, in the vicinity of the Cape of Good Hope, and off South Georgia (an island of Antarctica).

(c) *Caperea,* to which only one species belongs: *Caperea marginata,* or the pygmy right whale, which has no economic importance.

2.   The *Eschrichtidae,* which comprises only the *Eschrichtius glaucus* — our gray whale of Baja California, which is found near the American and Korean coasts. The gray whale has no dorsal fin. There are ventral furrows, numbering two or four.

The gray whale reaches a length of between 35 and 45 feet and weighs between 24 and 37 tons. Its baleen measures 11 to 13 feet. In color, it is black, or slate, and its skin is mottled with grayish patches of barnacles. Sexual maturity is attained at four and one half years, and gestation lasts between eleven and twelve months. A single calf is born every two years.

3.   The *Balaenopteridae,* of which there are two genera:
(a) *Balaenoptera,* comprising the following species:
   - *Balaenoptera borealis,* or Sei whale;
   - *Balaenoptera acutorostrata,* or lesser rorqual:
   - *Balaenoptera edeni,* or Bryde's whale; and
   - *Balaenoptera physalus,* or finback whale (also known as the common rorqual). It was the *Balaenoptera physalus* with which *Calypso*'s divers had several encounters. The finback whale measures 60 to 75 feet in length and weighs about fifty tons. Its back is grayish, and its white underside shows between 30 and 60 ventral furrows. There is a clearly distinguishable dorsal fin, rather high and triangular in shape.

The finback whale travels in schools of 20 to 100 individuals. It feeds on plankton, crustaceans, and small fish.

This species mates during the winter, and the period of gestation lasts between ten and twelve months. The male attains sexual maturity at five years; and the female, between three and eight years. Physical maturity, however, is not reached until the age of fifteen.

(Right) The odontoceti.

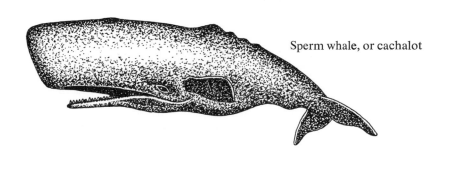
Sperm whale, or cachalot

Bottlenose whale

Killer whale, or orc

Pilot whale, or blackfish

Narwhal

Bottlenose dolphin

Pygmy sperm whale

Porpoise

0   17.5′   35′

Full-grown specimens may remain without breathing for from twenty to fifty minutes.

The finback whale has been one of the principal victims of whalers, and it is estimated that 90 percent of the species has been destroyed. In 1955, there were still approximately 110,000 specimens in the Atlantic; today, however, they probably number no more than 30,000.

Balaenoptera musculus, or blue whale (also known as the sulphur-bottomed whale), is the largest of the cetaceans and the largest animal that has ever existed on earth. It reaches lengths of between 80 and 100 feet, and the largest specimen known weighed 112.5 tons.

The blue whale winters in tropical waters, and spends its summers in polar seas. The skin is slate blue, and its throat is deeply pleated by approximately 100 furrows. Blue whales travel singly rather than in schools, and they are able to remain underwater for periods of ten to twenty minutes. Their basic food is krill.

They mate during May and June, and gestation lasts eleven months. One calf is born every two years. Sexual maturity is reached at the age of four and one half years.

The blue whale was the most avidly hunted of the great cetaceans because it yielded the greatest quantity of oil. In 1930, it was estimated that there were between 30 and 40 thousand blue whales in the Antarctic. Today, the most optimistic estimate sets the number at 2000, and perhaps fewer.

The blue whale is now a totally protected species.

(b) *Megaptera,* of which there is only one species: *Megaptera novaeangliae* — the humpback whale of our Bermuda expedition. The humpback whales and the gray whales are the only species to live in coastal waters.

The humpback's average length is 40 feet; its average weight: 29 tons. The upper part of the body is black, and the throat and chest are white. It is recognizable by its large white flippers, which measure a third of the length of the body. There are from 10 to 25 furrows on the neck and underside. Crustaceans are its staple diet.

Gestation lasts ten months. Sexual maturity is attained at the age of three; but full physical growth is not reached until the tenth year. A calf is born every two years.

During the 1930s, the Antarctic's humpback population was estimated at 22,000. At the present time, there are probably not more than 3000 specimens in the Antarctic. In the northern Pacific, however, there are an additional 5000 humpback whales.

Humpback whales are a protected species today.

The Odontoceti

The *Odontoceti* are toothed cetaceans. The number of teeth varies greatly by species, from the Goosebeak whale (or Cuvier's whale), which has two, to the dolphin with its 260 teeth. There are five families of *Odontoceti,* which include the majority of the species of cetaceans:

1. The *Monodontidae,* comprising two genera:
    - *Delphinapterus,* the beluga whale found especially in the arctic seas around North America (see Glossary); and
    - *Monodon,* the narwhal (see Glossary).

2. The *Delphinidae,* which contains nineteen genera:
    Steno, Sousa, Sotalia, Stenella, Delphinus (the common dolphin — see Glossary), *Grampus, Tursiops, Lagenorhynchus, Feresa, Cephalorhynchus, Orcaella, Lissodelphis, Lagenodelphis, Phocaena* (the common porpoise — see Glossary), *Phocaenoides* (Pacific Dall's Porpoise), *Neomeris* (Southeast Asian finless black porpoise), *Pseudorca, Orcinus* (killer whale), and *Globicephala* (the pilot whale, or blackfish, encountered by *Calypso*'s divers).
    Blackfish or pilot whales have rounded heads, the upper part of which projects over the upper jaw. They are between fourteen and twenty-five feet in length and are, as their common name indicates, wholly black. They have a dorsal fin, and between seven and eleven teeth in each jaw.
    Pilot whales travel in schools of several hundred individuals who follow a leader-whale blindly.
    Their main food is squid, which they pursue during their migrations. During the summer, they are found near the coasts of Newfoundland. They winter in warm waters, where they give birth to their young.
    Gestation lasts twelve months. The mating season is in the autumn. Males mature sexually at three years, and females at six years.
    Blackfish are the principal whale resource of Newfoundland, and between three and four thousand of these small whales are slaughtered there every year.
    The killer whale is another member of this genus to travel in schools. This mammal attains a length of about 20 feet and a weight of one ton. It is black, with white markings on its underside extending from the lower jaw to the middle of the stomach, and with another, smaller white spot above the eyes. The jaws each contain between 20 and 28 teeth. Killer whales prefer warm-blooded prey: seals, dolphins, and even baleen whales. They mate

between November and January, and gestation lasts between eleven and twelve months. The mother nurses her calf for a year following birth.

3. The *Ziphiidae,* which characterized by a beak-shaped muzzle, include five genera:
    - *Mesoplodon* (beaked whales);
    - *Ziphius* (Cuvier's beaked whale, or the goose-beak whale);
    - *Tasmacetus* (Tasmanian beaked whale);
    - *Berardius* (giant bottlenose whale);
    - *Hyperoodon* (bottlenose whale — see Glossary).

4. The *Physeteridae* contain two genera:
    - *Kogia* (pygmy sperm whale)
    - *Physeter,* the most common species of which is
    Physeter catodon — the cachalot, or sperm whale.

Of all the *Odontoceti,* the cachalot is instantly recognizable because of its oblique spout. It has two blowholes, but the left blowhole is the only working one. The cachalot is characterized especially by its massive head and squared snout. The head accounts for one third of the cachalot's body length. Only the lower jaw has teeth, but what teeth they are: each one ten inches long and weighing over two pounds.

The sperm whale has no dorsal fin, but does have a sort of "crest"; nor does it have ventral furrows.

It is usually dark in color, with spots that lighten as it grows older.

The white cachalot is a literary celebrity in the person of Moby Dick, immortalized by Herman Melville. A white or albino sperm whale has been seen in real life only once, in 1951. It measured fifty feet in length.

The largest cachalots — always males — reach a maximum length of sixty feet. They weigh between thirty-five and fifty tons. They feed principally on giant squid, which they seek out in the great depths of the sea.

Sperm whales live in family groups, or harems, of 20 to 50 individual whales. One calf is born every three years. Gestation lasts sixteen months, and the calf nurses for twelve months.

5. The *Platanistidae* are the fresh-water dolphins generally found in the estuaries of large rivers. There are four genera:
    Platanista, the Ganges dolphin;
    - *Inia,* the Amazon dolphin;
    - *Lipotes,* found in China; and
    - *Stenodelphis,* the La Plata River dolphin.

APPENDIX II

Whaling

The hunting of whales is a very old human occupation, dating far back into recorded history. For men in wooded canoes, armed only with primitive harpoons, the whale must have been a frightening and deadly adversary. But when one remembers that paleolithic man earlier had hunted Mammoths with spears and weapons of flint, it should come as no surprise that man, the predator, later dared measure his strength against that of the great cetaceans. This is especially true when one recalls that, though the techniques of whale hunting changed and were improved through the centuries (as we shall see), the basic weapon by means of which man pitted his strength against that of the great whales remained essentially the same. It was always a harpoon, or spear, thrown by hand.

The Basques

The Middle Ages are the earliest period from which we know for certain the techniques and the extent of whaling. However, if we may believe Orosius' *Seven Books of History Against the Pagans,* written in the fifth century,* Norsemen were already whaling when Rome ruled the world. In any event, we know that the Basques were avid whalers before the twelfth century, and that they had very likely begun whaling as early as the ninth century. It was necessary for the Basques, as for any other whale hunters, to be as close as possible to their prey for them to be able to use their harpoons and lances effectively. But they had an advantage. Every year, the *Eubalaena glacialis,* or black right whale (which the Basques called *Sardako Balaena),* passed along their shores in migration. And this species was an ideal victim. Right whales are comparatively slow, timid and weak; and, unlike other species, they were relatively easy to hunt in small boats and not difficult to kill with the primitive weapons of the period. They also have another characteristic; after they are dead, they continue to float, while whales of other species sink. It was therefore possible for the Basques to tow their kill into shallow water, or even to shore.

The right whale brought wealth to the Basques. The hunters not only used the mammal's flesh for food, but melted its blubber and marketed it throughout Europe, where it became the principal fuel for lamps.

So courageous were the Basque whalers, and so proficient did they become, that, before long, there were few right whales remaining in the Bay of Biscay. (Indeed, today there are none at all.) The whalers therefore built larger boats and struck out into the Atlantic in search of the game that had deserted their own shores. The chase led them northward, through the terrors of storm and icebergs, to strange lands: Iceland and Greenland. They went as far as present-day Newfoundland and thus discovered the coasts of North America before the time of Columbus.† In the sixteenth century, they were hunting whales with such vigor in Greenland that, a century later, the right whale was no longer to be found in those waters.

The Basques not only risked the then unknown dangers of the North Atlantic in their ridiculously small boats for the sake of whale oil, but also

---

*The text describes the arctic voyages of Other, a Norse chieftan. The Histories were translated by King Alfred of England at the end of the ninth century.

†There is, in Newfoundland, a tombstone, bearing a Basque inscription, that dates from the end of the fourteenth century.

Whaling ship: the cutting up of a whale. Engraving by Piquet (1791). *Bibliothèque Nationale.*

developed the process of flensing and boiling by which whale blubber is converted into oil aboard a whaling boat. The discoverer, it seems, was a mariner from St. Jean-de-Luz named Sopite, who invented the oven on which this process is based. Up until that time, it was necessary for the whalers to bring their catch ashore for it to be processed. And, in fact, Dutch whalers continued to do so until the end of the seventeenth century, and simply stored the blubber in barrels aboard their ships.

The Eskimos

We have less information about other people who, along with the Basques, were early whalers. And yet, we know that there were such peoples. In Scandinavia, for example, whale vertebrae were used as stools. And

Whalers attacking sperm whales. From Thomas Beale's *Histoire naturelle du cachalot*, London (1839). *Bibliothèque Nationale.*

Boat thrown into the air by a whale. Lithography of Saint Aulaire, from *Campagne d'un baleinier autour du monde:* (1840). *Bibliothè*que Nationale.

recently, in Greenland, some very old Eskimo villages were discovered in which the houses were built of whale bones. It is possible, of course, that these were the bones of whales that had gone aground. But we know for a fact that the ancient Eskimos developed a technique of getting as close to the whale as they could in their skin-covered canoes, and then of driving a spear into the animal's lungs — a mortal blow. As a buoy, they used an inflated sealskin, which would float if the whale sank or dived.

The Eskimo inhabitants of the Aleutians used to dip their harpoons in a poison that was very likely derived from aconite. And the natives of Greenland and of Spitsbergen used a bacterial poison that made any wound mortal. (In Norway today, in certain of the fjords, whalers use rusted arrows covered with the blood of dead whales, which induces blood poisoning in any whale that is shot with the arrow.)

The Dawn of Modern Whaling: The Eighteenth Century

At the beginning of the eighteenth century, the English, Dutch, and Danes, with the collaboration of the Basques, outfitted whalers who began hunting at Spitsbergen on a large scale. The English, Dutch, and Danes, along with their Basque tutors, had no more idea of the limitations of the natural resources of the sea than had primitive man — or, for that matter, the whalers of the nineteenth and twentieth centuries. They hunted relentlessly, competently, with a single purpose: to kill as many whales as possible in order to realize the greatest immediate profit. It seemed to matter not at all — even if they were aware of it — that such wholesale slaughter must necessarily impede, or perhaps even eliminate, breeding; or that their happy hunting ground at Spitsbergen might, in a few years, be empty of game. And so, the same thing happened for the second time in a century: the whales disappeared.

The French, too, and particularly the Normans, were whaling during this period, but on a relatively small scale. During the last quarter of the century, under Louis XVI, France had no more than forty whaling ships.

The Japanese were, as always, the whalers par excellence. They had the same advantage as the Basques: whales in migration passed near their shores. By the end of the seventeenth century, they had perfected a new technique: whaling with nets — and the nets, of course, were enormous, and equipped with many empty barrels to serve as floaters.

This technique required no fewer than thirty boats, some to round up an animal and the others to handle the nets. Once the whale was trapped within the nets, it was harpooned and speared until a man could, with relative impunity, climb on its head and attach a tow line.

The Dutch were no less assiduous. In the eighteenth century, there were 400 Dutch whaling ships, manned by 20,000 seamen. They hunted especially in Davis Strait, between Greenland and Baffin Island. They were followed by the English; and, in 1750, there were twenty whaling ships operating in this region. By 1788, there were 252. And again history repeated itself: there were no more whales to be found.

The Golden Age

It was at this time that the New England seafarers discovered the extraordinary abundance of whales along the eastern coast of North America. After the Revolutionary War, a whaling fleet was built in the United States; and this fleet was to be the basis for the sperm-whale hunting which was to provide a chapter in American economic history rich in color, courage, and marvelous legends, and also in misery.

As soon as the right whale became rare along the American coast because of excessive slaughter, American whalers began hunting everywhere on all the seas for cachalots. The cachalot, or sperm whale, was a much more fearsome adversary than the right whale. It was larger, stronger, and had a reputation for diabolical ferocity. Terrible stories were told of its monstrous intelligence, and of the fate of hapless fishermen who had become its victims.

Until the eighteenth century, no whaler had dared pit his weak weapons against this formidable animal. But now, Americans were demanding more and more whale oil; and this market justified, or at least resulted in, new feats of daring on the part of the whalers. Spermaceti, the wax contained in a chamber of the cachalot's huge head, was bringing a high price; and every sperm whale furnished a ton of it. It was on the cachalot's spermaceti that the fortunes of many of America's celebrated families were founded.

The whaling ships left from Nantucket, from New Bedford, from Mystic. The hunt continued through all seasons of the year; and young whales as well as old ones were the targets. It was a massacre, in every sense of the term; but a massacre with elements of drama. In 1778, Thomas Jefferson was writing to the French minister: "The Spermaceti whale discovered by the people of Nantucket is an aggressive and ferocious beast which requires of those who would hunt it as much skill as courage." Soon, they would be called "fighting cachalots."

Four-year Expeditions

The whalers had also discovered a new victim, far away in the Antarctic: the *Balaena australis,* or southern right whale. Between 1804 and 1817, 190,000 whales of this species were slaughtered, and they became more and more rare.

The whalers had, of necessity, to turn once more to the redoubtable sperm whale. Beginning in 1820, the Nantucket whaling fleet was growing. There were fewer and fewer small sailing boats with one or two hunting canoes (often manned by Indians), which had to return to port after taking five or six whales. And there were more and more large three-masters of 500 tons, carrying five, six or seven whaling boats, and a crew of forty men. These "South Seamen," as they were called, were perhaps the sturdiest sailing ships ever built.

In this Golden Age of sailing whalers, only extended expeditions were feasible; for only lengthy voyages could discover and kill a sufficient number of whales to justify the expense of the ship. When they sailed from their home ports, therefore, the South Seamen were often not seen there again for three or four years; for, in principle, they did not return without a full load of whale oil.

In the building of these ships, no attention was paid to comfort; and hardly more to sanitation. The crew was composed, for the most part, not of professional seamen, but the unemployed and the unemployable, the flotsam and jetsam of the whaling ports. Professor Paul Budker tells us that "in 1860, an ordinary seaman on an American whaler was paid twenty cents a day, while on land an unskilled laborer was paid ninety cents a day. In other words, in the United States the lowest category of worker on dry land was paid at least two or three times more than a seaman aboard a whaler."

Among the seamen, the harpooners occupied a privileged position. Their quarters were not in the forecastle, with the ordinary seamen, but amidships, with those of the officers.

Food and water were always scarce. Before leaving the ship's home port, the captain always took aboard as large a load of supplies as the vessel was able to carry. This practice had a reason: the captain did not dare visit ports of call in order to take on supplies, for, when a whaling ship did so, a good number of its crew usually deserted.

It has been said that today's sperm whales are not as large as those of the nineteenth century. Today, they reach a maximum length of 60 feet; but, we are told, in Moby Dick's time, they were often 90 feet long. And, in fact, the Jonathan Bourne Museum at New Bedford, Massachusetts, exhibits a cachalot's jawbone 23 feet long. And, it is reported that, in 1841, Owen Tilton of New Bedford killed a male cachalot 91 feet 8 inches in length.

What is certain is that, when measured against the size of the ships of that time, these whales must have seemed enormous. This is particularly true when it is recalled that whales were usually sighted from high up in a ship's rigging, from the crow's nest. From that vantage point, a man was on constant watch for the telltale spout, which he announced with the famous whaler's cry, "Thar she blows!" This ritual formula was, and remains, the only proper way to notify a ship's captain that a whale has been sighted.

The Battle

As soon as the alarm had been given, the whaling boats were lowered into the water. These craft were never more than 30 feet long, and were unusually light. They were carried suspended from the ship by davits, ready to be lowered instantly even in bad weather. A whaling boat's crew generally comprised a coxswain, an officer, and five seamen. Two of the seamen rowed to port, with oars fifteen feet long. On the starboard side, two others, and the harpooner, rowed with smaller oars. They were supposed to come as near as possible to the whale — which, given the swell and the small number of oars, must have been extremely difficult.

When the boat had drawn near to the whale, the coxswain gave a signal and the harpooner dropped his oar and picked up his weapon, turned, knelt on the gunwale, and threw his harpoon, aiming to hit the animal near the eyes.

The harpoon was attached to a line coiled in a basket. When the harpooner scored a hit, the whale usually began to swim away so rapidly that the line, as it uncoiled, had to be sprinkled with water to keep it from burning.

After the whale had been harpooned, a long and sometimes dramatic struggle followed. The whale dived but, slowed by the weight of the whaling boat that he had to tow, he could not go down very deep. And, of course, he had to rise to the surface in order to breathe. One can imagine how dangerous the situation was for the half-dozen men in the whaling boat, being towed along at 12 or 15 knots. But the real danger had hardly begun, for the next move was the most difficult of all. The coxswain and the harpooner now changed places, which meant that they both had to crawl along the entire length of the rolling, pitching craft, the coxswain toward the bow and the harpooner toward the stern. (The protocol of whaling required that it always be an officer — in this instance, the coxswain — who gave the coup de grace,

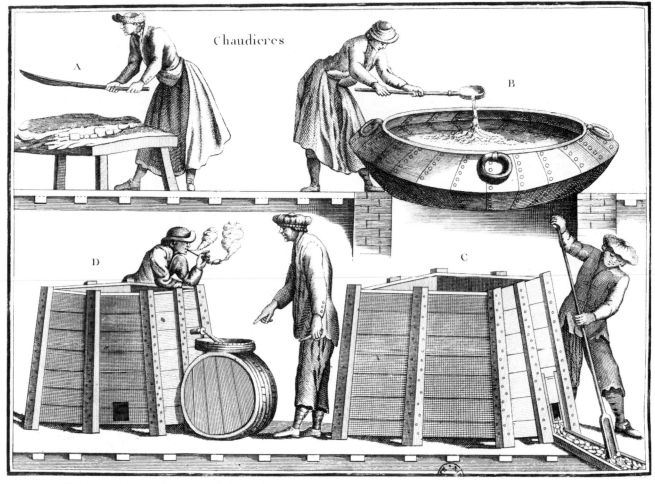

Kettles used to melt whale blubber, from Du Reste's *Histoire des peches, des découvertes des établissements des Hollandais dans les mers du nord.* An IX de la République. *Bibliothèque Nationale.*

the deathblow.) When this had been done, and as soon as the whale surfaced, the craft was once more brought close in, and the coxswain took a five-foot spear — sharpened on all sides — and attempted to plunge it into the whale head, as near to the eye as possible. If he was successful, he then rotated the spear in the wound.

At this point, no one could tell what would happen. The whale might smash the boat and its crew with a stroke of its mighty tail; or, if it was a cachalot, it might attack with its mouth and splinter the craft with one snap.

Most often, however, the whale was now mortally wounded, and blood was running from its blowhole into the sea, turning the water red around the boat. Then the men cried, "Flurry! Flurry!" which meant that the whale was in its death agony.

The enormous cadaver had to be towed back to the mothership, which often was by now so far away as to be out of sight. (It happened frequently that a school of whales was sighted and several whaling boats lowered at the

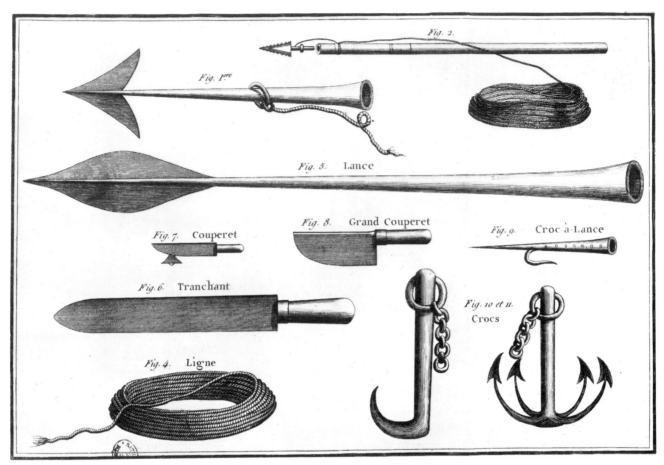

Harpoon, lance, and chopper. Du Reste, op. cit.

same time, so that it was not easy for all of them to make their way back to the ship with, or even without, their catch.) The whale was then tied to the ship's starboard, tail forward; and the butchery began. The men climbed onto the whale, despite the body's inevitable pitching and rolling, and began cutting away enormous slabs of blubber with their hooks. These slabs were passed onto the boat. As the men worked, the carcass was often surrounded by sharks, claiming a share in the spoils and ripping off pieces for themselves as they glared at the men working on the dead whale's back.

When the weather was good, this process lasted four or five hours. The flensing and boiling down of the blubber, however, took much longer. This was done on deck, in great kettles, into which the slabs of blubber were thrown. The blubber sometimes remained in the kettles for a day and a night, giving off an incredible stench and a suffocating smoke. No one slept until the job was done.

Occasionally, the whalers found an unexpected treasure: a ball-like substance, in the whale's entrails, that hardened on exposure to air. It was ambergris — a valuable substance used originally for medicinal purposes, and today in the manufacture of expensive perfumes. It is possible that the ambergris is a by-product of the sperm whale's diet of squid.

A Terrible Weapon

At this time, New Bedford, Massachusetts, was the undisputed whaling capital of the world. It happened, however, that the importance of whaling was already declining. Whales had been hunted so continuously that they were becoming harder and harder to find. Moreover, the commercial outlets for whaling products were slowly disappearing. Petroleum and electricity were replacing whale oil as the principal means of illumination.

Ironically, it was at the moment that whale oil was losing its importance that a new and terrible weapon was developed for use against whales: the harpoon cannon. Now, not only the right whales, the humpback whales, and the cachalots were in danger, but also the blue whales and the finbacks, whose size, up to then, had protected them.

Whales of sufficiently small size and sufficiently slow to be killed without great difficulty had become hard to find. In attacking larger and faster species, harpooners and whalers were now compelled either to face failure, or to take greater and greater risks. It was in the face of this dilemma that a Norwegian, Svend Foyn, marketed (1868) a harpoon designed to be shot out of cannon and containing an explosive head. This weapon had a pivoted crosspiece which was released upon discharge of the explosive, thus preventing withdrawal of the harpoon. The cannon also allowed a second line to be attached to the whale. Thus, the animal could be quickly brought back to the ship and secured to its side before it could sink. A later refinement was the pumping of compressed air into the whale after it had been harpooned in order to keep it afloat.

These new weapons allowed whalers to attack animals which, until then, had been considered too fast, or too powerful, to be hunted. Moreover, the advent of the steam engine made it possible for ships to approach to within 100 to 125 feet of whales — the ideal distance for a harpoon cannon. (A full-grown whale can swim at 14 knots; and, for a long time, motorized whaling boats' top speed was 10 to 12 knots.)

Svend Foyn's cannon quickly became indispensable, for whales — such as the right whale — that could be killed without it had more or less disap-

peared completely from the seas. What whalers now found on their expeditions into polar waters were, above all, finback whales. Even the most daring cachalot hunters had given up the chase late in the nineteenth century. But, in 1904, when a large number of them were discovered in the Antarctic, they began again — and this time, with the harpoon cannon and with more powerful and faster ships.

The End of an Age

At the beginning of the twentieth century, whale oil began to increase in value as certain manufacturers found uses for it. The whaling industry, now equipped with modern weapons and techniques, once more became profitable. New, fast whalers were commissioned, and factories were built in the Falkland Islands, at Newfoundland, etc. By 1904, the whalers were slaughtering the great schools of finback whales that had just been discovered in the Antarctic. Old cargo ships were anchored in protected bays, and to these were brought the carcasses for processing.

The resurgence of whaling, however, was short-lived. Little by little, the American whalers went out of business; and, one by one, the factories of New England closed their doors. In 1921, the American whaler *Charles W. Morgan* made its last expedition, and then was decommissioned. (The ship is preserved at Mystic, Connecticut.)

According to R. Clarke, the end of the sailing whalers came in 1925, when the *John R. Manta* and the *Margareth,* both schooners, were decommissioned at New Bedford.

But it was not yet over. In the mid-1920s, a group of Norwegians invented the factory ship — a ship equipped to take on board and completely process whales killed by smaller chasers. In 1925 and 1926, the factory ship *Lancing* was hoisting aboard, by means of an enormous ramp, the carcasses of the largest whales and flensing and boiling their blubber. This was the signal for a new massacre. In 1927-28, 13,775 whales were taken; and, in 1930-31, 40,201. By then, there were forty-one factory ships afloat. And the number of whales diminished accordingly.

The Antarctic was virtually empty of whales, and the Japanese and the

(Facing page above) Olaus, Magnus. Engraving from *Historia de gentibus septentrionalis* (1555). *Bibliothèque Nationale.*

(Facing page below) Olaus Magnus. Engraving from *Historia de gentibus septentrionalis* (1555). *Bibliothèque Nationale.*

Soviets turned once more to the North Pacific, where they found Sei and sperm whales. As the whalers of these two nations intensified their efforts, however, Americans, who had been among the most efficient hunters, gave up whaling altogether. Similarly, Great Britain, South Africa, Holland, and Norway were no longer maintaining a whaling industry.

Control

Beginning in 1931 and 1932, professional whalers, alarmed at the great decrease in the number of cetaceans, agreed to accept controls on the number of expeditions sent out each year. This was followed by agreement among whaling companies to limit the number of whales that each company was allowed to kill, the amount of whale oil that could be produced, and also the extent of the hunting season.

In 1937, the first international whaling agreement (called the London Convention) was signed by nine nations. Of rather limited value, it was in force until World War II. During the war years, however, whaling ceased almost entirely, and the various species of whales were thus enabled to increase their numbers somewhat. The whaling ships were either sunk or converted into tankers.

On February 7, 1944, a preliminary meeting repromulgated the provisions of the London Convention, and, in order to institute a standard unit of measure, established the Blue Whale Unit (BWU) — that is, a unit designating the quantity of oil furnished by one blue whale. This same meeting, on a purely arbitrary basis, lay down the following principle:

1 blue whale equals 2 finback whales equals 2 1/2 humpback whales equals 6 Sei whales. (These are the four species of baleen whale pursued by the whalers.)

In December 1946, the delegates of nineteen nations met in Washington, created the International Whaling Commission, and promulgated a new Convention. This agreement determines the dates of the opening and closing of the whaling season, prohibits the taking of a female accompanied by a calf, establishes minimum sizes of whale that may be taken (according to species), and, finally, sets up an annual "quota" (expressed in Blue Whale Units) of whales.

Certain species of whale were completely protected under the terms of the Convention; that is, they may not be hunted under any circumstances. These are the right whale, the gray whale of California, and the humpback whale. The International Whaling Commission decides which species are to be protected.

A whale hunt. Engraving by Piquet (1791). *Bibliothèque Nationale*.

In addition, a natural preserve was set up for whales, in which all whaling is forbidden. This is the largest preserve in the world: the arctic region between longitude 70 and 160 west.

Enforcement of the Commission's regulations is assured by the presence, aboard every factory ship and in every whaling station on land, of at least two inspectors.

"Since the end of the war," writes Professor Budker, "the whaling industry has subsisted above all on reserves of common rorquals. Blue whales and humpback whales complement these reserves, but the number of them taken is not large." At the present time, since blue whales and humpback whales are totally protected species in the Antarctic, the only species hunted in those regions by the Soviets and the Japanese are the finback and the Sei whales.

The End of the Massacre

An estimate reveals that, at the present time, there are approximately 220,000 large cetaceans in the sea; that is, whales belonging to the species that were most hunted. Of this number, 75 percent are finback whales; 15 percent, blue whales; and 10 percent, humpback whales.

For the past quarter-century, the International Whaling Commission has actively met its responsibilities. A scientific committee studies every aspect of the conservation of the various species. Of all the nations adhering to the Commission's rules and regulations, only three are still actively engaged in whaling: Norway (in a very small capacity), the Soviet Union, and Japan, who divide between themselves most of the annual quota of whales.

The twenty-third session of the International Whaling Commission, held in Washington during the summer of 1971, was of special importance. It was decided to abandon the Blue Whale Unit system since it was detrimental to certain species. Henceforth, quotas will be established for individual species — a system strongly urged for several years by the Commission's scientific committee. The last quota authorized was 2300 blue whale units, which was 400 units less than that of the preceding year.

Moreover, the United States has placed on its list of "endangered species" eight species of whales; which means that no whaling permits will be issued for any of these. This enlightened legislation has served to reinforce the fundamental determination of the International Whaling Commission to protect marine fauna with every means in its power. Similar legislation has recently been enacted which forbids the importation onto American territory of any product derived from an endangered species.

Illustrated Glossary

Amphipoda

An order of crustacean, subclass Malacostraca, division Peracarida. The carapace is always present, even though it may not always be distinct. The first thoracic segment, and occasionally also the second, is united to the head. Amphipoda are laterally compressed: *Gammarus, Talitrus, Caprella.* The *Cyamidae,* or whale fleas, are related to *Caprellidae.*

Apnea

Suspension of breathing of more or less long duration.

Aqua-Lung®

The Aqua-Lung,® or self-contained underwater breathing appartaus (SCUBA), was designed in 1943 by Jacques-Yves Cousteau and an engineer. Émile Gagnan

The principal characteristic of this apparatus is that it is an "open-circuit" device; that is, the used air is expelled directly into the water, and fresh air is provided not in continuous fashion, but whenever the diver inhales.

The air itself is stored in one or more air tanks (or "bottles" or "cylinders")

which are strapped onto the diver's back. Its flow is controlled by a regulator, which delivers air when the diver inhales and which assures that the pressure of the air corresponds to that of the water surrounding the diver. When the diver exhales, the used air is fed into the water by means of an exhaust located under the hood of the regulator. Two flexible tubes run from a mouthpiece to the regulator; one is for inhalation, the other for exhalation.

This simple and safe apparatus, entirely automatic and easily mastered, has, in effect, opened the doors of the sea to man and made it possible for a large segment of the public to experience the thrill of diving. The invention of the AQUA-LUNG,® therefore was a decisive step forward in man's conquest of the sea, and even in the history of human progress.

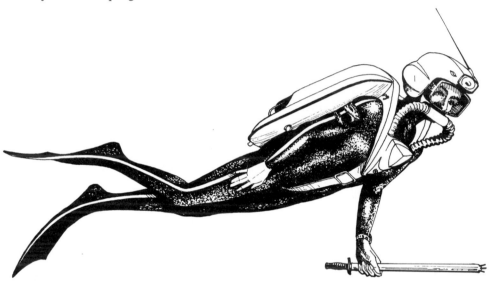

The Cousteau-Gagnan SCUBA.

The Cousteau-Gagnan independent diving unit was a revolutionary departure from the old "hard-hat" heavy diving rig, which most of us recall from the movies of the thirties. The hard-hat apparatus (so called because of the heavy copper helmet that it included) was complicated to use, uncomfortable, and dangerous. Moreover it required a long period of training, and it limited the diver to a small area of bottom. If, in the past twenty years, man has truly been able to go down into the sea, it is because of the independent diving gear — and its accessory equipment, such as the "fins" invented by Commandant de Corlieu, the mask, and the weight belt used to control buoyancy — which has proved its value as a means of exploration and scientific research even more than as a piece of sporting equipment.

Yet, even though man has now learned to operate autonomously in the sea, he is still susceptible to two of the dangers with which the hard-hat divers had always to contend: rapture of the depths, and decompression accidents. (See these two entries in the Glossary.)

Asdic

Acronym for Allied Submarine Detection Investigation Committee. It is an ultrasonic detection device which enables a ship on the surface to locate a submerged submarine. Like radar, it was developed by the British on the eve of World War II.

Automatic Camera with Edgerton Flash

The automatic marine camera was developed by the Center of Advanced Marine Studies of Marseilles on the basis of a design by J.-Y. Cousteau. Essentially, it consists of a camera installed on a trailer which is towed along the ocean bottom by *Calypso*. It is automatic in the sense that it begins operating as soon as it touches bottom. The apparatus is equipped with an electronic flash designed specially for the "Troika," or trailer, by Professor Harold Edgerton of MIT. Both camera and flash are battery operated. The automatic camera and Edgerton flash permit us to take close-ups of the bottom.

Balanus or Barnacle

A fixed crustacean, division Entomostraca, subclass Cirripedia. They are usually known as barnacles, or acorn barnacles.

Barnacles live on the shores of every part of the globe. Another type of barnacle, the ship or goose barnacle, attaches itself to flotsam in the sea, and, especially in the days of wooden ships, to ships' bottoms. They feed on micro-organisms from the water, which they filter through their modified limbs. The larvae are free-floating.

Beluga

The Belugae, or white whale, is a toothed whale, which belongs to the family Monodontidae, genus *Delphinapterus*. It inhabits the arctic seas of North America, but it is also found occasionally in shallow coastal waters and in bays.

The Beluga is between 12 and 14 feet in length and weighs slightly less than a ton. It has no dorsal fin. A young Beluga is dark gray, but it becomes lighter as it matures until its skin is yellow-white.

Belugae travel in schools of about ten individuals. They feed in shallow water, on fish, squid, and crustaceans; and they themselves are an easy prey for killer whales.

The female matures sexually at three years, when she is about eight feet long. Gestation lasts fourteen months, and birth takes place between March and May. The young white whale is approximately five feet in length, and it grows at the rate of three feet a year for the first two years of its life.

The Beluga is protected by a layer of blubber four to eight inches thick. When melted, this blubber produces about 200 liters of oil for every animal.

The word "Beluga" is somewhat confusing, since it is also used to designate the white sturgeon which is the source of caviar. The name became current in the nineteenth century, and came from the Russian word *bieluha,* white.

Blowhole

The blowhole is the whale's nostril. There are, in fact, two blowholes, but, so far as the sperm whale is concerned, only one of them is a working nostril. This organ has no connection with the whale's mouth.

Within the blowhole (the opening of which is controlled by a powerful muscle), there are inflatable air pockets on either side of the opening. Two internal "lips" control exhalation and contribute to the modulation of sound. In addition, a fleshy lamella, shaped like a tongue, makes it possible for a whale to close the blowhole more or less tightly.

Bottlenose Whales

The bottlenose whale, *Hyperoodon,* is a toothed whale of the family *Ziphiidae.* It is found in the North Atlantic in summertime, and, in winter, it migrates southward, sometimes as far as the Mediterranean.

Adult males reach a length of about 30 feet, and females of 25 feet. A female 20 feet long weighs about 2.5 tons.

The color of the skin varies from black to gray, and becomes lighter with age. Bottlenose whales not yet fully mature are often spotted with yellow and white. Males have only two teeth, located at the tip of their snouts.

These mammals are able to remain under water from ten to twenty minutes when they are feeding; but, when they are harpooned, they are able to stay much longer than that without surfacing.

They travel in groups of four to twelve individuals, and feed chiefly on squid and cuttlefish.

The gestation period is approximately twelve months. A new-born bottlenose whale is about 10 feet.

An adult male 30 feet long and with a 20-foot circumference may yield as much as two tons of oil and over 200 pounds of spermaceti similar to the spermaceti of the cachalot.

Cachalot or Sperm Whale

The word *cachalot* was already in use in the mid-eighteenth century. It probably is derived from the Portuguese *cachalotte* ("big head"), or from the Spanish *cachalote.*

(See Appendix I, "The Cetaceans")

Cephalopoda

A class of the phylum Mollusca which includes four subclasses: Decapoda, Octopoda, Nautiloids, and Vampyromorphes.

The Decapoda have ten legs equipped with suctions cups, such as Spirules with internal shells, the cuttlefish, the Teuthoidae, and the squids (the commom edible squid, *Chiroteuthis* and *Architeuthis* — the giant squid which is the cachalot's favorite food).

The Octopoda have eight arms, all equipped with suction cups. This subclass includes the octopus which lives in coastal waters, the Eledon which lives farther out to sea, *Ocythoe* (the female of which weighs several pounds, while the male is tiny), and the Argonaut (or paper nautilus), the female of which secretes a shell-like enclosure which she uses as a nest.

The Nautiloids are found in the Indo-Pacific region. They have external shells, of which they occupy only the last section. This is the only subclass without suction cups.

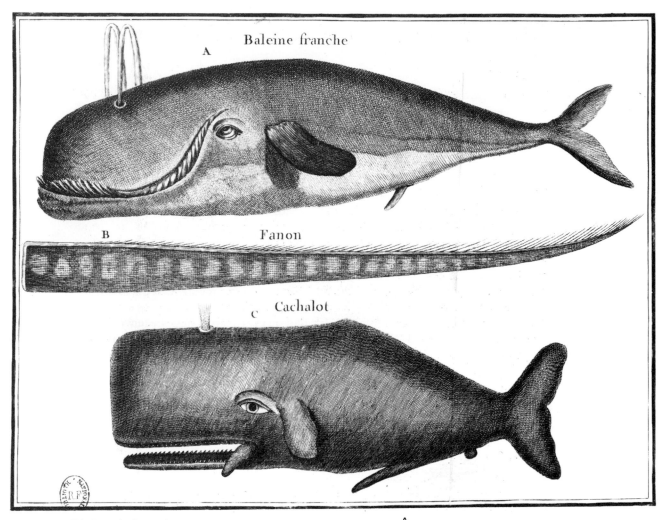

A Baleine franche

B Fanon

C Cachalot

Right whale and sperm whale. Du Reste, *Histoire des pêches, des découvertes des établissements des Hollandais dans les mers du nord.* An IX de la République. *Bibliothèque Nationale.*

The Vampyromorphes are fantastic beings with enormous eyes and luminous organs. They are veritable living fossils, only recently discovered.

Chiroptera

Chiroptera are bats, an order of mainly nocturnal animals highly specialized for flying. Their wings are formed of large membranous planes stretched between the elongated digits of the fore limbs.

In flight, the bat emits a constant series of ultrasonic cries which it uses to determine, by the amount of elapsed time before the echo returns, the direction and distance of the objects reflecting the sound. These sounds are also used to detect prey.

Clam

The common name of the *Venus mercenaria,* an edible bivalve or two-shelled mollusk that lives buried in sand or mud.

Coryphaena

There are two species of *Coryphaena: Coryphaena hippurus,* and *Coryphaena equisetis.* The first is commonly known as the dolphin fish, and the second as the pompano dolphin — confusing names, since *Coryphaena* are not related to the true (mammal) dolphins. Both are beautifully colored fishes of the open tropical oceans.

Decompression Accidents

Decompression accidents during dives are caused by the fact that gas from the diver's air tends to go into solution in the diver's blood. If the diver rises to the surface too quickly, this gas comes out of solution in the form of bubbles in the blood stream, which may impede circulation. The result is decompression sickness, (the bends), which is more or less serious depending upon the speed of the diver's ascent, the depth from which he began the ascent, and the amount of time spent at that depth.

Decompression sickness may be prevented by timing the ascent in such a way that the gas is diffused normally. And, for that purpose, tables have been worked out that indicate the number and duration of the pauses that a diver must make during his ascent, according to the depth that he has reached and the time spent at that depth.

Dolphin (Common)

The common dolphin is a member of the family *Delphinidae*, genus *Delphinus*. It is found in all warm and temperate seas, and occasionally in cold waters. The dolphin travels in schools of about twenty individuals.

The size of the dolphin varies from five feet to eight or nine feet, rarely more, and it normally weighs about 160 pounds.

The color of its skin runs from brown or black on its back to white on its underside. A darker streak runs from the periphery of the eye to the snout.

The common dolphin feeds in shallow water on fish and cephalapods.

The gestation period lasts about nine months, and the calves are born during the spring.

DSL

During World War II, sonar devices detected mysterious layers at various depths and in very diverse regions in the seas. These were labeled "Deep Scattering Layers."

Observation revealed that these layers rise toward the surface during the night, and sink during the daylight hours. It transpired that these layers were made up of marine fauna — animals that were photographed by Professor Harold Edgerton of MIT, from aboard *Calypso*, by means of a special flash apparatus developed by Professor Edgerton. The principal constituents of these layers are copepod crustaceans, jellyfish, and siphonophores.

Echo Location

A method of orientation used by several animals, including bats and birds as well as cetaceans. The animal directs itself according to the echo that it receives of a sound that it makes.

Flippers

Flippers are the pectoral fins of cetaceans. X-rays of these members show the bones of five "fingers" (except for finback whales), a "wrist," and an "arm." This is usually interpreted as evidence of the whales' land origins.

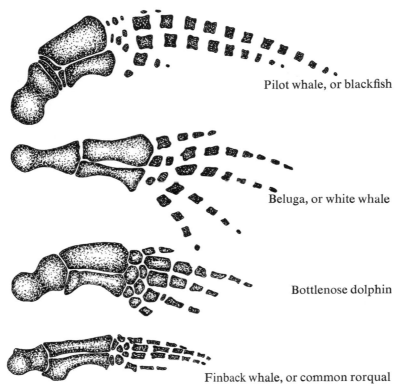

Pilot whale, or blackfish

Beluga, or white whale

Bottlenose dolphin

Finback whale, or common rorqual

X rays of the flippers of various cetaceans. Note that the finback whale has only four "fingers."

Harpoon

The harpoon has been used since the dawn of history for fishing and hunting. In primitive times, it was made of wood or bone, with one or two rows of barbs.

The *harpé*, as the Greeks called it (the word was derived from a Semitic term, hereb) is depicted on monuments dating from the third millenium before Christ. And in the language of the Basques, those intrepid hunters of whales, the word *arpoi*, taken from the Greek root, means "to capture alive."

The present form of the harpoon is described in a text dating from 1474.

An important modern development was the addition of a pivoted crosspiece to the head, which prevents a harpooned animal from shaking the weapon loose.

Jonah

The fifth of the "lesser prophets" of Israel, who lived in the eighth century before Christ. According to the Bible narrative, Jonah, in order to avoid fulfilling the Lord's command to predict to the inhabitants of Nineveh the destruction of their city, took passage on a ship. The ship was soon overtaken by a storm and was in imminent danger of sinking.

Jonah, convinced that the storm was a punishment for his disobedience, and wishing to avoid the loss of the ship and its crew, advised the seamen to throw him overboard. They did so, and, as soon as Jonah was in the water, he was swallowed by a whale.

The prophet spent three days in the stomach of the animal, where he took the opportunity to compose a canticle which is preserved to this day. At the end of the third day, he was vomited onto a beach.

Jonah had learned his lesson. He went immediately to Nineveh and carried out the Lord's orders.

The Book of Jonah, which forms part of the Old Testament, relates these adventures. The methods of modern biblical criticism, however, have revealed that the Book of Jonah was written, in all probability, long after the time of Jonah himself.

Krill

Krill *(Euphausia superba)* is a small crustacean Schizopod between two and three inches long. It is, in effect, a shrimp-like creature found in coastal waters, with an orange head and appendages and a green underside. This green color, which is visible through the thin stomach wall, is caused by the algae on which the krill feeds.

This crustacean, which produces a form of plankton, lives in cold water, and is much more common in the Antarctic than in the Arctic. It multiplies with extraordinary rapidity during the antarctic summer and covers the water with a reddish-brown layer — a layer which is usually about forty feet thick, but sometimes reaches a thickness of 3000 feet.

The krill matures at the age of two years.

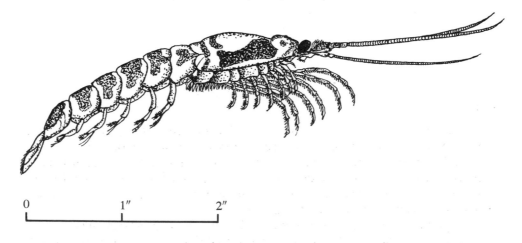

0   1″   2″

The krill (*Euphausia superba*), a small crustacean on which whales feed.

Level Reef

A level reef is a coral plateau, more or less long and unbroken, that extends along a shoreline or on top of another reef that is completely surrounded by water. Level reefs are found in shallow water in tropical seas.

Leviathan

The whale has always astounded man by its size and its monstrous appearance. The Leviathan, a sea monster, had its origin in Phoenician mythology, but it is commonly known through its place in the Bible.

Yahweh, in order to give Job an example of his power, describes the Leviathan: "From the depths of the sea came whales like islands, and the hideous Leviathans rising up on the sand with crocodiles twenty cubits in length. Man is before the sea like a child before a Leviathan's lair."

In the book of Isaiah, it is said "On that day the Lord, with his great and strong staff, will lay low Leviathan and slay the whale that is in the sea."

Some have thought, with good reason, that the biblical description of Leviathan referred to the cachalot. The spouting is described as "a smoke which rises from its nostrils as from a boiling kettle. In its neck, power has taken up its abode; and terror goes before him."

Not all commentators are agreed on the nature of the Leviathan, and some identify it with the crocodile rather than with the whale.

Here is the (negative) description given in the fortieth chapter of Job:

"Leviathan, too! Can you catch him with a fish-hook, or run a line around his tongue? Can you put a ring through his nose, or pierce his jaw with a hook? Riddle his hide with darts? Prod his head with a harpoon? You have only to lay a finger on him never to forget the struggle or risk it again. Any hopes you might have would prove vain, for the mere sight of him would stagger you."

And, in Isaiah, the Leviathan is a symbol for the powerful pagan nation that is to submit to Yahweh.

Minisub

There are several types of minisubs, or diving saucers, designed by Captain Cousteau and developed by the Center of Higher Marine Studies at Marseilles.

The *SP-350,* a two-passenger vehicle. It is equipped with a cinematographic camera, a still camera, a hydraulically operated pincer and lift, and a storage basket. The SP-350 has been used in more than 600 dives.

The *SP-1000,* or sea-flea, carries only one man but is designed to be used in conjunction with a second SP-1000. It has two exterior cameras (16mm. and 35mm.), both controlled from within, and tape recorders for recording underwater sounds. It has been used in over 100 dives.

The *SP-4000,* or Deepstar, is capable of diving to 4000 feet. It was built for Westinghouse and was launched in 1966. Since then, it has participated in over 500 dives. It is a two-passenger vehicle, with a speed of three knots.

The *SP-3000,* presently being tested at sea, was built for CNEXO. It is expected to attain a speed of three knots, and will carry three passengers.

Moby Dick

The most famous of the works of Herman Melville, *Moby Dick* is devoted to the subject of whaling as practiced by whaling ships of the nineteenth century.

The book is the story of the contest between Moby Dick, a great white sperm whale, and Captain Ahab, who has sworn to kill the whale. The work is also a poetic and symbolic representation of the eternal battle between man and evil incarnate as "the beast."

Ahab, who wishes to establish order in the world, finally is defeated and dies a victim of the monster. The forces of evil have won the victory. This pessimistic conception of human destiny is expressed in magnificent language that owes a good deal to the Bible, to Shakespeare, and to the English writers of the eighteenth century.

Moby Dick had no particular success during Melville's lifetime. It was only after World War I that its fame spread. In 1956, John Huston made a film of the book.

Herman Melville's own life was only slightly less an adventure than Captain Ahab's. He was born in 1819, in New York, of a family of eight children. At the age of thirteen his father died, and he was obliged to earn his living for the next years as a bank employee, a clerk, and a schoolmaster.

In January 1841, he signed onto the whaler *Acushnet,* whose destination was the South Pacific by way of Cape Horn. In July 1842, as the ship was taking on provisions at Nuku Hiva in the Marquise Islands, Melville deserted. A month later, he signed onto an Australian whaler, the Lucy Ann, the captain of which was wholly insane.

Life aboard the *Lucy Ann* was even worse that on the *Acushnet,* and Melville deserted once more, this time at Tahiti, along with a large part of the crew. Taken prisoner, he escaped to the neighboring island of Eimo. There, after two months, he became a seaman on a Nantucket whaler, the *Charles and Henry,* which took him to the Hawaiian Islands. In August 1843, he enlisted as a seaman aboard the U. S. naval frigate *United States,* which, fourteen months later, put into Boston.

Melville's seafaring life had lasted three years and nine months. With two desertions on his record, he certainly cannot be offered as the very model of a seaman or sailer. Nonetheless, he returned to the United States with his mind filled by an incomparable, though rapidly acquired, experience. He immediately began writing, and, a few years later, two works appeared simultaneously in New York and London: *Typee* (1846), and *Omoo* (1847). They were both successful.

His next book, *Tuesday,* was a total failure. He left New York in 1850 and went with his family to Arrowhead, near Pittsfield, Massachusetts. There, he wrote *Moby Dick,* his masterpiece which, when it was published, was almost completely ignored. His later books fared no better.

In 1866, Melville fell ill, and he accepted, in order to live, a job with the Port of New York Customs Bureau. After having two volumes of poetry published at his own expense, he died in 1891. He would be forgotten until thirty years had passed.

Narwhal

The narwhal is a toothed cetacean of the family *Monodontidae.* It inhabits the arctic seas, keeping to coastal waters and occasionally venturing into the mouths of rivers.

Its length varies from 10 feet to 16 or 17 feet — not counting its spirally twisted tusk, slightly to the right of the snout, which may grow to a length of 9 feet. The tusk is found only in the male.

The narwhal has no dorsal fin, but only a slight protrusion, or dorsal "crest."

Contrary to what is commonly believed, the narwhal's tusk is not used to break ice, nor as a weapon. It seems likely, in fact, that it serves no useful purpose at all.

In other times, the tusk was thought to be the "horn" of the unicorn, and was very highly regarded for the medicinal powers attributed to it. The purveyors of these "unicorn horns" were Norwegian fishermen who hunted the narwhal in Iceland and Greenland.

The narwhal travels in groups of six to ten individuals, with the females often being separated from the males. They eat cuttlefish, crustaceans, and fish.

The gestation period is unknown. The calf, at birth, measures four and one half feet in length, and remains with the mother for a time.

Observation Chamber

Calypso was originally a minesweeper, and it was necessary to modify her considerably for her new career as a marine research vessel. Among the other changes made, a "false nose" was added to the prow — that is, a metallic well that goes down to five feet below *Calypso*'s waterline and ends in an observation chamber. The chamber has eight portholes, through which we are able to observe and film anything in the water, even when *Calypso* is moving.

Observation Deck

What the text refers to occasionally as *Calypso*'s "crow's-nest" is not a crow's-nest in the classical sense. That is, it is not a platform atop a mainmast, but rather a raised metal platform built as far forward as possible so as to constitute an upper deck. It serves two purposes: it supports our radar antennae, and it provides an excellent vantage point for observation.

Observation Lumen

A research expedition by the Cousteau team, in the Mediterranean, the purpose of which was to determine the horizontal propagation of light at depths of 25, 50, 100, 150, 200, and 250 meters. The minisub SP-350 was used on this occasion.

Phototropism

Phototropism is a term used to describe a tendency of plants and animals to grow or move toward a light source. It is this response which causes newly germinated seedlings to grow upwards toward the light where their leaves and later their flowers will be in the best position for the life processes to continue.

Phytoplankton

Phytoplankton is a term used for the minute plant life which floats in the surface waters of the oceans. It is made up exclusively of unicellular forms: diatoms (which are plentiful in cold and temperate seas), dinoflagellates (in warm waters), coccolithophores, Cyanophycae (or blue algae), etc. Its development depends on the sun's light, which by photosynthesis builds up the organic matter in its tissues. Phytoplankton is essential to the life of the oceans, for it is the food source for the animal plankton (zooplankton) which in turn nourishes the larger animals, such as the blue whale.

Pinnipedia

An order of animals containing three families:
Otaridae: sea lions, furred seals;
Odobaenidae: walrus;
Phocidae: seals and sea elephants.

The Pinnipedia are mammals living partly on land at the edge of the sea, although they are beautifully adapted for life underwater. They feed on fish and crustaceans and are found in all seas except the Indian Ocean. They are most common in the polar seas.

Porpoise

The porpoise is a toothed cetacean of the family, *Delphinidae*, genus *Phocaena*. It is found from the Arctic Ocean to the west coast of Africa, and also on the west coast of Mexico. It varies in length from four feet to six feet, and its average weight is about 160 pounds.

The porpoise's skin is white on its underside, and almost black on its back. Its blade-like teeth number 54.

Porpoises travel in couples and also in schools of a hundred or so. They swim only a short distance beneath the surface, and rise to the surface to breathe every fifteen seconds. Their diet consists of small fishes that swim near the surface.

The porpoise's deadliest enemies are the shark and the killer whale.

Mating occurs at the end of spring and during the summer. The gestation period is eleven months. At birth, the baby porpoise is approximately half the length of its mother.

At certain epochs of history — at the time of Henry VIII, for instance — porpoise meat was regarded as a great delicacy.

Pygmy Sperm Whale, or Pygmy Cachalot

The pygmy sperm whale belongs to the family *Physteridae,* genus *Kogia,* and inhabits the Atlantic, Pacific, and Indian oceans.

It reaches a length of 9 to 13 feet. Its dorsal fin, situated in the middle of its back, is sickle-shaped. Its tail spread is about two feet. The average weight is between 400 and 700 pounds. Its head, which accounts for one sixth of the total body length, resembles that of the porpoise.

Little is known about the habits of these cetaceans. We know that they travel in schools, migrating to polar waters in summer and to temperate and warm areas in autumn and winter, where their females give birth. The mating season is quite long. The gestation period is about nine months. A 10-foot female's calf weighs approximately 175 pounds and is six feet long.

Rapture of the Depths

Rapture of the depths is a form of narcosis induced by the presence of nitrogen, and seriously impedes a diver's reasoning processes. The depth at which it affects a diver depends upon the individual. Some divers experience its symptoms at, say, 135 feet, while others are affected only at greater depths and later — sometimes too much later.

A diver's threshold of susceptibility can be raised considerably by replacing the nitrogen in his breathing mixture by a lighter gas, such as helium.

Siphonophores

Siphonophores are Cnidaria of the class Hydrozoa. They are exclusively marine animals and are able to float. They are fragile, transparent, and often magnificently hued in iridescent colors.

Siphonophores sometimes look like jellyfishes but are in fact hydrozoan colonies that are not fixed, but free-floating. The individuals of the colony therefore develop in such a way as to be capable of performing special and distinct functions. The axis of the colony is a stolon, at the end of which is an air-filled membrane (the pneumatophore) that serves as a floater.

Siphonophores feed on forms of marine life that they capture by means of venomous filaments — a weapon effective enought to be dangerous even to man.

Siphonophores reproduce by means of eggs, and also by budding in the form of medusae.

Sirenia

Sirenia are an order of aquatic mammals whose forward members have evolved into pectoral fins, and who lack hind legs. The tail is flattened horizontally.

There are two living families: the *Halicoridae,* or dugongs, and the *Manatidae,* or manatees; a third, the Rhytines (Steller's sea cow), was killed off by man in the eighteenth century.

The dugong lives in the Indo-Pacific region, in the Red Sea, and in Australian waters. It averages eight feet in length and weighs about 450 pounds.

Dugongs live alone or in small schools and feed on algae and on seaweed growing in shallow water.

The female has well-developed mammary glands.

The flesh, oil, and leather of the dugong is highly regarded in some parts of the world, and for this reason the animal has been hunted extensively. There are many places where their numbers have been greatly reduced.

Three species of manatee exist and are found on the West Coast of America, in the Tchad River basin, and on the coasts of Africa. They also enter rivers and their estuaries.

Manatees are somewhat larger than dugongs, reaching a length of about 14 feet and a weight of 1500 pounds. They are strictly vegetarians and feed on water plants that they pull out with their upper lip.

Manatees live in small groups, and are threatened with extinction, at least in certain areas, since they have neither defenses against man nor any natural timidity.

Sonar

Sonar (Sound Navigation Ranging) is an apparatus of underwater detection and communication. It is, in effect, the marine equivalent of radar, and is based upon the reflection of sound or supersonic waves.

Spermaceti (See Tank.)

Sperm Whale (See Cachalot. Also, Appendix I, "The Cetaceans.")

Spout

The whale's breath is the classic means man has of discovering a whale's location. When a cetacean rises to the surface to breathe, it gives off, through its one or two blowholes, a spout which is visible from a distance. It is, in fact, a whitish spray which acts as a marker for whaling ships. This spray cannot be attributed solely to the con-

Spouts of various whales.

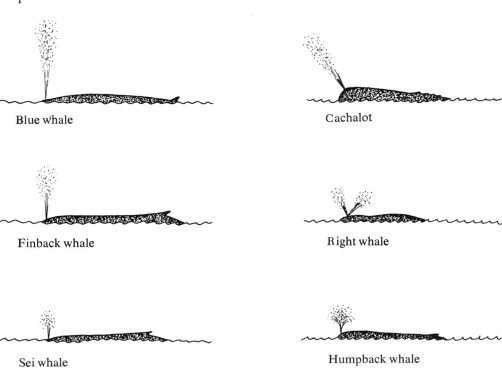

Blue whale

Cachalot

Finback whale

Right whale

Sei whale

Humpback whale

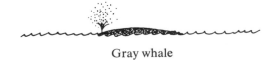

Gray whale

densation of water vapor in cold air, for it is visible even in tropical waters and climates.

As there is no passageway between its mouth and its blowhole, a cetacean cannot blow water out while exhaling.

Paul Portier, a French biologist, has offered the following hypothesis: the expansion in the open air of air which has been compressed in the thorax of a whale causes the condensation of the water vapor when the whale exhales.

F. C. Fraser and P. E. Purves have noted the presence, in the whale's lungs, of very small drops of oil and of mucus, which may explain the visibility of its spout. This oil in the whale's respiratory tract may also have a part in the absorption of nitrogen.

Each species of whale has a particular kind of spout. That of the blue whale and of the common rorqual is a single geyser that rises from 18 to 30 feet. The right whale's spout is double. That of the sperm whale is single, and emerges from the blowhole to the left of the whale and at a 45°angle.

Squid

The squid is a Cephalopod and a decapod — that is, it has ten arms, equipped with suction cups — and belongs to the family Teuthoidae.

The squid that forms the basis for several common dishes is only about eight inches long. It is this species that, at certain seasons of the year, group by the hundreds of thousands for their mating ritual — an event that was the subject of one of our films: *The Night of the Squid*.

Chiroteuthis, characterized by its extraordinarily long tentacles and slender body, is noted for its swimming ability.

Architeuthis, or giant squid, is the natural prey, and the natural adversary, of the cachalot. It is probably the basis in fact for many legends concerning marine monsters — sea serpents and, especially, the "Kraken" of the Norwegians. And, in fact, its size lends itself to this sort of interpretation, for its body may be twenty feet long, and its tentacles reach a length of perhaps forty feet.

Little is actually known about Architeuthis. It lives in the great depths of the oceans, at 10,000 to 12,000 feet, and rises to the surface only at night. Specimens are taken alive only rarely, and then with great difficulty.

Tank

A "tank" is a cavity in the forward part of the head of a cachalot (and of certain other toothed whales) which contains an oily substance, not unlike wax, called spermaceti. The biological function of this substance has not been clearly established.

The tank may hold as much as five tons of spermaceti, which is of a quality superior to ordinary whale oil.

Tegea

A lens which is installed on cameras in order to increase the size of the area that they may film. The apparatus has been adapted for use on a special camera, with a corrective lens, for underwater filming.

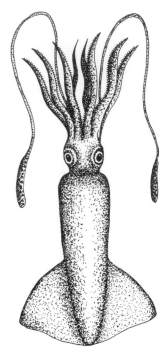

Giant squid.

Zooplankton (Animal Plankton)

Zooplankton is concentrated in the well-lit surface of the sea. (See DSL, Deep Scattering Layer). Herbivorous animals feed in that layer, as do carnivores.

Zooplankton make vertical migrations. At night, they occupy layers near the surface, and, during the day, sink deeper into the sea. In certain cases, light itself causes certain species to sink.

Among the zooplankton are the Radiolaria, Acantharia, Foraminifera, Cnidaria, Ctenaria, and a large number of crustaceans and mollusks.

Engraving from Rondelet's *Histoire complète des poissons* (1558). *Bibliothèque Nationale.*

Bibliography

Budker, Paul. *Baleines et baleiniers*. Paris, 1955.

Fitter, Richard. *Les animaux sauvages en voie de disparition dans le monde*. Paris, 1970.

Matthews, L. H. *The Whale*. London, 1968.

Norris, Kenneth S. *Whales, Dolphins and Porpoises*. Univ. of Calif., Los Angeles, 1966.

Riedman, Sarah R. and Elton T. Gustafson. *Home Is the Sea: For Whales*. New York, 1966.

Ruspoli, Mario. *A la recherche du cachalot*. Paris, 1955.

Slijper, E. J. *Whales*. London, 1962.

Walker, Ernest P. *Mammals of the World.*, Baltimore, 1968.

Walker, Theodore J. *Whale Primer*. New York, 1962.

Photo Credits

The documents reproduced in this volume are from the following sources:

Bibliothèque Nationale, Paris: 29, 247, 271, 272, 277, 278, 280, 283, 288, 300.

Roger-Viollet: 272.

Photographic Service, Embassy of the United States, Paris: 17.

Collection Jean-Horace Chambon: 197.

The photographs published in the present work were taken by Georges Barsky, Ron Church, Philippe Cousteau, François Dorado, Frédéric Dumas, Albert Falco, André Laban, Dr. Claude Millet, Yves Omer, Jacques Renoir, and Ludwig Sillner.

Several of the photographs taken on the surface of the water are from the private collections of members of *Calypso*'s team.

We should like to express our special thanks to M. Jean-Horace Chambon for his kindness in allowing us to photograph, and reproduce here, the two engraved whale's teeth from his personal collection.

Index